THE CONC

THE CONCEPTS
OF ETHICS

BY

SIDNEY ZINK

NEW YORK
ST MARTIN'S PRESS INC
1962

MACMILLAN AND COMPANY LIMITED
London Bombay Calcutta Madras Melbourne

THE MACMILLAN COMPANY OF CANADA LIMITED
Toronto

ST MARTIN'S PRESS INC
New York

PRINTED IN GREAT BRITAIN

CONTENTS

v

CONTENTS

INTRODUCTION

THE ethical theorist tries to understand the concepts we use in our everyday ethical decisions and judgments. Some of these concepts are perfectly fundamental: such are value, obligation and responsibility. It is the explicit or implicit presence of one of these concepts in a judgment which enables us to identify the judgment as ethical. These concepts involve others. In understanding value we are driven to determine its relations to desire and to pleasure; and in understanding responsibility we must analyze will, choice and intention. I propose, then, to investigate these concepts and their interrelations.

In my view ethics concerns events or objects which can be known. But the problem of knowing these things is not, like the problem of knowing other events and objects of an empirical science such as chemistry or zoology, one of obtaining experience of new phenomena. We are well acquainted with the phenomena; the problem is to understand their relations. Whether this understanding involves new 'observations' it is not now necessary to decide. What is involved is, at any rate, very different from what we usually think of as 'observation'. It is like what is done by the theoretical rather than the experimental physicist. The method is not to gather anything new but to re-examine what we have.

What we have are thoughts about these things — value, obligation, responsibility. And the conspicuous and viable form in which we have these thoughts are as modes of verbal expression. In elucidating these concepts and their relations I shall continually refer to the way we talk about them. However, my objective is to elucidate not just the way we talk about these things, but the way we think about them. There is a distinction; still, to do one is to do the other. One cannot talk clearly on an extended scale while not thinking clearly. One can, in a confused state of mind, utter a clear sentence, but, as Plato showed, one cannot write a clear paragraph or engage in a clear dialogue. Further, one cannot think at all without words or symbols. Thus the elucidation of thought is the elucidation of words, phrases and sentences.

The method of treating philosophical problems by a conjoint analysis of what we think and how we speak is, I think, the dominant philosophical method today. The method, understood quite generally, is as old as Plato, but in recent times it has been given a new self-consciousness and rigor by the work of G. E. Moore and Ludwig Wittgenstein. (Moore's influence is especially prominent in the pages that follow; he is responsible not only for the mode of philosophic method so widely practiced, but also for the way in which many current problems in ethics are posed.) To what degree their methods are alike is a tempting question which cannot be broached here. Briefly, however, Moore typically referred to 'common sense', to what the ordinary person must think, while Wittgenstein typically referred to ordinary language, to the way the ordinary person talks. But both have in common a stress upon the particular case — upon elucidating and testing a philosophic proposition by considering what this proposition comes to when its terms are taken in the way that we ordinarily take them, and applied to the sorts of particular cases to which we would ordinarily apply them. Some recent writers — O. K. Bouwsma comes first to mind — have concentrated their efforts almost exclusively on the detailed analysis of particular cases. Others, such as Nowell-Smith, have directed their attention mainly to the verbal expressions we use in dealing with a subject. Both, I think, are proper and useful. I think that a reference to verbal expressions is most to the point when there is reason to believe that a philosophic puzzle has been generated through the looseness and ambiguity of language, as on the question of responsibility and 'free will'. Whereas a reference to concrete cases is most to the point when one wants to confirm or criticize a general doctrine, as the 'teleological' or 'deontological' theories of obligation. However, both methods are appropriate in both sorts of treatment. In treating responsibility one will want to consider particular cases in which we do hold persons responsible; as in treating obligation one will want to ask how we use the word 'obligation'. And finally, one will want to ask how this word interacts with other words when we are speaking of obligation generally, as well as when we are speaking of some particular case of obligation. One thing which the method would exclude as profitless, and which I hope I have excluded, is the formulation of general principles which are not supported either by the way we talk or by their capacity to explain what we think about concrete cases.

Sometimes, then, I shall refer to what people do or would 'say', and sometimes to what people do or would 'think'. I use the latter when there seems either no particular problem about the form of verbal expression, or any light to be gained from analyzing it — when most light is to be got from directing attention chiefly to the actual phenomena themselves in the form of either an unusual or a decisive case.

A principle of thought and language which I presuppose is that members of a language community understand the basic concepts in the same general way, but that no one understands them fully. The philosopher has the opportunity and the inclination to reflect more about them and to advance their general understanding a little or a lot.

The absence and the need of more understanding of the basic ethical concepts is seen in the paradoxes and contradictions about them which sometimes come to the surface. On any given occasion the ordinary person feels no strain in his handling of these concepts. He can express what he thinks with fair readiness and point. But if he comes to compare what he says on different occasions, he can feel puzzled, for he seems to contradict himself. And it may happen that the puzzlement breaks out in a single very perplexing moral problem, which has elements that bring in both of his contradictory views. Telling examples of these discrepancies are on the questions of 'Relativism' versus 'Objectivism', 'Hedonism' versus 'Stoicism', 'Subjective' versus 'Objective' Obligation, 'Free Will' versus 'Determinism'. In an easy-going mood the ordinary man may say: 'Good is relative' or 'Value judgments are merely a matter of opinion'; but then when speaking of a particular question, say Hitler's persecution of Jews, he will denounce this in the strongest language, as 'Hitler was an evil man'. Similarly, at one time he will be inclined to say that of course 'Pleasure is good', and in another context that of course 'If a thing is good we ought to pursue it'; but then if one asks, 'Do you mean that one ought to pursue pleasure, and his own pleasure?' he will not know what to say. Another case. He says that 'A person ought to do what he thinks right'. But he also thinks persons sometimes mistake right for wrong. The two notions thus commit him to saying, 'A person ought sometimes to do what is in fact wrong'. One final case. He may say at one time that 'Nothing happens without a cause' and at another that 'A person is free to choose'. Further, the difficulty takes on practical poignance when he considers what ought to be done about persons convicted of crime. He may not know what is right — whether we ought to punish the person because he was 'free to choose' or whether we ought to try to help him because 'he couldn't avoid doing what he did'.

I shall attempt to show that these paradoxes arise from overlooking distinctions of meaning in our concepts, and that an analysis of their meanings enables us to resolve the puzzles.

The first and last examples above, and especially the last, show that the questions, though 'merely theoretical' in mode of treatment, are not so in final result. However, it is a common view among present analytic philosophers (whose general method I pursue) that philosophic analysis can be done without any practical commitments; that the ethical theorist can do meta-ethics without doing ethics; that he can explain how such concepts as value and obligation are related without saying what is good or obligatory. There is a truth here. And there is a healthy desire to specialize the theoretical work so as to do it better. But there is also an error, and perhaps an unhealthy desire to avoid taking a stand. The ethical theorist can avoid a stand on the more particular questions for ethical decision, but he cannot avoid a stand on general questions. To continue with the above examples : if he holds the deterministic view that no human actions are avoidable, and if he thinks that persons are not responsible for things they cannot avoid, then he is practically committed to refusing ever to judge any person responsible. This result is a highly general one, but it is no less practical for being general, and the more important for being so. Again, if the theorist maintains that pleasure is something which is good, and that people are obligated to pursue pleasure, then he is committed to recommending that they sometimes pursue their own pleasure. Finally, if he argues that value judgments are not expressions of knowledge but expressions of feeling (or attempts to arouse feeling), then he is committed not to presenting value judgments as if they were claims to knowledge. If value judgments are not claims to knowledge, then the theorist who knows this is committed, when he utters sentences about value, to making sure that the persons to whom he makes these utterances understand them for what they are. And this would require some pains, for ordinary persons are under the impression that value judgments are true or false.

Now, of course, in saying that the ethical theorist is practically committed to all these things, I am committing myself to a judgment both about the nature and the value of ethical theory. To say the theorist is committed in these ways is to say what the theorist *ought* to do. A theorist ought not to advance a theory which he doesn't believe ; and he ought to try to get people to understand and believe his theory ; and he ought not to act contrary to what he believes. These, obviously, are propositions not about what is a good theory and not even about what is a good theorist, but about what is right action. To assert that a good theory is a true one, and that a good theorist is a theorist who holds a good theory, is to assert technical propositions about the nature of theory and not ethical propositions carrying an implication as to what any human being ought to do (as it would be if we said that it is good to construct theories). But it is an ethical proposition to say that if the theory is true, and if it is the sort of theory, as ethics is, on which one can act, then one ought to act on it. Thus a theorist who would agree that he has the practical commitments I say he has, could agree to this only if he agreed with this general ethical principle. And he *might* disagree with it. The theorist will have to reflect and see whether he does. My way of urging that he does not is to cite what people in general think about this matter, and what he as a member of this group thinks about it as shown by the way he and others generally talk. People generally, and the theorist too, think that a person ought to practice what he preaches — that if he believes a theory to be true, then on the appropriate occasions he ought to act on it. Thus if we mean by a meta-ethics one that remains quite pure of practical commitments, there is no such field. Nor is there any need for this esoteric word-form 'meta'. It may be that there can be a pure logic or mathematics, but there cannot be a pure ethics. We can say what we need to say with the word 'theoretical'. Ethics is, like logic and aesthetics, more or less theoretical and philosophical. It is the more theoretical, and the less practical, as it has less to say about general sorts of ethical problems, such as the rightness of capital punishment, divorce, advertising, etc., and as it has less to say about completely particular ethical problems, as what a person ought to do in a particular case. The present essay has nothing directly to say about such things, except by way of illustration. It is a work in theoretical ethics. But, even on such specific topics as the above, it does carry *some* implications, even if only as to the sort of reasons which are relevant to their solution.

A word now — and a very inadequate one — about debts. I believe that a great debt which without this mention would probably go unnoticed is to John Dewey. I was so early saturated with his work that it is impossible for me to say how much I owe to him. Although I found — and find — much to resist in Dewey, my stress upon the flexibility of ethical rules and upon a plurality of values stems from him.

My explicit concern in the following pages is almost

entirely with writers influenced, as I am, by G. E. Moore. I am indebted to the authors of many books and articles who are mentioned here scantily or not at all. To keep the lines of my analyses clear I have considered in detail only those works which I feel to be directly relevant to the points I want to make. This means that no explicit mention is made of writers who do not share fundamental assumptions of this essay or who do not pose problems in a way useful for my purposes. I have learned from them nevertheless. And those whom I do discuss I often charge with mistakes in so positive a manner that my references to them often conceal the real benefit I have gained from them.

Another matter. I have broached a number of large topics which I have touched very lightly — for example, desire, punishment, rights. My excuse is that I have had here to treat these in the course of another topic. I am as painfully aware as the reader will be of the much fuller consideration which these topics call for.

Finally, I want to give thanks to Rudolph Weingartner for reading the book in manuscript and suggesting many improvements in clarification. I am also grateful to Robert Connolly for his cheerful labor in preparing the Index. Above all, I want to express indebtedness to my wife for steady encouragement and help.

CHAPTER I

VALUE

1. *Terminology*

THERE are some differences in the way we use the terms
'value' and 'good'. The most obvious difference is that
'value' is used exclusively as a noun, for which the corresponding adjective is 'valuable'; while 'good' is used
primarily as an adjective. However 'valuable' does not
mean quite the same thing as 'good'. 'Valuable' suggests
'good to possess', or 'good to use'; while 'good' cannot
similarly be analyzed in terms of 'valuable'. We would
call some things 'valuable' — diamonds, water, popularity
— which we should hesitate to call 'good'. And we would
call some things 'good' — an act of courage, a right choice,
or an experience of pleasure — which we should hesitate
to call 'valuable'. There are other things which we would
speak of in both ways, as both valuable and good — for
example, friendship, truth, health. But these are things
which are good to possess. We do not speak of a 'valuable pleasure' or a 'valuable act of courage', for we cannot
strictly possess these but can only experience the pleasure
and perform the act of courage. We would speak of a
'good pleasure' and a 'good act of courage', and we would
speak of a 'valuable habit of courage' or a 'valuable life'
for we could have or possess these latter.

Another difference is connected with this. 'Valuable'
suggests a relation or potential relation to one for whom
the thing is valuable, while 'good' does not. This also
comes out in that 'value' also serves as a verb, 'to value',
while 'good' has no verb form. Further, at least a possible
analysis of 'to value' is 'to believe good' or 'to appreciate
as being good'; while we cannot similarly analyze 'good'
in terms of 'to value'. One might say with some plausibility that 'to be valuable' is equivalent to 'to be valued'
or 'to be capable of being valued' by someone. Further,

B　　　　　　I

one use of the expression 'valuing' a thing is 'to believe it is good' or 'to appreciate it as being good'. By contrast we cannot analyze 'good' in terms of a belief about value or about anything else. The upshot of all this is: (1) the term 'value' suggests a relation or potential relation to a person who judges value, while 'good' does not; (2) 'good' seems a more basic term, 'value' being analyzable in terms of it, but not the converse.

However, because 'value' has three grammatical functions while 'good' does not, 'value' is a more usable term than 'good' for a general ethical inquiry. Also value is more general in another way, in that it is used to name a greater variety of things. Thus we speak of 'value terms' and of 'value characteristics' to refer to all the features which ethics considers. However, 'good' also has special advantages. 'Good' has an opposite, 'bad', while the only opposite of value is the artificial term 'disvalue'. In the light of this the best procedure seems to be to use the terms primarily with reference to the meaning they have in common, which meaning is most directly expressed by 'good', and to use one or the other of the two words according to the demands of the particular contexts.

2. *Occasions and Uses of Value Judgment*

We make value judgments on two quite different sorts of occasion. I shall call one occasion 'practical' and the other 'theoretical', though these terms are not perfectly accurate. The practical occasion is one in which we want to decide what to do, and in which we want to make the best decision; so we try to estimate the value of the possible alternatives. On these practical occasions judgment is comparative. We judge not just that a thing is good or very good or bad, but that one thing is better (or much better or somewhat better) than others. Such occasions are practical in that the judgment is made in the interest of action. Some change in the world is expected to follow as a result of the judgment. These practical occasions can differ in seriousness. The judgment can be decisive for the entire future of an individual or a community, or it can affect only an evening's pleasure.

There are other practical value judgments which approach to theoretical ones. Judgments by the official judge of a competition, as a 'beauty' contest or a skating contest, are practical in that, as a result of judgment, the winner is awarded a prize. However, the judgment is not practical for the judge. Unless his professional career happens to depend on people's approving his judgment (as that of a professional umpire), the judgment is, from the judge's standpoint, a mere theoretical appraisal of merit. So far as no action or choice on the part of the judge results from the judgment, we might call such judgments 'practical-impersonal'.

Plainly, our main concern in making value judgments is with the practical-personal sort. This is not to say that the need to make choices is prior, and the judging of value secondary. For the making of choices is hardly separable from the judging of value. It might seem that we would never have thought of judging value if we were not confronted with choices. On the other hand, it would seem that certain occasions would not present themselves as occasions for choice if we did not regard the alternatives as differing in as yet undetermined degrees of value. We only represent the occasion as one for choice because we assume that there are alternative possible actions which differ in value. But this question of priority aside, it is clear that our chief use for value judgments is as a basis for choice.

However, this is not the sole use, or sole authentic use, of value judgments, as some writers have claimed. We often judge the value of things just out of an interest in their value, and not to guide our choices or the choices of others. If we have seen a play, it is natural to ask whether it is a good play, and if good, whether better than other plays of a given class — of the author, of the genre, of the period. And this may lead by natural steps into asking all sorts of questions of comparative value: about contemporary plays generally, or contemporary art, or the tragic as compared to the comic form, or literature as compared to visual art, or the activity of art generally. We do not have to think about these things; but we sometimes do.

And though our appraisals here may somehow and eventually affect our choices, this is not their purpose. For
instance, we might, as a result of the discussion of the play,
decide to see no more plays. But the making of such a
choice, rather than being the motive of the inquiry, is an
unforeseen result of it. When the inquiry began, we did
not see that we had a choice to make. It was not that the
occasion for choice instigated the value judgment, but that
the value judgment instigated the occasion for choice.
Having arrived at certain value judgments, we can recognize
occasions for choice which were unrecognized before.

Nor is the point here dependent on the peculiar case of
aesthetic judgments. People who are interested in practical
affairs and material goods can discuss the relative merits of
various commodities in a perfectly disinterested way. They
can ask whether one sports car or vacuum cleaner or fishing
reel is better than another when they have no thought of,
and no means for obtaining, either of the things whose
value is assessed. Publications such as *Consumers Research*,
which rate commodities, are read not merely by prospective
purchasers but by persons who are just interested in such
matters as whether one brand of vacuum cleaner is better
than another. For such an inquirer these judgments are
purely 'theoretical' or 'contemplative'.

One other sort of value judgment is even more decisively
separated from a choice-guiding use. We sometimes judge
things which are not conceivable objects for anyone's
choice, as historical or fictional figures. One might object
that still such figures have general qualities which may
appear in other persons, and can be cultivated or chosen in
them or in ourselves; hence the judgment here is choice-
guiding. To this there are several replies. The most
obvious one is that we judge the value of these objects quite
spontaneously, with no thought of making or influencing a
choice. Further, we judge such objects in their nature as
concrete individuals and not merely as clusters of general
qualities. Finally, we judge the value of objects which we
explicitly recognize would be good to choose but which we
are unable to choose — for example, an expensive painting,
a yacht, a trip to the South Pole, an additional ten years of

life, a younger body, a saintly character, universal fame.

In his *Language of Morals* Mr. R. M. Hare flatly maintains the contrary. He holds that the 'primary function of the word "good" is to commend' (p. 127), and that 'when we commend or condemn anything, it is always in order, at least indirectly, to guide choices, our own or other people's, now or in the future' (p. 126). Thus: 'We only have standards for a class of objects, we only talk of the virtues of one specimen as against another, we only use value-words about them, when occasions are known to exist, or are conceivable, in which we, or someone else, would have to choose between specimens. We should not call pictures good or bad if no one ever had the choice of seeing them or not seeing them (or of studying them or not studying them in the way that art students study pictures), or of buying them or not buying them' (p. 128).

Now it is true that we only have standards for a class of things which it is conceivable that we could make a choice of. But this is just because there is nothing which we could not conceivably have some choice concerning, even if the choice were only one of giving or not giving it our attention. The fact that things we call valuable could always be possible objects for choice does not show that choice-guidance is the primary use of value-words. If we can apply a value-word to a sort of thing, then that sort of thing could, at least in principle, be chosen in some respect. To show the primacy of choice, what needs to be shown is that on every particular occasion of the use of a value-word the thing judged could be chosen. And this cannot be shown.

If Hare means in the above passage that we do not praise particular pictures to people who we think may never have a chance to see these pictures, then this is just false. A person back from Europe may praise these things to persons who he thinks will never go to Europe. Indeed, when one praises such things he usually does not consider whether the hearer can duplicate his own experience. Further, one may, as a form of cruelty, praise the thing to someone just because the person has no possibility of choosing it. One might praise pictures to an enemy who had gone blind. Let us suppose that one ought not to do this, but the present question is not what is the right use of value judgments, but what is their 'primary' use.

The question when ought we to make value judgments is an interesting and special topic, or rather two topics: (1) when ought we to form value judgments? and (2) when ought we to express them? One might argue that a person ought to form such a judgment only when he has a choice of his own to make, and that he ought to express it only to another person who has such a choice. Moralists have frequently and no doubt rightly exhorted us to curtail the number of our value judgments. Many of these judgments are designated as 'gossip', and with respect to them perhaps we ought to follow the advice of Epictetus: 'If a man wash quickly, do not say that he washes badly but that he washes quickly. If a man drinks much wine, do not say that he drinks badly, but that he drinks much.' But I think no one has recommended that we restrict value judgments solely to the guidance of choice. Of course if Hare is right, no such restriction would be required, for it already exists. But we can see that this would be a restriction, and an unnatural and pointless one. It would deprive us of a harmless pleasure, and it would deprive future choices of the enlightenment that comes from having speculated on the values of things.

3. *Can Ethics be a Science?*

No doubt a primary consideration in the minds of those who regard value judgments as purely practical is that we cannot construct a science of values after the fashion of other sciences. But it is well to be clear why this is so. The differences between ethics and the scientific fields of knowledge are often exaggerated.

The peculiarity of ethics conceived as a science providing general principles and particular descriptions is that it has but one or two basic properties or predicate terms (named by 'good' and 'right') and that it cannot quantify these. Though ethics can say that one thing is better or more obligatory than another, it lacks a unit by which to express this quantity exactly. Fields which we call sciences have available either a great variety of properties which can serve as possible predicate-terms (as, for example, zoology) or they have a few properties whose relations are capable of mathematical formulation (as physics and perhaps economics). Ethics, however, can only state that general sorts of things or particular things are good (or right), or that some particular thing is in some undetermined degree better (or more obligatory) than some other. The moralist is reduced to making either very general statements or very particular statements. The first seem utterly vague, the latter utterly unsystematic, and both unclear in application to new cases. Nor do we have quite specific principles to explain the exceptions.

In a mature science, when one of its principles does not hold, the variation can be explained by another principle. To take a crude example, if aspirin does not remove pain the physician can apply another principle which explains that aspirin does not cure a pain of this particular sort, because aspirin affects such and such conditions whereas this pain has different conditions. The assumption of the scientist is that whatever elements and relations do exist in a particular case will not be peculiar to the case. Whenever any connection exists in a given case, this connection, if formulated quite precisely, will hold in general. Its not seeming to hold in general is just owing to our failure to perceive the subtler elements and relations which are present in it. Moreover, the scientist has evidence for this assumption, for he does discover ever more principles and is able to provide an ever more complete account. The value theorist cannot do anything comparable. The clear sign that he cannot is that no one has ever attempted a complete systematic exposition of substantive value principles.

A moralist may say things like: Love is good, or supremely good; pride is bad; hate is bad. Or he may describe in great detail, as does Dostoevski in his novels, the goodness or badness of a particular person. But the first seems too exclusively abstract to count as scientific knowledge, and the second too concrete. Even writers such as Nikolai Hartmann, who think that a more systematic knowledge of values is available, still recognize the

narrow limits of such knowledge. Hartmann writes:
'Thus, for example, brotherly love is evidently higher in
value than justice, love for the remotest higher than
brotherly love, and personal love (as it appears) higher than
either. Likewise bravery stands higher than self-control,
faith and fidelity higher than bravery, radiant virtue and
personality again higher than these. But it is more difficult
to say how, for example, truthfulness, wisdom and faith
stand to one another in relative height; it is the same with
the basic motives running through all the more special
values, such as universality and individuality, likewise
purity and fullness of life, pride and humility, and so on.
It may be that these values stand on the same plane. But
even this cannot be definitely known. The materials are
too heterogeneous. We cannot bring them near enough
together to decide.' [1] Further, though Hartmann believes
that values are ideal essences systematically related, he is
completely unable to show us any convincing number of
systematic relations, as is evident in the dubious examples
above. It is far from clear that the values mentioned above
do relate to one another in the ways he claims. It at once
strikes us that we can think of negative instances, of cases
in which an act in the interest of brotherly love would be
higher than an act of personal love, or an act of self-control
better than an act of bravery, and so with the other value
comparisons. Any ranking which we attempt seems liable
to such exceptions.

This in itself would not be fatal, could we discover
principles by which to account for the exceptions. It might
occur to us that Hartmann's ranking will hold, if we
recognize that each of these qualities of value differs in
quantity, so that whenever in a situation a value lower on
his scale seems superior to a higher value, this is because
there is a greater quantity of the lower value. This is
indeed plausible. We could imagine cases where, say, the
higher value (assuming it is higher) of personal love is
inferior to the value of brotherly love, just because there is
so much brotherly love involved. For instance, we can
think of a case where there is a conflict between a person's

[1] *Ethics*, tr. Stanton Coit, vol. ii, p. 387.

brotherly love for the members of a community and his love for a particular person (King Edward VIII confronted this choice) and in which we think a choice of the alternative involving brotherly love is the right one. It might seem, then, that a value hierarchy such as Hartmann's could stand, subject to the proviso that the values so ranked are assumed to be in equal amounts.

The scheme is empty none the less. For we have no principle for commensurating any two such values. We have no common unit by which to measure the two, and to determine, say, how much personal love is equal to how much brotherly love. This makes the discernment of the ranks of ideal value essences a somewhat (not entirely) idle exercise. Values such as personal love and brotherly love always actually exist in some given amount or degree; they never, by definition, exist as purely ideal. Further, their quantities are essential to their worths. If, then, we lack means for measuring these quantities so as to translate degrees of quantity into degrees of height, there will be little point in stating quite generally (or 'ideally') that one particular value is higher than another, other things being equal. It makes no sense because perhaps other things are never equal, and if they were we would not know how to determine it.

The extreme feebleness of our capacity for correlating different dimensions of value appears most plainly in regard to pleasure. For there can be no doubt that at least two sorts of quantity affect the value of a pleasant experience, its intensity and its duration. But we have no way of translating a quantity of one of these into a quantity of the other, or hence for saying how much in duration we should be ready to give up for how much of an increase in intensity.

We conclude that we cannot possess scientifically systematic knowledge of value. Any value scheme must be vague and imprecise. Further, these traits attach to values whether or not values can be known in any objective fashion by persons. For supposing that standards of validity in value judgment are relative, either to each person or to groups, such that the individual is not concerned to bring his judgments into accord with those of others, he will encounter the same difficulties in any attempt to construct a value system. He will be as unable to arrive at any purely personal method of commensurating different value dimensions as he would be to arrive at some method that would satisfy others. This point has importance, for some people seem to think that if our judgments of value are vague and imprecise, then these judgments must be relative to a person or group. But these judgments are vague and imprecise, whether they are relative or objective.

4. *Are Ethical Sentences Declarative?*

A more reasonable conclusion here would be that value judgments cannot be asserted at all. If all that can be said can be said clearly and precisely, then we cannot say things about values. Our language has value words, which we do use. But their use, according to the skeptical position, is not cognitive. We use these words and make value judgments, not (or not primarily) to *describe* a thing, but to express or evoke a certain feeling (as approval or disapproval) about it. Such is the view of C. L. Stevenson in his justly famous *Ethics and Language*.

According to Stevenson, what distinguishes ethical terms, such as 'good' and 'right', is that they have a strong 'emotive meaning'. By 'emotive meaning' he means a dispositional property of words to evoke in their hearer an emotional response. Thus when we make an ethical judgment which predicates one of these terms of an object or event, the term lends to the judgment an emotive force fitted to influence the hearer. To say that a thing is 'good' is to tend to arouse a feeling or attitude of approval of this thing in the hearer. This utterance is not at all like a descriptive or logical statement, as saying the thing is heavy, yellow, colored, visible, extended, sensory. 'Good' is not primarily the name of a 'property' at all. Of Moore's view that 'good' is the name of a particular sort of quality, Stevenson says that this quality is 'an invisible shadow cast by confusion and emotive meaning' (p. 109). Thus these ethical terms do not, on the Stevensonian view, stand for something which we know about things, but are tools for expressing and evoking feelings.

The crucial question here is whether this emotive use
of ethical terms is their primary one. We must concede
to Stevenson that people often do use ethical terms in an
emotive way; and Stevenson concedes that in some cases
our use of these terms is not emotive. What remains for
dispute is whether this emotive use is, as Stevenson claims,
the distinguishing feature of ethical terms.

First, though we do use these terms to express our own
feelings and to arouse the feelings of other persons, we use
non-ethical terms in the same ways. We may say 'Smith
is a bad man' to cause our hearer to shun him, or we may
produce the same effect by mentioning certain facts about
Smith, as 'Smith speaks inaudibly, coughs incessantly, has
a nervous tic, and seldom washes', or: 'Smith took a lot
of money from friends and relatives, spent it all on wine,
women and song, and is now asking the same people for
more money to support himself and his latest mistress'.
Nor, of course, are emotively arousing statements confined
to statements about people. 'That bear has killed several
people' or 'That wire is high voltage' or 'That bomb is
about to explode' — would tend to produce emotion in
their hearer, though there is no reference either to ethical
properties or to persons. Thus while ethical terms and
statements may be used emotively this does not distinguish
them from other sorts of terms and statements, unless it can
be shown that ethical terms can be used in no other way.

Stevenson agrees that an ethical term can be used in other
ways. Sometimes, he says, ' "good" has much the same
use as "effective", as in the context, "Wearing oilskins is
a good means of keeping dry in a storm" ' (p. 83). And:
' "Good" sometimes has the same use as "almost universally approved", or "approved by members of our community" . . .' (pp. 83-4). I rather doubt that 'good' is
used in this second way, unless in a technical way by a
sociologist; and the first use is plainly non-ethical.
Stevenson does describe a way in which ethical terms
acquire a particular descriptive meaning. But this meaning
is something which is not discovered but only assigned by
the user of the term as a device for persuasion. This
method is called by Stevenson 'Persuasive Definition' and

is said to constitute one important category of ethical discourse.

'Persuasively defining' an ethical term consists in 'assigning' to the ethical term a special descriptive meaning, while leaving unaltered the term's old emotive meaning. The purpose is to cause a hearer to shift the attitude of approval (or disapproval) which is evoked by the emotive meaning of the ethical term to this new set of descriptive qualities. For example, a speaker, to persuade a hearer to approve of a third person whose 'culture' has been questioned, declares that 'In the true and full sense of the term, "culture" means *imaginative sensitivity* and *originality*' (p. 211), which the person in question possesses, despite other lacks (as in formal education and manners) which are generally thought parts of 'culture'. In this way the 'semi-ethical term' 'culture' is provided with — 'assigned' — a new descriptive meaning as part of a persuasive process. And Stevenson argues that ethical theorists who have proposed definitions of basic ethical terms — as Mill in defining 'good' or Plato in defining 'justice' — have been doing essentially the same thing. Thus what is most constant and ethically central to ethical terms is, according to Stevenson, the emotive meaning. Any descriptive meaning such terms have, turns out either to be non-ethical, as when 'good' is used in the sense of 'effective', or a rather arbitrary creation of an individual user.

The question then is just whether we are referring to anything when we use such a term as 'good'. The answer is that surely we must think we are if this term is to have the emotive force which Stevenson makes so much of. The reason that we can persuade a person to do a thing by saying the thing is good is surely that he recognizes that if it is good then he ought to do it (and may even like doing it). Plainly we will not ordinarily persuade him nearly so well by saying that we want him to do it, or by urging or commanding him to do it. Stevenson agrees that this is so, and explains it by saying that the emotive meaning of 'good' is indefinable, hence its emotive effect cannot be so well produced by any other term. But the question is why the term does have its special effect. It has it, surely,

because we think that things may be good, and because we
want things which are good. It is true that we cannot
provide an exact equivalent of the emotive force of 'good'.
Nor, quite probably, can we of any other word. But we
can see that the sort of model given by Stevenson as at
least approximating to the meaning of good has effects
completely different from the effect of 'good'. The dis-
parity between, say, 'Lincoln is a good man' and 'I
approve of Lincoln; you do so as well', is radical. Saying
the thing is 'good' does suggest that one approves of it,
and saying this also tends to elicit the approval of others.
But this is just because we tend to approve of what we
think *is* good. Merely calling a thing by the name 'good'
would not tend to express or arouse our approval; it is
only thinking it is good that can do that.

Moreover, it is obvious that we sometimes use an
ethical term merely to explain and not to convince. One
may say that he did an act because it was the best thing in
the circumstances and yet be quite indifferent whether his
hearer approves of his action. Again a person may confess
having done something wrong even while hoping that his
hearer will not disapprove of it, and even perhaps hoping
that he will convince himself that the act was not really
wrong. Or a speaker may honestly tell a person that a
possible act is wrong while hoping that the hearer will do
the act. He may even say, without contradiction, 'I know
it is wrong but I would like you to do it'.

The inadequacy of the emotivist account of ethical
terms comes out in yet another way. Ethical problems
and judgments occur quite as fundamentally in personal
deliberation as in social disagreement. And when a person
is trying to decide what to do, he is not concerned with
expressing his feelings or influencing himself, but with
deciding what is good or right. He is trying to *know*
something, rather than trying to *feel* something. Feelings
are, of course, very important in personal decisions. And
a person may try to influence his feelings in various ways.
He may try to understand how he feels, or he may try to
work up certain feelings in himself. But neither of these
is what is distinctive of personal decision. A person's

understanding of his feelings is distinct from his judging their worth. He may try to understand them because he believes that he has acted badly through a failure to understand them, or because he believes that the best thing he can do under certain circumstances is to express his feelings, or to act on the basis of his deepest desire (if, for example, he is choosing a wife or a vocation). In these cases the deliberator (a) will be trying to *know* his feelings, and not to express or influence them, and (b) he will be using ethical terms not in their effect on his feelings but as predicates of his feelings. It is also true that a person may use ethical terms to arouse his feelings and to goad himself into a particular course of conduct. He may repeat to himself that a given action is bad in order to intensify his repugnance to doing it, and to help counteract a strong temptation. But in these cases again the ethical judgment of the act's badness is distinct from and prior to the use of this judgment to influence feelings. And this attempt at self-persuasion is less a part of the deliberative process of reaching a decision than it is a subsequent attempt to enforce this decision. It is only in this secondary phase that ethical terms are employed for their emotive force.

It is really quite absurd to describe the deliberation involved in reaching a personal decision as a process of self-persuasion, in which the deliberator attempts to influence himself by using the emotive powers of ethical words.[1] It is not entirely without plausibility to suggest that this is a process of reaching an 'agreement of attitude' in the sense of arriving at a harmonizing of one's desires. An ethical egoist might hold such a theory. But this is not Stevenson's view. For the egoist's deliberative problem would be just to *know* what would satisfy his desires most harmoniously, while for Stevenson the ethical deliberation

[1] Plainly the phrase 'self-persuasion' is figurative, since persuasion involves two selves. The metaphor here consists of personifying two tendencies or desires of the self, and thinking of them as exerting persuasion on each other. But this is not an accurate picture. For the person himself, which is not identified with either of these conflicting tendencies, is the chief agent in deliberation. If we wanted to represent the matter both figuratively and in terms of persuasion, a more accurate metaphor would be of the self as an arbitrator or judge before whom the conflicting tendencies appeared, addressing their persuasions then not to each other but to him.

is not concerned just to get such knowledge but to exert
influence. We can make sense of our wanting to move
other people in certain ways — ways, perhaps, which correspond with our desires. But we could have no motive at all
for wanting generally to move ourselves. A desire to influence always presupposes some other desire. But there
is no other constant desire which could account for our
deliberating always with the end of moving ourselves. To
want to move someone, one has to want to move him in a
certain direction. We could not want to move ourselves
until we had found some direction in which to move. Our
concern in deliberation is to find this direction by finding
out what is good or what we want.

5. *Are Values Simple?*

Thus our way of using ethical language suggests that
value terms do refer to a knowable feature of things, and
that our business in ethical deliberation is to know this
feature as well as we can. Let us call this the doctrine of
the objectivity of values. The doctrine has many aspects,
and has been attacked in a number of ways. Its chief
advocate in this century has been G. E. Moore, who upheld
the doctrine in a highly original way in his great *Principia
Ethica*. However this doctrine has been linked, both in
Moore's treatment and by other writers, with a number of
more special and dubious views, as that value is (1) a
property, (2) simple, (3) intrinsic, (4) non-natural. All of
these characterizations of value raise questions. I shall
argue that value is rightly called a 'property' but that it is
more confusing than illuminating to ascribe these other
features to value, and that the objectivity of value does not
entail any of them.

The term 'property', interpreted in its most elementary
sense, refers to any feature of a thing which can be signified
by the predicate of a true or false assertion. The question
whether value is a property is then the same as the question
whether value is a feature which is meaningfully assertible.
And if value is assertible then it is knowable. All these
features stand or fall together — the features of being a
property, assertible, knowable, objective. If value has any

one of these features, it has all the rest. What has, I think, sometimes caused confusion has been the restriction of the meaning of 'property' to the meaning of 'attribute of an independent substance'. But properties may be of various sorts : they may belong to substances or enduring objects, to events or processes, to momentary states of substances, to other properties, to relations. In particular, if value is a property, it may belong to a state, such as pleasure, or to a quality of a person, such as courage, or to a relation, as to the relation of a desire to an object. At any rate, I shall use 'property' in this broad sense, such that the question whether value is a property turns on whether value is meaningfully assertible and knowable. This is the crucial question, and we shall consider it in detail in the succeeding sections, particularly in Sections 6 through 10. But let us now take up the other features which Moore asserted of value, starting first with 'simplicity'.

Moore wanted to show that value is a fundamental or primitive concept, not analyzable or definable in terms of any other concepts, either valuational or non-valuational. Other value terms, such as 'right' and 'beautiful', are, he held, analyzable in terms of the primitive value concept of good, but good is perfectly 'simple' and unanalyzable.

He urged this in *Principia Ethica* by an argument which has come to be called the 'open question argument'. The contention is that whenever an analysis or definition of the meaning of 'good' is proposed, 'it may be always asked, with significance, of the complex so defined, whether it is itself good' (Section 13). The point here is that if the proposed definition of good (suppose this definition to be 'pleasure') were such that the defining term ('pleasure') fully exhausted the meaning of the term defined ('good'), then it would be senseless to ask whether pleasure were good. Moore grants that it is conceivable that everything which is good may also have some other property (such as 'pleasant' or being 'the object of what one desires to desire'), but he holds that we can always recognize that any two such things would be at most only uniformly connected and not identical. Analogously, we may find that a particular color is uniformly connected with certain physical conditions, but this would not show that the color was just its physical conditions. The question, then, is whether any other term or set of terms provide the sort of exhaustive analysis of the meaning of 'good' which would enable us to dispense with the term 'good', except perhaps as an exact synonym and abbreviated symbol for this other defining term or set of terms. Moore's contention is that we cannot: 'good' cannot be just another symbol for 'pleasure' or for 'what we desire to desire'; otherwise the statement 'Good is pleasure' would be equivalent to 'Pleasure is pleasure', and the question 'Is good pleasure?' would be equivalent to 'Is pleasure pleasure?'

Now one might in reply claim, as Bentham surely would have claimed, that the statement is a tautology and the question is, ultimately, senseless. And to the rejoinder that the question does not seem senseless, he might reply that the senselessness of a question is relative to the knowledge of the questioner. 'Is "I" (the Roman numeral) identical with "1" (the Arabic numeral)?' is not senseless when asked by someone who does not know the meaning of one of the symbols. Similarly, the objector might say, the question whether good is pleasure is not senseless for one who does not know that they are the same. Towards this rebuttal Moore's stand must be that the question whether good is pleasure (or anything else) is significant even for one who knows both what good and pleasure are.

This stand does seem a strong one. For we do seem to be familiar with both good and pleasure (and with the meaning of other terms offered in definitions of good) and we do seem to recognize that, however uniformly any allegedly defining property may be connected with good, this property is not just the same as good. However, such an 'argument' is evidently a pattern for refuting proposed definitions of 'good' rather than being itself a positive refutation of all of these definitions. The refutation is carried out only as particular definitions of 'good' are proposed and as the 'open question argument' is successfully applied to them. The argument can never conclusively show that 'good' is 'simple' and incapable of analysis, unless it can be shown, as surely it cannot, that

C

all possible analyses have been presented and proved defective. The result at this stage is that the unanalyzability of good is an hypothesis for which we have some positive evidence and no negative evidence.

However, for the unanalyzability or 'simplicity' of value Moore suggests another argument which does, I think, have more finality. The argument is that, if a person did not know what value was, we could not hope to break up the notion of value into other notions so as to make him understand it. If we could bring a person to know what value is, we could not do so by the method of analysis. We should have to teach him in the same way that we would teach him to know a color he had never seen. We would show him the color — 'define' it 'ostensively'. And it would be better to say not that we were teaching him what value is, but that we were offering him an experience of it. We might, however, go on to teach him things about value, as that the word 'value' is the name for the object of what he is experiencing. We might also teach him to distinguish fine shades of value. But this would presuppose that he already possessed a rudimentary knowledge of value. Thus if we mean by a thing's being simple that it can only be known in direct experience, and not through experience of other things or through verbal symbols, then it is true that value, like yellow, is simple.

Mr. S. Toulmin in his *Reason in Ethics* has denied that we do explain value by pointing to instances. He writes : 'Suppose, then, someone says to me, not "cochineal is red", but a sentence which on the face of it is very similar, "meekness is good". If I do not understand it, how can he make me ? Will he point out to me instances of meekness, and hope to make me understand good in the way which would be effective if one were teaching "red"? Hardly!' (p. 18). But why this 'Hardly!' Someone who thought meekness is good might do just this. Further, though he might do other things, such as to describe consequences of meekness or to point out its similarities to other good things, he would reply finally upon presenting in their concrete detail actual instances of meekness and hoping that the person will see the goodness in them.

Toulmin gives another equally odd reason to show that value is not a directly perceived simple property. He says that even a supporter of the objective doctrine will deny that 'good' shares all the logical properties of the simple qualities. He says that the objectivist will insist : 'Goodness is not a vague notion like the simple qualities — we don't mark off the "good" from the "indifferent" and the "bad" in the way we mark off the "blue" from the "yellow" and the "green", or the "tall" from the "middling" and the "short"' (p. 18). But it would be only a very foolish objectivist who talked this way. There is nothing in the objectivity of values which requires that the line between the good and the indifferent be perfectly sharp, or that we can be perfectly sure where a thing ceases to be indifferent and is of definite value. The odd thing is that Toulmin should attribute such a view to the objectivist.

It is, however, misleading to compare the simplicity of value, as Moore did, with that of a particular color. Value is a very general term, and if it refers to something which exists, must stand for a general category or class of existence, like the term 'color' or 'visible' or 'sensuous', and not like the term 'yellow', which stands for a particular species of the general class of 'color'. If the comparison is with the specific yellow, then the other term of the comparison should be a specific value, such as courage. Both the general category and the specific variety are alike in that the only source of knowledge of either is direct experience, not conceptual analysis. But suggesting that value is like a specific sensory quality suggests that value will be equally plain and obvious to observation. One of the chief grounds of objection to the Moorean view has been just that we do not encounter this quality of goodness. But obviously we could not encounter it in the form in which we encounter a particular sensory quality, any more than we can encounter the general feature of color in this way.

The general concept of yellow is, of course, an abstraction from particular yellows, just as the concept of color involves abstraction from particular yellows, greens, blues, etc. But the particular yellow is concrete in a way that the yellow's coloredness, or one of its dimensions of hue, saturation, or brightness, is not. We do seem to perceive the 'yellow' directly, while we do not with similar directness perceive the characteristic of being a color, or of being something sensuous. Similarly with a specific value, for example courage. In such a particular instance we do seem to perceive the value directly. We can no more conceive perceiving the courageous act and not perceiving its value than we can conceive perceiving a yellow object and not perceiving the yellow. But it is not at all clear whether or how we grasp the general characteristic which unites these cases to other members of the same genus. There is no need to hold that we perceive them directly. They may be explained as discoveries of a more complex and secondary conceptual act. And we may want to conclude that the general category does not exist at all in the authentic way in which the particular instance exists. But this is another matter. The point is that if values exist, then they, like colors, appear both in particular and general modes, and have whatever sort of existence and cognitivity are proper to these modes.

6. *Are Values Observable?*

A question which has been thought related to this question whether value is 'simple' is that of whether value is 'observable'. Professor Richard Brandt in his recent *Ethical Theory* takes a view such as that of Moore to 'imply' that value words refer to unobservable properties (pp. 183-4). And Brandt argues that there is no reason to believe there are such properties. But he, like others who think it makes no sense to talk of 'observing' value, does not say what he means by 'observe'. Everything turns on this.

Evidently we ought to understand by 'observable' something more specific than 'knowable'. We ought to mean at least 'knowable directly and not merely by inference'. But by the latter we may understand 'knowable in the form of sensation'. And what is knowable in the form of sensation is itself a sensation. Obviously a value is not a sensation, nor knowable in the way in which sensations — as concrete colors, odors, tastes, etc. — are knowable.

(This is another reason why it was a mistake to analogize value to 'yellow'.) So if we mean by 'observe' 'have a sensation of', then value is not observed.

However we also use 'observe' more widely, as when we say that we can observe the results of experiments, or more specifically, that we can observe degrees of temperature or size, etc. But plainly we do not apprehend these common dimensional characteristics of sensory qualities in just the same way that we apprehend the total sensation to which the characteristic attaches. Likewise with the complementarity of several colors and the harmony of several sounds. Plainly we do not know these in just the way we know the single qualities to which these characteristics attach. It seems best to say that we have a 'sensation' of a particular colored area or duration of sound, but not 'sensations' either of the dimensional characteristics, such as brightness and loudness of the concrete sensory quality, or of relational characteristics such as complementarity and harmony of several such qualities. But it might be appropriate to say that we 'observe' such characteristics. And if we 'observe' these, we might also wish to say that we 'observe' the value of things. One might say, 'Having observed what a good person he was, I decided to seek his friendship'. In any event, the important point is that any evidence that would serve to show that value was unobservable because not known as a sensation would work equally to show that properties which are the common currency of science are likewise unobserved. And if this is so, unobservability is no obstruction to knowledge.

It may appear that there is one difference between the knowledge of a dimensional characteristic of sensation and a value characteristic, namely that the presence of the dimensional characteristic can be inferred as certainly present where the sensation is present, while no such necessary relation holds between the presence of value and any other characteristic or set of characteristics. But this is not so. What can be inferred from the perception or knowledge of the existence of a color is that it will have some *degree* of extensity or size or brightness, etc. We can neither perceive nor necessarily infer its specific degree of extensity. Similarly, there are at least some characteristics knowledge of whose existence allows us certainly to infer the existence of some degree of value or disvalue. If we know that a state contains pleasure, then we can be certain that the state has some degree of goodness or badness — we know that what is pleasant cannot be devoid of value or disvalue.[1] Now it would appear (and at any rate I shall not question) that value differs from a dimensional characteristic such as extensity in that value and disvalue are opposites while largeness and smallness of size are not. However, dimensional characteristics of other sensations do appear to be opposites — for example, hot and cold, sweet and sour, bright and dark; and the principle holds equally of these, that we can certainly infer that in the existence of the sensational characteristic the dimensional feature will be present, while we cannot certainly know what its specific degree will be. This is even more patently true of dimensional characteristics such as harmony and discord, which adhere to several sensations.

Still, it may be urged that we can directly perceive the dimensional characteristic of the sensation, and indeed that we cannot avoid perceiving it; while we cannot directly perceive the value characteristic. But it is far from evident that we can directly perceive the former in a way in which we cannot directly perceive the latter. If one does always, in perceiving a sensation, perceive its dimensional characteristics, then plainly one does not always know that he perceives them; and it could be maintained equally plausibly that he perceives the value characteristic, only he doesn't know he does. In truth, there seems no reason to say we perceive anything in this sort of unconscious way. The fact of the matter is that a perceiver of the sensation is able to become aware of the dimensional characteristic, as is also the perceiver of the pleasure able to become aware of the value characteristic. Perhaps this awareness never occurs except through an act of comparing two sensations or two value carriers, such as pleasure, with respect to the dimensional and value characteristic. (If so, it might be best to call both of these abstract relational characteristics.)

---

[1] The specific argument that pleasure is good comes in Chapter III.

At any rate it is plain that we cannot perceive a specific degree of a sensation's dimensional characteristic except by comparing it with either a standard or with other particular sensations. It is the same with respect to value. We conclude, then, that there is no sort of evidence showing that we perceive such features as size, temperature, harmony, etc., which would not show equally that we perceive value.

Critics have seemed to suppose that value, if observable at all, must be observable *either* as is a sensation *or* in some highly special way going by the name of 'Intuition'. Moore used the term to refer 'merely' to what is 'incapable of proof'; but the term does to most persons suggest something more recondite. However, there is no need to postulate a special faculty for knowing values, any more than a special faculty for knowing such things as the brightness of colors or the harmony of sounds. Value characteristics are not quite like any other characteristics, and are not known in just the same way. But the thing is to see how they are known, not to invent or pick a name for this way.

7. *Is Value Relative?*

We have now before us the central thesis that value is an objective property, and it will be well, before taking up the other features of value, to consider the major misunderstandings and objections to which this thesis has been liable. First, the misunderstandings.

All or almost all of the objections to the objective doctrine which are based on misunderstanding, are sometimes put in the form of the thesis that: 'Values are "relative"'. But this doctrine includes several sub — or variant — doctrines.

The name of Relativism is probably most closely associated with a very common but really absurd doctrine, which I shall call Subjectivism. The view is that the truth of value judgments is relative to the judgment of a particular judge, either a social group or an individual. On this view, for a judge to say a thing is good means that he *thinks* it is good. But this is absurd. For judgments are about objects; they are not about the judge's thought. In order that the judge have a thought, his thought must be about something. And to have a thought of what is good, he must suppose that what is good is not identical with his thought of it. No one who judges that 'X is Y' means by 'Y' his thought of 'Y'. The only thought involved is his thought that 'X is Y'. The absurdity can be put formally as involving an infinite regress. If 'Y' is the thought of 'Y', then this second 'Y' will also be the thought of 'Y', so that the first 'Y' will now be the thought of the thought of 'Y', and so on to infinity.

We may now turn to the more plausible versions of Ethical Relativism. These largely consist of denials of doctrines which may be mistakenly identified with that of the objectivity of values. The chief of these doctrines which are denied I shall call the doctrines of Value Independence and Value Absoluteness. I shall consider first the denial of Value Independence.

This variety of Relativist holds that nothing is good except some state, relation, or quality of men (or of men and animals). Advocates of this view, as Spinoza and Santayana, have seemed to want to put human beings in their place, and to impress on us that this place is nothing special, that 'the universe has no more interest in us' than in other things. Santayana expressed this by saying that the ferocity of the tiger and the placidity of the oyster have no more value or disvalue to the 'universe' than has the rational happiness of man.

But first, it is hard to know what to make of statements which refer to the interests or values of the universe. More important, if the point is that values are satisfactions of interest, this does not show that values cannot be objectively known. They obviously can be known if we can know what satisfies interests. The question whether values will be what satisfies some limited range of interests, as those of men (not animals), or those of particular men, is a further matter. If values exist, then perhaps they only exist where men exist, either as states or qualities or relations to men. And if values can be known, perhaps men are the only knowers of them. (I shall comment on this later.) But this would not tend to show that values are not objective properties.

A quite different doctrine sometimes intended by the 'relativity' of values is the denial of the doctrine of value absoluteness. It holds that value principles (as that 'One ought to keep his promises') are not absolute, universal, or inviolable, but are merely general, and subject to exceptions. I shall later recommend this view. But it does not at all entail a denial that values are objective properties. That the act of keeping a promise is not always right or good does not entail that, when it is right or good, this value characteristic is not an objective property of the act. Any more than the fact that not all oranges are sweet entails that the sweetness, of an orange which is sweet, is not an objective property of the orange.

A similar version of the Relativity doctrine is that the values of particular kinds of things, such as material objects, temporal events, or mental states, are different when the broader situations in which they occur are different. A diamond, or event of violence (human, as a murderous rage, or non-human, as an earthquake), or state of satisfaction, may be good in one situation and bad in another. But again, that this is so does not imply that value is not an objective property. It may indicate only that value is a property of something very complex. Let us call this view about value that of the Situational Relativity of values. I shall also argue that this view is true.

This fact of situational relativity seems to have sometimes been confused with another thing which has also been sometimes intended by the 'relativity of values', and which is actually the chief ground for maintaining that values cannot be known. This is the fact of disagreement in value judgments. It is a fact, and an obvious fact, that people disagree, and disagree with lamentable persistence, in what they think good and bad, right and wrong. It is no doubt often the case that a value disagreement could be removed by a clear and complete delineation of the actual object of the disagreeing judgments. Sometimes an object, act, or feeling is judged differently by observers because they do not describe in the same way the situation of which these things are parts. The objectivist would hope that such complete description might, together with other improvements in apprehension, eventually remove all value disagreements. But in any case it is clear that the two things — the situational relativity of values and value disagreement — are distinct. And it is only the fact of disagreement which opposes the thesis of value objectivity. It opposes this thesis, moreover, not by positively contradicting it, but by constituting negative evidence for which the objectivist must somehow account. The noncognitivist or skeptic will use this fact to argue that there can be no cognitive object which is in dispute among the persons holding divergent judgments, while the cognitivist will argue that the disagreement indicates only that some of the disagreeing judgments are mistaken. We shall consider next this matter of the possibility of mistake in ethical judgment.

8. *Are there Mistakes about Values?*

We are now ready for the more formidable arguments which are offered to show that we cannot know values as objective properties of things in anything like the way that we know other properties. These arguments are briefly that (1) people persistently disagree about values, (2) people do not admit mistakes about values and (3) there is no test for determining mistake and removing disagreement. I believe the first argument is strong. But I shall try to show that the other arguments are weak, and that any strength they seem to show is borrowed from the first argument. Finally, I shall offer a sort of pragmatic argument for the doctrine of the objectivity of value.

A major argument which has been used to show that value is not something which can be known is that people will not recognize mistakes about values as they recognize mistakes about other things. In particular it has been argued that a person will not recognize that he is making a mistake in value at the time that he is making the mistake, while a person will recognize that he is making a mistake about color at the very moment when he is making the mistake. Nowell-Smith writes in his *Ethics*: 'But the one thing I cannot say is ...: "This type of conduct still seems to me to be wrong; but it must really be right, since everyone says so". And this is precisely what the colour-blind man does say in such a case' (p. 59). But if Nowell-Smith means that *no one* would *ever* say 'This type of conduct still seems to me wrong; but it must really be right, since everyone says so', then Nowell-Smith is surely wrong. A person might perfectly well say this, and say it seriously. For he might well believe that his judgment is somehow deficient, and in a way that the judgment of most persons is not. Nowell-Smith goes on to say that a person might admit that he has been mistaken in a past value judgment, and also admit himself 'to be morally blind in a dispositional sense' (i.e. 'recognize a general incapacity to see moral truths until someone else points them out to us') (p. 59). However: 'What we cannot do is admit that our present moral view *is* in fact mistaken. For to admit this would be to abandon the moral view in question. A moral view is, as we shall see, a principle that we adopt, an affirmation that we are prepared to make; and to make an affirmation and at the same time to admit it to be false is a contradiction-in-use like "It's a horse, but I don't believe it is" or "It's a horse but that isn't true"' (p. 60).

Any persuasiveness carried by this argument that color and moral judgments differ in this particular way depends upon an ambiguity in the term 'view', the term being taken in one sense in the case of color judgments and in a different sense in the case of moral judgments. When we speak of a 'view' with reference to color we ordinarily mean by the term a sensation or perception; and it is somewhat odd to say that one has a sensation or perception which 'is mistaken'. Whereas when we speak of a 'view' with reference to morals we ordinarily mean by the term a moral principle; and it is not so odd to say that one holds a general moral principle which there are grounds for believing 'is mistaken'. That 'view' is ordinarily taken in these different ways is fairly obvious. One does not ordinarily speak of his 'color view', but of his 'view of *a* color'; whereas one does ordinarily speak of his 'moral view', and of this as the equivalent of his 'view of morals'. The reason for this is that we are not inclined to think of ourselves as adopting a principle of color judgment, as we are accustomed to think of ourselves as adopting a principle of moral judgment. Thus, if one were to say that his 'view of a color' were mistaken, the person might seem to be saying that the particular *sensation* he is having is not the sensation he is having. However, he might explain his statement so that it makes sense. He would do so if he said that his present perception of the color of an object does not give an accurate report of the color which he has reason to believe the object has. Plainly a person may have reason to think that his present perception of a color 'is mistaken'; no less than he may have reason to think that his perception of what is morally right in some situation 'is mistaken'. Further, a person may have reason to think that his general mode of color apprehension leads him to make mistakes in color perception; just as a person can have reason to think that his general mode of moral apprehension leads him to make mistakes in moral perception. Of a person's elementary color perceptual apprehension or 'view', as of his elementary value apprehension or 'view', he can say that this color or moral view 'is' mistaken. Further he can say that he will adopt as a principle of behavior a different color or moral 'view'. The color-blind person may say, 'I still see the two colors as the same, but everyone else says they are different, so I suppose I must be wrong'. Similarly a person with unconventional moral views may say, 'I can't see the difference between a white lie and a black lie (or perhaps, between sexual intercourse within marriage and outside marriage), but everyone else says there is a difference, so I suppose I must be wrong'.

The difficulty here is aggravated by a failure to notice another distinction, between 'is mistaken' and 'must be mistaken'. There is an oddness in saying (for both colors and values) that 'My view, in the sense of a principle I adopt, *is* mistaken'. But there is no oddness in saying, 'My view, in the sense of a principle which I hold, *must be* mistaken'. To say that 'A principle which I hold *is* mistaken is in effect to say that 'I refuse to hold this principle'. But to say that 'A principle I hold *must be* mistaken', is just to say: 'There appear to be strong reasons for thinking that I ought to abandon the principle'. A person can say quite consistently that a principle which he holds 'must be' mistaken; what he means is that he has held the principle but is considering abandoning it. Here again the cases of color and value run parallel. A color-blind person who has used his own perceptions as his principle for describing colors of things, and who then discovers the peculiarity of his judgments, might say that his principle 'must be mistaken'. And when he had definitely decided to change his principle, he would say, not that his principle 'is' mistaken, but that he has given up his old mistaken principle. One who discovered a peculiarity in his value principle might do the same.

The 'is' form, somewhat curiously, suggests greater certainty, and is based on a different kind of evidence, than the 'must be' form. To say that a thing 'is' such and such is to suggest either that its knowledge is of the most direct and unquestionable sort, or that its evidence is of such a reliable sort that doubt would be extraordinary. On the other hand, to say that a thing 'must be' such and such is to suggest that doubt has arisen or might arise, and that there is indirect evidence adequate to allay this doubt. The way we ordinarily talk is to say that a thing 'is'; this form is not adopted however when this direct knowledge is lacking. The 'must be' form is adopted when there is indirect evidence that the thing 'is'. Thus it would not naturally occur to a person to say that a thing's color 'is' brown, when the sensible apprehension through which he directly knows color reveals the color of the thing as red. But it would be natural for the person, in the light of the indirect evidence of other people's testimony, to say that the thing's color 'must be' brown. Likewise a person can admit that he 'must be' mistaken about his moral view. For example, suppose that a person held the unorthodox moral view that monogamous marriage is wrong; that he arrived at this view through his own experience and general inquiry; and that he held that this view, despite its unorthodoxy, was quite certainly true. Suppose now, as a result of psychoanalysis, he discovers that certain unconscious desires influenced the formation of this moral view.

Such a person might at one stage admit that he might be mistaken and at a later stage admit that he must be mistaken.

It would be unrealistic and over-formal to assert that as soon as the person admits that his moral view must be mistaken, he no longer holds that moral view. It would be to overlook the complexity of moral belief and degrees of moral assent. Borderline cases abound in the holding of moral views. Probably at any given time and for any given person there are some moral principles which he rejects or holds with an extreme simplicity and definiteness. There may be a moral principle which the person thinks plainly *is* mistaken, and another moral principle which the person thinks plainly *is not* mistaken. But towards other moral principles he may have all degrees of doubt and certainty. And about one such principle the person may admit that he 'must be' mistaken in adhering to it, while yet he does not take the decisive step of giving it up. This is a particular kind of moral conflict. It is a conflict not merely between different values, one or more of which the person must decide to sacrifice, nor merely between an intellectual moral belief and a contrary behavioral disposition or habit, but between contrary bodies of evidence as to right moral belief. Faced with this conflict the person may experience the serious moral doubt which takes the form of his thinking that his moral view 'must be' mistaken, while yet he is not so absolutely certain that his view is mistaken as to let it go. Similarly an observer may think he sees at some distance a flying saucer, yet think that he 'must be' mistaken, yet still not be absolutely certain that he is mistaken.

It is true that people more readily admit mistakes about colors than about values. People disagree about colors, but they do not persist in disagreement. However it is not at once clear what this shows.

A part of this admission and agreement may be verbal. We can see why persons who do not actually know that they have made a mistake, and who have made no improvement in knowledge, may be willing to admit a mistake about color when they would not admit a mistake about values. To admit any mistake is somewhat humiliating. It is the more humiliating, the more serious the mistake ; and mistakes about moral principles are the most serious. Vanity suffers in admitting a defective ability to perceive colors. But a person's pride is identified very much more strongly with his moral principles. Further, to change moral principles and conduct is harder than to make the practical adjustments required by an acceptance of the normal distinctions of color. Thus there are emotional sources of resistance to the admission of moral mistakes which are not present in the admission of color mistakes. Accordingly the greater reluctance to admit a moral mistake may indicate only the operation of these emotional factors, and not a difference in the corrigibility of the two sorts of knowledge.

Evidently a person's change of his color judgment could constitute a change in his knowledge of color only if it occurred in one of two ways : (1) if it were a change in his color perceptions as a result of a change in his visual capacities, either through a removal of his color-blindness or through a change of the environmental circumstances, as his point of view or the illumination. Or (2) if the person came to recognize a mistake not through a different visual perception but through making certain inferences. This is in fact the way that we think of a color-blind person as concluding that he is mistaken. We suppose that he reasons somewhat as follows : '(1) There is evidence that capacities for discriminating sense qualities do differ among persons, for I myself have found that my capacities for discriminating certain qualities, as differences in pitch and timbre, have grown in acuteness ; (2) there is also evidence that sense qualities generally are correlated in uniform ways with physical events perceptible by vision, as the different sound-qualities are produced by different instruments ; and in particular, qualities of color which I can perceive are roughly correlated with a certain range of recorded wave lengths ; (3) there are more distinctions of wave lengths than I can observe colors, while other persons can uniformly assign names to different colors which are uniformly correlated with these smaller differences of wave length ; (4) hence it must be that these persons are perceiving colors which do exist but which my cruder sensibility cannot detect'.

Now we should not hesitate to call the result of such reasoning based upon such experience, genuine knowledge. We would call it not perceptual but rational knowledge. But it is rather peculiar. For it is knowledge about perception which is obtained by reasoning and which cannot be verified in perception (that is, in the perception of the person for whom it is knowledge). The case is not like inferring that a deer exists because there are deer tracks, for the person could perceive a deer; nor is it like inferring that a God exists from the signs of his work, for no person can perceive God. One of the curious features of this knowledge is that it depends on the perceptual knowledge of someone else. The color-blind person can know by inference that a particular color exists only on the assumption that other persons know this color in direct perception. His inferential knowledge assumes that some persons have capacities for knowing which he does not have, and that consequently such persons can know things, or know them in a way, which he cannot.

One might be inclined to say that what he knows is not that the particular color in question exists, rather what he knows is that other persons know that it exists. And knowing that someone else knows a thing is not the same as knowing it. Knowing that someone knows the principles of organic chemistry is not the same as knowing these principles. Nor is knowing that someone knows that opium exists like knowing on the basis of one's own experience that opium exists. The difference plainly is that in knowing in this way that a thing exists one does not quite know what it is that exists. The person who has not experienced opium may know that it exists, but does not know what it is (though he may know many things about it — many of its causes and effects, etc.). Likewise the color-blind person who knows that a particular shade of color exists still does not know what that color which exists, is. Let us call this a sort of knowledge, but let us be clear as to what sort of knowledge it is and is not.

Then, we are less impressed by the docility of the color-blind person who talks like the rest of us. This does not mean that he knows like the rest of us. Nor are his mistakes in knowledge so corrigible as they have been represented. But granting that they are perfectly corrigible there is nothing to indicate that the corrigibility in color judgments is more genuine or complete than the admission of mistake in moral judgments.

However, Mr. Toulmin has argued that the way in which explanation leads a person to change his judgment is radically different in the case of judgments of color and value. Toulmin says that scientific explanation differs from ethical explanation in that the scientific explanation cannot change the experience it explains, while the ethical explanation can change this experience. He writes : 'The sun still looks red at sunset, although we know that it is not really red ; physics may explain why a stick looks bent, when it is really straight, but it cannot stop the stick looking bent. . . . The relation between a "moral experience" and the corresponding ethical judgment is different. The schoolboy who discovers that he has been given his colors as a result of favoritism and not merit, no longer gets the same satisfaction out of them . . . the soldier who discovers that his superior officer is using him to feather his own nest, no longer feels it his invariable duty to obey him. An ethical argument — in answer to the question, "Is this *really* good (right, obligatory) ? " — may, that is to say, change the corresponding experiences (our feelings of satisfaction or of obligation)' (p. 127).

There is truth in this, but it does not show the difference that Toulmin asserts. Let us try to give a more detailed statement of Toulmin's view here. In the moral case what happens is that (1) the person first judges that an act is right ; then (2) discovers new features of the act ; then as a result of (2), (3) changes his mind and now judges the act not right ; then (4) as a result of (3) feels differently about the act, which he now judges differently. Thus if we mean by his 'experience' of the act what occurs in (4), then his 'experience' is different. But now what about the case of the red sunset ? The person (1) judges it red ; then (2) is provided with new facts about it ; and as a result of (2),

D

(3) judges it not red; but (4) continues to 'experience' it as at first, namely red. The two accounts are parallel except in the fourth stage. But what is obvious is that the notion of 'experience' is construed quite differently in the two cases. By 'experience' in the color case we mean simply the perception of the feature being judged; while by 'experience' in the moral case is meant the feelings about the feature being judged. In both cases the judgment changes. But in only one case, according to Toulmin, do the feelings change. But this is not true. It may happen that, as a result of one's judgment that the sunset is not really red, one no longer feels the same about the sunset — it may no longer give one the same satisfaction or thrill, it may no longer seem beautiful or glorious, like a fire kindled by a god. Also, it may happen that, despite the changed moral judgment, one continues to feel the same about an act or event. The soldier may still feel that it is his duty to obey the officer, even though he knows it is not his duty — just as the person may still 'feel' the sunset is red even though he knows it is not really red. Both may admit that their previous judgments were wrong, and assert that they now 'know' that the sunset is not really red or the act really obligatory, though their feelings conflict with the judgment.

There is this difference in the two cases : the scientific explanation, if it is rightly formulated, is seen not to bear at all on the perceptual sensation which is simply had. The explanation does not propose to correct this perception. It is not like the sort of reasoning which leads a color-blind person to admit mistake in his color judgment. Here too the person, while changing his judgment as a result of the explanation, would not change his experience. But his inability to change is recognized as a defect, and as making an incompleteness in his knowledge. While his failure to change his experience of the sunset, when he obtains new knowledge about it, marks no deficiency in his mode of perception or any incompleteness in his knowledge. It is different in the ethical case. The ethical explanation does bear on the apprehension of the ethical feature, which is right; and the explanation proposes to correct this appre-

hension. Thus the explanations do have different effects
in the two cases.

But that is because they are two quite different sorts of
explanation. The scientific account does not point out an
error in our previous or usual mode of apprehension, but
rather provides certain additional information about the
thing apprehended which explains how this apprehension
arises and what different apprehension we would have
under different conditions ; while the ethical account does
not explain the source of our apprehension, rather it brings
out an error in this apprehension based on ignorance of
relevant features of the thing apprehended.

The difference between the two sorts of explanation can
be brought out in this way. The scientific account relates
to the natural perception as (not an ethical, but——) a
psychological account relates to the unreflective ethical
apprehension. A psychologist might explain how we
arrived at this apprehension, but this would not necessarily bear on its correctness ; just as the physicists' and
physiologists' account of our natural perception of color
explains its causes but need not bear on its correctness.
And the correlate to an ethical explanation which corrects a
value apprehension would be, in the case of color perception, not a physical but an epistemological explanation.
But such an explanation of the perception of the sunset
would show us that there is nothing here to correct.

The cause of the apparent difference which Toulmin
finds is that in the case of colors he is contrasting a scientific
account with a natural apprehension, while in the value
case he is contrasting a philosophical account with a natural
apprehension. These two sorts of account relate in entirely
different ways to our primary apprehension. There is no
discrepancy in the fact that the scientific explanation does
not change our perception of color, or that the ethical explanation does change our perception of value.

This difference also is explained by the fact that the
'simplicity' of color is not at all like the ultimacy of value.
We cannot 'explain' a thing's color by analyzing its perceptual parts or elements, for it has none — it is itself
elementary. But a value, in at least most varieties, is not

similarly elementary. It belongs, at least often, to a complex occasion, and we explain it, as in the case of the soldier's duty, by analyzing the elements of the occasion. However there is a variety of value which is somewhat like the sunset's color, namely that of pleasure. Suppose a person experienced a pleasure in the exchange of affection with a particular person and perceived it as of a particular value. Now suppose particular elements of the value occasion were brought to his notice such that he then *judged* the pleasure bad. He might still continue to engage in this pleasure and 'experience' it as good, even while judging it bad, just as the person continues to 'experience' the sunset as red, even while judging it not red. Both cases involve a similar error, namely a failure to distinguish two quite distinct objects of judgment. The perceiver of the sunset should not judge that the sunset is not red; he should only judge that other elements involved in the occasion of the color are not this same color. Likewise the perceiver of value should not judge that the pleasure is not good, but that other elements involved in the occasion of the pleasure are not good.

When an absolutely elementary object of knowledge is involved, such as color and pleasure, then it is true that *knowledge* of these is not the most direct or effective way to change our perception of them, though knowledge may readily change associated feelings about them or our 'experience' of them. The direct way our 'experience' of these simple elements can be changed is through a change in our own experiential ('perceptual') capacities. To change our perception of the sunset's color we can change our visual powers, and to change our perception of the immediate value of a pleasure we can change our modes of pleasure response.

Still, mere knowledge can also change these perceptions. Psychological experiments show how our preconceptions of what colors objects 'ought' to be (that is, what colors are usual or standard) can lead us to perceive objects as of these colors when they are in fact not in these cases so colored. Similarly our preconception that a particular pleasure is 'bad' can lead us to perceive it as bad. This

knowledge can influence our perceptions of the most
elementary contents both in the case of color and value.
But in both cases when it does so it leads us, not to correct
our mistakes, but to make them. That this is so I cannot
fully support here, for I cannot in a treatise on ethics
consider in detail our knowledge of sensory properties.
But I shall, in the chapter on Pleasure, try to show that we
do perceive value in our experiences of pleasure, and that
later supposed corrections of these elementary judgments
are a result of confusing the value of the pleasure with the
value of something else associated with it.

We have then, I think, shown that people do acknowledge mistakes about value, and acknowledge the correction
of mistakes, in ways not basically different from the ways
in which they recognize and correct mistakes in other
matters, such as judgments of color. This is not to assert
that our apprehensions of value are quite like our apprehensions of other things. The crucial question is whether these
apprehensions are so different as to force us to conclude
that the apprehensions in which we grasp other things can
provide knowledge while our mode of apprehending value
cannot. So far we have encountered no such radical
difference. It remains to consider other aspects of our
value apprehensions which might be held to constitute such
a difference. We shall first consider an interpretation of
value judgments and value mistakes which would show this
difference to be radical; then we shall consider what I
believe to be the strongest objection to the view that values
can be known, namely that for the correction of value
mistakes we lack a decisive test.

9. *Is there Contradiction in Ethical Judgments?*

Toulmin gives an account of the change of value judgment, and the admission of mistake, according to which
the change and admission do not involve our perceiving
any value property at all, but involve only our reasons for
the judgment. Toulmin agrees that value judgments may
contradict each other (and are in this sense cognitive), but
he asserts that the contradiction concerns not the predica-
tion of a value property of the thing judged but rather the

reasons for the conflicting judgments. 'Suppose that one man says "O is X" and the other says "O is not X". If "X" is a word for a property, say "red", we may say that one man is attributing to the object the property of redness and that the other is withholding it. . . . Now let "X" be "right"; we may again say that, since there is a real contradiction, one must be attributing to the object the same predicate that the other is withholding. . . . However . . . "Rightness" is not a property; and when I asked the two people which course of action was the right one I was not asking them about a property — what I wanted to know was whether there was any reason for choosing one course of action rather than another; and provided they are arguing about the reasons for my doing different things, we are perfectly justified in talking of a genuine contradiction between "N is right" and "No, not N, but M". The idea . . . that, if one man attributes the predicate "X" to anything and another withholds it, they cannot be contradicting one another unless "X" stands at least for a *property*, is a fallacy. All that two people need (and all that they have) to contradict one another about in the case of ethical predicates are the *reasons* for doing this rather than that' (pp. 27-8).

This view that the contradiction resides not in the conclusion, but in the reasons, leaves scope for two or three sorts of contradiction: (1) in the truth of these reasons, or (2) in the force of these reasons as establishing the conclusion, or possibly (3) in whether there are any reasons. Toulmin does not say in which of these the contradiction resides. But none would be adequate to account for our actual contradictions. First, in order for a premiss to be a reason it must be such that when it is true, and the inference valid, the conclusion is true. Where there are reasons, then there must be true or false conclusions. But any conclusion which is true or false can be contradicted. Thus if there can be any kind of contradiction about ethical reasons, there must also be contradiction about ethical conclusions. Thus ethical contradiction could not be reduced to contradiction about ethical reasons.

Further, it is obvious that we would not be interested

in ethical reasons if we were not interested in ethical conclusions, and it would never strike us that we were contradicting each other in our reasons if we did not think we
were contradicting each other in our conclusions. The fact
is that we can contradict each other in our ethical judgments
without offering any reasons. Moreover, it is usually only
after we have contradicted each other in this way that we
begin to look for reasons. And we look for these reasons
only on the supposition that we are in contradiction, and
in the hope of resolving the contradiction. Thus what is
in fact central to ethical contradiction is a contradiction in
the conclusions, not in the reasons. And if reasons for
ethical conclusions are true or false in virtue of predicating
properties of things, it may also be that ethical conclusions
likewise are true or false in virtue of predicating the value
properties of right or good of their objects.

It would seem to be the complexity of the occasion of
value which has led Toulmin to his special account. This
complexity is such that there are good-making characteristics of things and events which are more elementary for
knowledge than the goodness which they 'make'. Thus we
might be inclined to say that reference to these characteristics are only reasons on the basis of which we conclude that
a thing is good, rather than its value being itself a further
attribute. But this is a mistake. The criteria for saying
that a thing is of a given sort are not merely reasons for
a conclusion; they are reasons for believing that another
perhaps more complex property is present. Compare the
relation of symptoms of a disease to the disease. The
patient's symptoms are reasons for diagnosing his disease
as of a given sort, but these symptoms are not the only
properties which are attributed to the patient. We can also
believe that he has the disease ; and this is not just the same
as believing that he has symptoms of the disease. Similarly, to believe that a thing has certain properties which
tend to show, or even conclusively show, that it is of value,
is not the same as to believe that it is of value. For we can
believe this without having deduced it from these reasons,
and we can believe these reasons while we remain unwilling
to believe that the thing is good. Nor can this be explained

by the reasons in such a case being not good enough — not being conclusive. For reasons in ethics, as symptoms of a disease, are as such never conclusive; they do not necessarily entail the conclusion, in the way that the premises in a mathematical argument entail a conclusion.

10. *Is there a Test for Values?*

Let us now consider the objection that value is not an objective property because, though persons do admit mistake in value judgment, the admission has no adequate basis, for there is no general test of the truth of the judgment.

We find that this point reduces to the old fact of disagreement. A person may have what he regards as a decisive test of a value judgment. For example, he may have a private oracle. But those who will not agree with him in his value judgment will probably likewise not agree with him as to his test. And ordinarily we count a test as a test only if it is generally agreed to be such. A test enables us to increase our knowledge of a thing, both in respect of our certainty about its identity and in respect of its specific properties; but the providing of certainty is the primary feature. A test is used not chiefly to extend our knowledge, but to pin it down. The virtue of the test is that it substitutes for judgments which we count doubtful, judgments which we count certain, or more certain. But a primary source of doubt is disagreement among observers; so that a test which will remove doubt must remove disagreement. Obviously the test can do this only if the observers agree that the proposed test is a genuine test. Thus, again, the crucial matter is that of agreement. It is not that the disagreement comes from our having no test, so much as our having no test comes from our disagreement.

It comes back then to this. The position of the non-objectivist is: Where people cannot agree more than they do in value judgments, there can be no object of knowledge. The position of the objectivist is: Where there are admissions of mistakes there must be a possible object of knowledge. How shall we decide which of these features to take as our final mark of whether a thing can be known —

the presence of uniform tests and ultimate agreement or the presence of a belief in the possibility of mistake ? In other sorts of alleged knowledge this choice does not confront us, for where there are judgments that we think possibly mistaken there are also means by which we can agree on the actuality of mistake. Only in ethical judgments do we find ourselves thinking both that some of them must be mistaken but also that we cannot establish or get agreement that they are such. In science we can either agree as to what is the case, or agree as to how we could settle the question, while in value judgment we often disagree and cannot agree on a test by which to remove the disagreement. Hence we are forced to decide. Shall we say that value judgments are not claims to knowledge, since we cannot get agreement on them ; or that they are claims to knowledge, since we think they are sometimes mistaken ?

Perhaps we need not decide ? We might treat values as a borderline case, and say that in one respect value judgments are like claims to knowledge, while in another respect they are not. But there is a decision to make, namely whether we shall try to get more agreement in our value judgments. All value theorists seem to agree in this value judgment, that it would be generally good to have more agreement in value judgments. Well, if we think values are knowable, we will have more hope of getting agreement, and make more effort to get agreement, than if we think they are not. And we will be more likely to get agreement if we try to get it. There is then a pragmatic advantage in adopting the objectivist hypothesis. By trying in the concrete to obtain the agreement which would prove the hypothesis true, we are most likely to succeed in proving this. And if we do not succeed, still we will have obtained more of an end universally recognized as desirable than if we assumed that the cognitivist hypothesis were either false or unverifiable.

11. *Is Value Intrinsic?*

Let us now consider whether we are able to describe further features of value, and in particular those, with which Moore has been much concerned, of being 'intrinsic' and 'non-natural'. Moore thought that the question whether value is intrinsic is crucial, and indeed that when people speak of the objectivity of value what they really have in mind is that value is intrinsic. However, he seems to regard this feature as something unnecessarily special and complex.

By 'intrinsic' Moore meant 'depends solely on the intrinsic nature of the thing in question', so that 'it is *impossible* for what is strictly *one and the same* thing to possess that kind of value at one time, or in one set of circumstances, and *not* to possess it at another' (*Philosophical Studies*, p. 260). This necessity is not causal, but *a priori*. In the case of subjective predicates such as feelings (which of course are not 'intrinsic'), Moore says that it is conceivable that there might be causal laws necessarily connecting a value, such as beauty, with a particular kind of feeling. However, the principle of intrinsic value does not assert this kind of causal necessity. For the causal necessity would hold only in a universe with stable causal laws, while the above necessity would hold in any universe with causal laws of any kind. This sort of *a priori*, non-causal, necessity is not peculiar to values; it applies equally to yellow or to a content of pleasure. 'Suppose you take a particular patch of colour, which is yellow. We can, I think, say with certainty that any patch exactly like that one, *would* be yellow, even if it existed in a universe in which causal laws were quite different from what they are in this one' (pp. 268-9).

But it is not at all clear just what this 'necessity' or 'intrinsicality' are, and Moore repeatedly admitted as much. Moore, however, thought the necessity was not purely logical; while, if we exclude causal necessity, it is hard to see what kind of necessity other than purely logical is left. When he says that any patch of yellow, exactly like another patch of yellow, would be yellow even in a universe with different causal laws, the question is what is meant by the 'patch of yellow'? There are two possibilities. It could mean a patch of some material which was yellow; but the yellowness of a material will certainly

depend upon the causal laws affecting that material. Or it
could mean just an expanse of yellow color, considered
merely in its character as colored and in no other way.
But on this interpretation the necessity is logical. It is true
by definition that one expanse of yellow color which is
exactly the same (except numerically) as another expanse
of yellow color will be of the same color. To say that one
thing is the same as another (except numerically) is to say
that any feature (except number) which one has the other
also has. Thus to say two color expanses are the same
(except in number) is to say that they have the same
features, including the feature of specific color. This sort
of necessity is just the necessity of the entailments of our
concept of 'same, except in number', and it applies to
everything of which we use this concept and not in a
special way to value or color or pleasure. If the 'intrinsic'
character of value thus consists just in the application of
this principle to value, then there is nothing at all special
about value's being an intrinsic character.

Further, the force of this point that value is 'intrinsic'
and that the sameness concept is applicable to it, is just
that value is objective. The point of Moore's principle —
that 'it is impossible for what is strictly one and the
same thing to possess that kind of value at one time, or in
one set of circumstances, and *not* to possess it at another' —
is that a value is such that it really does belong to a certain thing, or to a certain set of characteristics, and consequently that if anyone rightly judges that this thing has this
value then this judgment will be binding for all persons
and all time.

There are other senses of 'intrinsic' which we should
consider. But first we must examine here the trait of value
Moore called its 'non-naturalness'. Both the 'intrinsicality' and the 'non-naturalness' of value concern the
relation of the value characteristic of a thing to its other
characteristics.

It is evident that only certain of the characteristics of a
good thing are relevant to its goodness. For example, if it
is a good act to give $1.00 to charity, the giving of this
money in cash or check, or handing it over with the left

hand or the right hand, would not usually affect the act's goodness. While its goodness would usually be affected by its being for $100.00 rather than for $1.00 and by its being handed over at an early rather than a later date. Let us call these relevant characteristics 'good-making characteristics'. The questions are (1) how are they related to the characteristic of goodness, and (2) how are the good-making characteristics and the characteristic of goodness related to the thing to which they belong.

Let us first deal with the second question. As to the difference between these two sorts of characteristics, Moore calls the characteristic of being good 'non-natural', in contrast, for example, to 'yellow' or 'pleasant', which are 'natural' characteristics. A natural characteristic of a thing is one which a complete description of it must mention or which is entailed by the characteristics which are mentioned.[1] A non-natural characteristic is one that need not be mentioned in a complete description. Let us say, then, that a non-natural value characteristic is not descriptive, while the natural characteristic is descriptive. The two kinds of characteristics are related to each other in that the value characteristic is 'dependent' on or 'derivative' from certain natural characteristics '. . . in the sense that, if a thing is good . . . then that it is so *follows* from the fact that is possesses certain natural intrinsic properties, which are such that from the fact that it is good it does not follow that it has those properties'.[2] However, Moore found these notions very puzzling both when he first wrote about them in 1917 and when he later reconsidered them in 1942. He was naturally puzzled by value's being 'intrinsic' and 'dependent on the intrinsic nature of a thing' while yet not 'descriptive' of this thing. Indeed he found this so puzzling that in his first version he said that value was 'intrinsic' but not an 'intrinsic property'; later he thought this expression awkward and chose to say just that value was an intrinsic property but a non-natural one. In both cases he explained the difference between the two sorts of properties by saying that the value property was not de-

---

[1] *The Philosophy of G. E. Moore*, ed. P. A. Schilpp, p. 587.
[2] *Op. cit.* p. 588.

scriptive, and in both cases he confessed that the account was 'vague and not clear', for he could not 'specify the sense of describe in question'. However he thought the value property to be of an importantly different kind from the natural properties, and that a solution of this difference was to be found in the different way in which, in one sense, we use the word 'description'.

But in any ordinary sense of the word 'description', a complete description would have to mention or imply the thing's value. We do continually mention value terms in describing things — whether persons or material objects, events, or states of things. Further if a person does describe a thing and fails to mention its value, we may specifically request an account of its value. Consider our purpose in describing. This purpose surely is to provide knowledge of the thing described. And we would not think a person could know the nature of, say, an artwork such as Renoir's *Bathers*, or of an individual such as Lincoln, or a state such as pleasure, or a commodity such as steel, while knowing nothing of its value. Whatever else a 'complete description' or 'complete knowledge' would include, it would include this. We might think of a description in a narrower way, namely as providing just sufficient information to enable us to identify the thing. Then of course a complete description would not have to mention the thing's value, but neither would it have to mention all of its natural properties. It may be this sense of description which misled Moore.

We can return now to the concept of 'intrinsic value'. The term 'intrinsic' here may suggest two sorts of notion, both of which cause confusion. (1) One is the notion of 'essential'. But in fact value is not essential to any kind of substance. (2) The other is the notion of a *kind* of value : 'intrinsic' as opposed to 'extrinsic'. But neither can 'intrinsic' designate one kind of value among other kinds. I shall take up these two senses of 'intrinsic' in turn, and then the concept of (3) good of a kind.

(1) The most common sense of 'intrinsic' would seem to be that in which it is roughly equivalent with 'essential'. Moore suggests this in using 'intrinsic' in the phrase

'intrinsic nature', explaining an 'intrinsic property' as one which 'depends solely on the intrinsic nature of the thing'. Indeed the concepts of 'intrinsic' and 'nature' seem to entail each other, as do the concepts of 'essential' and 'nature'. Also, the concept of 'essential' in respect of a thing's nature entails the concept of 'unessential'. It makes no sense to speak of attributes which are 'essential' to a thing's 'nature' unless we think this thing has some attributes which are unessential. Finally, we apply these concepts primarily to (a) concrete substances (b) which are members of a kind, in virtue of which the thing's nature, and the attributes essential and unessential to this nature, are defined. We do not speak of the 'nature' of an attribute, relation, event, or of an individual substance which does not share a nature with other substances.

Thus to say that value is an 'intrinsic property' is to suggest that it is a property of a kind of substance. But value does not seem to belong only to substances, and it has been disputed that value belongs to substances at all.

On reflection, it seems very doubtful whether value is a property of at least any very large number of the material substances which none the less we do unreflectively describe in value terms. Indeed a bit of reflection leads us to conclude that either no material objects are good or bad in the genuine sense, or at any rate that only perhaps two classes are, namely persons and aesthetic objects. And we may go on to exclude even these. We may conclude that only states of persons or complex events including persons have value. (This will be discussed in Section 13 of this chapter.) But even if value is felt to belong to a concrete individual substance, it seems to belong to it not in virtue of its being a general kind of substance, but rather in virtue of the particular set of attributes which it happens to combine.

However, a thing conceived as merely particular cannot have intrinsic or essential attributes, for we distinguish essential from unessential by the concept of the general class to which a thing belongs. But in fact there are no kinds of natural substances to which value is essential, as there are kinds of things to which other attributes are essential. There are no kinds of substances about which

our decision whether to call it a thing of this kind would
depend on our deciding whether the thing had value (or
value in a certain degree), as our decision whether to call
a thing a member of a kind — say a man or a fish or a
living organism — would depend on our deciding whether
it had some other attribute in a certain degree.

There are concepts which entail the concept of value,
and we might say that to these classes of things value is
'essential'. We would call a thing a 'virtue', or a specific
sort of virtue such as 'courage', only if it had value (or
value in a certain degree); and there are other terms, such
as 'pleasure', about which there is still dispute as to whether
the concept entails value. But value is not an attribute
essential to any kinds of things which are concrete substances. Value is 'essential' to the concept of these attributes or states of substances (as virtue or pleasure), but
not to the concept of the substances to which they belong.
For these substances can exist without these valuable attributes or states. It follows that, since these attributes and
states cannot exist apart from the substances to which they
belong (while these substances can exist without these
valuable attributes and states); and supposing nothing
exists which is not a particular substance; value would
not be 'essential' to anything which exists. But of course
value may still exist, as belonging to a *particular* event or
substance which is characterized by one of these general
attributes such as virtue or pleasure.

It is true that we do sometimes refer to certain attributes
as 'essential' to a particular individual. But this, like the
use of 'essential' with reference to qualities, relations and
states, is an extended use. What comes to mind by 'essential to the nature of the thing in question' is 'essential to
the thing in question as a member of a kind'. And so far
as 'intrinsic' suggests 'essential', the notion of 'intrinsic
value' is misleading, for it suggests that value is intrinsic
to certain general natures.

(2) In its standard ethical use, however, the expression
'intrinsic' is opposed, not to 'unessential', but to 'extrinsic'. But in this sense also the term encourages confusion.
'Extrinsic value' is used in a way in which it must mean

conduciveness to — that is, being a cause of — something which is or may be of intrinsic value, or to something which is also of extrinsic value. The distinction between 'is' and 'may be' (and between 'sometimes', 'often' or 'always') is important, as is also the distinction between being extrinsically valuable as a direct means to a thing of intrinsic value and being so as a means to another thing of merely extrinsic value (and hence being only indirectly a means to a thing of intrinsic value). The same sort of material object is conceived as being able to function in all of these sorts of ways. For example, bread may be thought of as something which is usually a cause of value, while guns are less often a cause of value. And bread may be thought of as something which is a cause of health, which is conceived as itself of extrinsic value, or of pleasure, which is conceived as of intrinsic value. Whenever we speak of bread or guns as 'good', either in general or in particular cases, it is 'extrinsically good' which is meant.

The phrase, however, as also the correlative expression 'intrinsically good', is misleading. For 'extrinsic' and 'intrinsic' suggest two parallel classes of a single genus, while in fact the first term stands generally for something which is a cause of the second.

It is true that a thing which is a cause of good may also be itself good. For example a pleasure may be itself good, and may cause another pleasure. Likewise a virtue might be conceived to be good both intrinsically and as a cause of other good things, such as pleasure or virtue. But we do not call things 'extrinsically good' in so far as they both are causes of good and are good intrinsically, and it would not be appropriate to do so. We had best use the phrase to mean simply 'cause of good', and try not to let it confuse us. I shall henceforth use it in this sense. I shall also have to make use of the expression 'intrinsic value', but it is to be remembered that it is used only in order to make explicit that what is being considered is not 'extrinsic value'.

Other expressions synonymous with 'extrinsic value' do approximate explicitness about the causal relation to value indicated by the term 'extrinsic value'. These are the expressions 'instrumental value' and 'of value as a means' (or 'good as a means' by contrast to 'good as an end' or 'good for its own sake'). These expressions, however, are misleading in another way. For to call a thing an instrument or means is to suggest that we can control it to cause value, while we do want to call things extrinsically or instrumentally good which we cannot control, for example a shower or a day of sunshine. Here then is another division among things extrinsically valuable.

To summarize: things which are 'extrinsically valuable' or of 'extrinsic value' (that is, causes of value) may be: (1) 'direct' or 'indirect'; (2) 'usual' or 'occasional'; (3) 'simple' or 'complex' (complex in being of value as well as causing value); (4) 'instrumental' or 'uncontrollable'.

The concept of 'extrinsic value' may be confused with another important practical concept, namely the concept of a 'good of a kind'. This likewise is a slippery notion. For a thing which is a good instance of a kind might seldom be good at all, as, for example, a 'good lie' or a 'good robbery'. The thing so described may belong to a class which is generally bad, both extrinsically and intrinsically, and may be itself bad in one or both of these ways. What we mean by the expression 'good of a kind' is something that could be rendered entirely without any use of value terms, namely by 'paradigm case' or 'having all or most of the features, and in a high degree, of a kind'. We might thus describe a person as a 'good gambler' or 'good duellist' even though we thought gambling generally was neither itself good nor a cause of good.

The explanation for our use of good in this dispensable and even perverse way would seem to be the following. Almost any class of thing will on some occasion be of use as a cause of something good. This is so even of things which are of the worst sort — lies, robberies, murders. On some occasion one of these things will be extrinsically good. Second, when such a thing is of use, the thing which will be most of use ('best to use') will be the thing which is a model instance of its kind, an instance which is the best of its kind. If good can be served by telling a lie, then quite probably good may be best served by telling the best lie.

E

Thus it may be that we call any model instance a 'good of a kind' because any kind of thing may be extrinsically good, and usually the instance of most extrinsic good is the most perfect instance of the kind. The notion of 'good of a kind' would thus depend on the notion of extrinsic good, and in particular of instrumental good. That this is so is evidenced by the fact that we do not call things good of a kind when the kinds of which the things are members are regarded as intrinsically good. We would not speak of a 'good act of virtue' or 'good act of courage' or of a 'good saint'. And if we speak of a 'good pleasure' this suggests that we do not think of the pleasure as something which is itself good.

To sum up this section. In Moore's notions of the 'intrinsicality' and 'non-naturalness' of value we have been able to retain as defensible only the principle that value is objective. And we have seen that other senses of 'intrinsic value' are misleading, one in suggesting that value may be an 'essential' property of a kind of thing, the other in suggesting that there are two parallel classes of value, 'intrinsic' and 'extrinsic'. This last sense of 'intrinsic' is, if not the least misleading, at any rate the least dispensable. We need a term which will convey, as does 'extrinsic' value, 'cause of value'; and, because we ordinarily and often speak of 'value' loosely to mean just 'cause of value', we also need a term which will make explicit, as does the expression 'intrinsic value', that the value under consideration is value itself and not its cause. We shall, then, with this warning, continue to use the expressions with these meanings.

12. *The Situational Relativity of Value*

Our positive results to this point come largely just to the assertion that value is an objective property. For the rest we have been engaged in clearing up and supporting this doctrine. We have, however, observed certain other features of value along the way which I now want to state in a more positive form.

We have already called the feature of value which consists in its dependence upon particular situations the 'situational relativity' or 'variability' of value. The point of the expression is that value cannot be universally predicated of kinds of things. There is no single characteristic or single recurrent complex of characteristics which can be said always to make good the things to which they attach. The principle which Moore asserted of judgments of extrinsic value is also true of judgments of intrinsic value, they can be true only generally, not universally.

This doctrine would seem to be the one which Dewey has wished to express in saying that the good is always unique. But this is not quite accurate. Intrinsic values do recur in similar objects, events, qualities, relations. Life would be more frustrating than it is if this were not so. What is true is that we cannot be sure that the value which has been generally associated with a particular sort of thing may not in some situation fail to be associated with that thing, through some element being present here which was not present in the other cases. And this may occur in the case of things intrinsically good no less than of things extrinsically good.

This feature of value is sometimes expressed in misleading ways. Suppose a stone which apparently is devoid of value halts a person's slide down a slope; or suppose that the same stone, because of its unusual color and shape, is at some time perceived by someone with pleasure. These facts might be expressed by saying that the thing 'became of value' or that the thing 'was of value in a particular relation'. And the general principle might be stated that anything 'may become of value' or 'is of value in a particular relation'. But these expressions are not accurate. The verb 'become' suggests the undergoing of an internal change and not merely a change of relation. We say that a tree 'becomes' tall or that a stone 'becomes' broken, worn, dark. The stone does not change in a similar way to 'become' valuable. Similarly, to say that a thing 'is valuable in a given relation' is less accurate than saying that the thing is a cause of value or is the object of a good experience.

We will no doubt go on using the misleading expressions, and there is no harm in it, so long as we understand these expressions as meaning the same as the more accurate expression. However, these expressions do encourage the notion that value is not objective. They suggest that value is a property of a concrete substance, while at the same time suggesting that it is not a real property of it, but only a property it may develop, or a property it may have in some particular set of circumstances. A great deal of the confusion as to whether value is objective or is a property arises from confusion as to what it is a property of, and from the notion that if it is objective it must be a property of a substance rather than of an experience or a complex event.

This doctrine of situational relativity will be opposed by two opposite groups — the skeptics and the absolutists. Let us consider the argument of each.

The skeptic will ask, 'How, if the value of a thing, as aesthetic enjoyment, depends upon the situation, can we say that in general it is valuable? Aren't we restricted to saying only that in some individual cases it is valuable? Surely we must say not that aesthetic enjoyment has value, but that some particular cases of aesthetic enjoyment have value.' This is indeed what we must say, if we will speak with strict accuracy. But the thing to notice is that in this respect principles concerning values are no different in kind from principles concerning other properties, as that bread nourishes or water refreshes. These statements are true only under certain conditions; and we could never state all of these conditions. For these conditions include the absence of all negative conditions that would prevent the principle's holding, and we can never hope to state all of these. Further, if we attempt to include all of these conditions in a single law, the formulation becomes a mere tautology. Thus there is nothing peculiar in our inability to state unconditionally such a value principle as that aesthetic enjoyment is good.

It is true that ethical principles are probably subject to more exceptions than any other sort of principle. Practical principles are in reliability midway between the principles of science and the rules of an art such as the drama. They are somewhat like rules of cookery or rules of home-medicine. They presuppose a greater number of conditions

than other principles, and these excepting conditions are
even less capable of exhaustive enumeration. But this is a
difference of degree. Further, these differences of degree
exist among ethical principles themselves. No doubt Moore
was led to select aesthetic enjoyment and personal affection
as great intrinsic values not just because their value is
greater than that of other values, but also because it is more
invariable. For example, there are doubtless fewer occasions on which personal affection is not good than occasions
on which sense pleasure (which also has considerable claim
to be an intrinsic value) is not good. But there is nothing
amiss in asserting ethical principles to the effect that both
of these are good. We must remember that these principles
are subject to exception, but we also must remember this
in the case of non-value principles.

This feature of value principles was clearly stated long
ago by Aristotle, who advised us not to look for the same
degree of exactitude in all subject-matters. Ethical principles are merely general and probable — not, like the
principles of mathematics, universal and necessary. And
this fact about ethical principles has a consequence of
paramount importance for ethical judgment and deliberation. Plainly principles that are true only for the most part
cannot provide direct or certain decisions. What they do
is to acquaint us with connections that may exist in the
given situation. It is our task as deliberators to survey this
situation as something individual and try to determine what
particular value potentialities actually exist in it.

Still, many would dispute that the value of anything is
relative to a situation which includes other objects, hence
that the value of anything is dependent upon the particular
relations into which it may enter. The objector may agree
that this principle is true of every single concrete object
which has ever existed or will ever exist, but assert that it
is not true of general kinds of complexes of objects which
may be defined. Moore took this view in *Principia Ethica*.
He there said that the task of Ethics was just to make
universal judgments of what sorts of things are intrinsically
good (Section 17); and he said that two such outstanding
intrinsic goods are aesthetic enjoyments and the pleasures

of personal affection. He described both of these as
'organic wholes', involving several constituents. Aesthetic
enjoyment must include (a) an appropriate feeling towards
the beautiful object (Section 114) and (b) a cognition of the
object's beautiful qualities (Section 115); personal affection
must include, besides both (a) and (b), (c) the *existence* of
an intrinsically good object. Since Moore was proposing
to offer here universally true judgments, he was implying
that every case of aesthetic enjoyment or personal affection
which has existed or will ever exist is intrinsically good.
Presumably he might have agreed that some such case
might have been extrinsically bad. But the judgment that
it was a cause of something bad would be independent of
the judgment that it was itself good. (For according to
Moore all judgments of extrinsic value differ from judgments of intrinsic value in that the former are only generally
true.)

But we can think of cases in which aesthetic enjoyment
or personal affection would be bad, and bad not as a means
but as constituting an element in an organic whole which
is intrinsically bad. We can imagine a person choosing to
enjoy beauty or love when he knew this was the wrong
thing to do. In such a case it is not that beauty or love is
a cause of what is bad, but that by experiencing them the
person cannot engage in something else which he knows he
ought to engage in. And so he can only experience them by
doing a bad act. (That there are bad and good intentional
acts will be argued in Chapter IV.) One may say that still it
is not the beauty or love itself here which is bad, but rather
the choice of experiencing it. But the point is that here
we cannot separate the value of the aesthetic enjoyment
from the value of the act of engaging in the aesthetic enjoyment. The former is a part of the organic whole which is
the latter. It is no use to say that the aesthetic enjoyment
would be good if we could separate it from the other
elements in the situation, in particular from its being an
object of choice. For here we cannot separate it.

What Moore seems to have overlooked is that these
sorts of organic unity (appreciation of beauty and love) are
themselves often complexes in a higher organic unity which

includes the further element of an act of choice. Moore did think that some acts of choice, specifically acts of conscientiousness, have some intrinsic value (Section 108). But there are cases in which the intrinsic value of conscientiousness can exist only at the expense of another intrinsic value, as beauty or love. Nor can one say that the problem here merely concerns the limitations of causes of existence, and that both would be good if they could both exist. There is nothing in the nature of the causal conditions which makes it impossible that the person conceive his duty as being to engage in the appreciation of beauty or love. The trouble, in the case considered, is that the person does not conceive of his duty in this way. Hence to realize the intrinsic value of beauty or love would be at the expense of realizing the other intrinsic value of conscientiousness. One might of course say that the right act here would be to go ahead and act unconscientiously so as to realize beauty. But that would not help the argument. For then it would still be true that in this case something else said to be an intrinsic value, conscientiousness, is not good.

Possibly the reason Moore supposed that universal judgments could be made of intrinsic values is that he momentarily forgot that choosing a good thing could itself be of intrinsic value (or the reverse). Virtue in general he regarded as the disposition to perform actions generally good as means. And he seems to exaggerate this point to the neglect of the facts that virtue sometimes consists (a) not merely in actions but in the *choice* of the action to perform and (b) in the choice of the *ends* of the action, as well as the acts which are the means to them; and that (c) the virtuous choice of means as well as of ends may have intrinsic value. He says that 'Practical Ethics asks, not "What ought to be?" but "What ought we to do?"; it asks what actions are *duties*, what actions are *right*, and what *wrong*: and all these questions can only be answered by showing the relation of the actions in question, as causes or necessary conditions, to what is good in itself' (Section 109). What he seems to overlook here is that an action which may be right or wrong in its relation of being a cause may also be good or bad in its relation or aspect of being chosen or intended. In the *Principia Ethica* he seemed to regard the intrinsic value which was present in conscientiousness as provided by 'the emotion excited by the idea of rightness'. In *The Philosophy of G. E. Moore*, however, he did say that an action of choosing a certain thing might be intrinsically good (p. 619). But if it can, then the choosing of one intrinsic value may be intrinsically good and of a different intrinsic value intrinsically bad.

13. *A Universal Condition of Value*

But if we cannot state sorts of things which are always good, or specify sets of conditions under which they are so, still it might appear that we can state certain necessary conditions of value, or state the general categories of existence within which value occurs. Indeed this has often been attempted.

One prominent theory, Hedonism, holds that nothing is good or bad except human feeling — in particular the feelings of pleasure and pain. Another major theory, often called the Interest Theory of Value, holds that nothing is good except as it has a certain relation to human interest or desire. Still another theory maintains that the sole thing that is good is the realization of personal selves. Thus each of these theories defines a universal condition of the occurrence of value. According to one, this condition is the existence of a feeling; according to another, it is the existence of a relation of an object to a human disposition; according to another, it is the existence of an enduring and changing self. Stated in other terms, these theories take the stand that value can only be a property of a single kind of thing — a feeling, a relation of an object to an interest, a self.

I shall discuss the first two of these views in detail in Chapters II and III. Here we note that all three theories agree in respect to one feature of this universal condition of value — namely the existence of human beings. They all agree that anything good must belong to a state, relation, or quality of a human being. Many ethical writers — for example, the early G. E. Moore, Nikolai Hartmann and

Plato — do not agree to this. Moore first considered good to be capable of existing independently of human beings. In *Principia Ethica* he presented the following case. 'Let us imagine one world exceedingly beautiful. Imagine it as beautiful as you can; put into it whatever on this earth you most admire — mountains, rivers, the sea; trees, and sunsets, stars and moon. Imagine these all combined in the most exquisite proportions, so that no one thing jars against another, but each contributes to increase the beauty of the whole. And then imagine the ugliest world you can possibly conceive. Imagine it simply one heap of filth, containing everything that is most disgusting to us, for whatever reason, and the whole, as far as may be, without one redeeming feature. . . . The only thing we are not entitled to imagine is that any human being ever has or ever, by any possibility, *can*, live in either, can ever see and enjoy the beauty of one or hate the foulness of the other. Well, even so, supposing them quite apart from any possible contemplation by human beings; still is it irrational to hold that it is better that the beautiful world should exist, than the one which is ugly? Would it not be well, in any case, to do what we could to produce it rather than the other? Certainly I cannot help thinking that it would' (pp. 83-4). Moore here does not give reasons for his conclusion; he instead paints a detailed picture which he finds convincing. But it is questionable whether the details help. The difficulty is not at all one of imagining a beautiful landscape. The difficulty is in conceiving a beautiful landscape which will by no possibility ever be present to human perception or even thought. Once we imagine that the landscape does exist, it is hard to suppress every glimmer of belief that throughout eternity *no* one can discover it. The question therefore is better considered abstractly: can we think anything good which has no relation of any sort to sentient beings? I think we cannot. It is hard to argue the matter, but the following argument may elucidate it somewhat. The belief that a thing would be good imposes on us some obligation to attempt to realize it, providing that we are able to realize it. But (contrary to Moore) we would not think that we had the slightest obligation to realize a good which, the moment it was realized, would have no relation of any sort to any sentient being. Therefore we can join the Hedonists, Interest Theorists and Self-Realizationists in asserting one universal condition of the existence of value, namely, that it relate in some way to some sentient being.

There remain two questions. One is whether it is sufficient for the existence of value that it relate to animals or God. As for God, it is doubtful whether he exists, but if he does, certainly we conceive value as existing in relation to him. With respect to animals, we do seem to believe that values can occur in relation to them. At least we think it is bad for them to suffer needless pain. Thus *some* sorts of value could exist if no human beings existed, so long as a God or animal existed. But it is hard to know about such values, nor are we very interested in knowing about them.

The pressing question is what are the more particular respects in which value can exist with relation to human beings. This will get detailed treatment in certain chapters which follow. I shall argue that value may be truly or falsely predicated of human beings in every dimension of their existence. (1) A particular person, as an enduring substance, may be good; as when we say that Socrates was a good man. (2) An enduring disposition, as Socrates' honesty or knowledge, may be good. (3) A momentary state, as a feeling of pleasure or a conscientious act, may be good. (4) A series of states, as a life or a period of life, may be good. (5) Finally, a relation of human beings to each other may be good. And of course these five kinds of things may also be bad.

It is also obvious that the values of these several sorts of existence are intimately connected, and that, generally, value in any one dimension tends to be associated with comparable sorts of value in the other dimensions. A person's goodness will depend upon the goodness of his dispositions and his acts. But he can be a good man (though not a saint) while doing a bad act, and while having at least one or a few bad dispositions. There is the same merely general correlation between a person's goodness and the goodness of his experience, his life, and his relations to other persons.

The lack of a strict correlation between value in these several dimensions gives rise to value conflicts and problems of choice. For instance, an activity, say of studying natural science, may have one degree of value as a pleasurable experience, another value as the exercise of intelligence, another value as a part of a successful life. Some experiences are better than others in pleasantness, some experiences involve better activities (are better things for us to do), and some experiences are better than others by virtue of their position in the more inclusive life pattern of experiences and activities. It may be that doing science is a less pleasant experience than reading a novel, exercises a less valuable disposition than collecting funds for charity, and, as an incident in a more inclusive system of experiences, is less valuable at a particular moment than studying history. These discrepancies present problems for choice. For example, a person often has to decide whether to obtain a particularly good experience or whether instead to develop a good disposition. However, there are also general value principles to provide guidance. It is a principle of common sense that it is better to choose what will promote one's enduring capacities or one's life in preference to what will provide merely a good experience of the moment.

Our serious concern with these problems of moral choice, and with discovering principles (however general and provisional) for right choice, supports the thesis I have been urging throughout this long chapter — that value is a property about which we attempt to make true judgments.

Since, as I believe, this view of ethical objectivism is the view of common sense, my support of the doctrine has consisted mainly in repelling attacks upon it and in clearing away confusions which stand in the way of its acceptance. Some of these confusions concern chiefly the way we apprehend value and the way we speak and think about it. In particular, I have tried to show that Prescriptivism (Section 2), Emotivism (Section 4), and other accounts less readily classifiable, as those of Nowell-Smith (Section 8) and Toulmin (Section 9), are based on such confusions.

Other confusions concern chiefly special features of value (genuine or presumed) and the bearing of these upon the objectivity of value. Some such features are the 'simplicity', 'observability', 'relativity', and 'intrinsicality' of value, treated in Sections 5, 6, 7 and 11. This line of inquiry (excepting the topic of 'intrinsic' value) culminated in Section 10, which attempted to focus in stark fashion the ultimate grounds on which one must decide for or against the doctrine that value is objective. (It would be idle, and foolish, to insist that the matter has been settled here. But I hope I have (mimicking Mill) presented considerations capable of determining the intellect to assent to ethical objectivism.) For the rest, I have tried to state the general limitations of value judgments (Sections 3 and 12) and the general areas within which value is found (Section 13).

The opinions of the last section, which are stated quite sketchily and dogmatically, run counter to hallowed theories which hold that value exists in some single state or mode. In the next two chapters I shall consider what I take to be the two most plausible of these theories, and in the case of each I shall try to show that value is not confined to the domain which the theory maintains. In Chapter II I shall argue that value does not exist at all, as the Interest Theory holds, in a relation of an object to an interest. In Chapter III I shall argue that pleasure, which the Hedonist claims is the sole thing which is good, is in fact only one kind of good thing.

DESIRE

ETHICAL theorists, like theorists of other sorts, have a deep desire for an explanation of their subject-matter which is perfectly simple and comprehensive. They would like to find a single principle to stand at the head and serve as the source of all other principles. Thus the most prominent theories have almost invariably named some one thing as the sole ultimate object of ethical knowledge and pursuit. There are both transcendental and naturalistic theories of this single good, and the accounts are of both highly theoretical and highly practical sorts. 'The Good' is conceived by Plato to be something beyond the world of time and sense; while religious philosophers conceive it to be God. More naturalistic accounts are the Stoic doctrine that the good is virtue and the closely similar Self-Realizationist doctrine that it is the realization of the self's potentialities. The thoroughgoing naturalists are divided between the Hedonistic theory that the sole good is pleasure, and the Interest Theory that it is any object of any interest.

I shall have nothing to say of the transcendental views; I think that they are the most obviously mistaken, but their mistakes are very general ones about the nature of knowledge, which is another topic. With the other views there a clear division between the Stoic and the Self-Realizationist theories on one side, and Hedonism and the Interest Theory on the other. What differentiates them is their degree of concern with virtue; the first holding that virtue is either the sole good or the chief element in the good, while the latter holds that virtue is not in itself a good at all. In the first group we can roughly include the more complex theories of Aristotle and Kant; for though both recognize that pleasure is involved in the complete good, they treat it as an element or aspect in a whole of which the chief constituent is virtue. Aristotle's major point is that the best pleasures are those belonging to the activities of the highest virtues; Kant's major point is that pleasure can complete a whole which is already made good by the presence of a Good Will, but that pleasure is not good apart from this. Both views are rather grudging admissions of the good of pleasure. (We shall consider their positions in more detail further on.)

I have already expressed the opinion that value can exist in the dimensions of action, as virtue; of experience, as pleasure; and of a person or a life, as self-realization. Reasons for holding these opinions will come out in the chapter on Pleasure. First I shall consider the Interest Theory, which constitutes an attack on all these views.

1. *The Interest Theory*

That value does not belong to objects, but arises only with our desire for them, is a doctrine which everyone is apt to hold at some time or other. The doctrine is a natural response to the fact of value disagreement and value change. The doctrine may arise as follows. In ordinary discourse we ascribe the predicates 'good' and 'valuable' to concrete objects. But in the face of the facts that different people do not say that the same things are good, and that our own minds change about what is good, it may occur to us that value cannot exist where it seems to exist. Once on this road we may travel it the full way to the skeptical conclusion that values do not exist at all, but are at most a kind of emotive expression. But if we do not want to go so far, we may welcome as a happy compromise the so-called Interest Theory, according to which values do exist, but only in relation to interest.

According to this theory, when I say that an object has value I am in some sense expressing my interest in that object rather than reporting my knowledge of it. I look at the object from the standpoint of my interest, rather than from the standpoint of my knowledge. From this last standpoint I see that I should not think of attributing value to the object if I were not interested in it. It is not that the object itself has value; it is the relational complex — the object-of-interest — that has value. Understanding

this enables me to understand how it is that people judge
the same object to have different values. These objects
do 'have' them — that is, people have different interests
in them. The objects participate in different relations, and
they 'have' and 'lose' value as these relations change.

The central argument for this view is, then, that it
explains the variations in the judgments which mistakenly
attribute values to objects. Once we see that values do not
belong to objects, we can allow that much of this variety is
not a case of really conflicting value judgments but of quite
compatible but diverse value relations. If Jones finds the
solitude of the desert fearful and Smith finds it sublime
this indicates that the desert both has value and lacks value
— it has value in relation to Smith's interest and lacks it
in relation to Jones' interest. This view, while it allows for
much 'relativity' of value, also allows for much 'objectivity'. For it holds that there are true and false value
judgments.

A value judgment is true if it attributes value to a
particular object in relation to a particular interest, and if
these objects and interests do exist in the way described.
Thus if someone (Smith or someone else) says that the
solitude of the desert is of value for Smith's interest in the
sublime, and if the desert is solitary and Smith does have
an interest in the sublime, and if the solitary does satisfy
the interest in sublimity, then the judgment is true. Likewise a value judgment can be in error either through
attributing (a) a property to the object which it does not
have, or (b) an interest to the person which he does not
have, or (c) a relation between this objective property and
subjective interest which does not exist. The special
evaluative problems are clearly those of (b) and (c), and the
central question for both is what interest is. Plainly interest
must be something distinct both from (1) the object of
interest and from (2) value and (3) the judgment of value.
And 'interest', whatever 'interest' may be, could not be
conceived apart from (1) an object in which it would be
satisfied ; but interests often exist when their objects do
not exist. When an interest's object does not exist, no (2)
value exists. Finally the interest is distinct from (3), the

judgment of value, for the interest is one part of the object
of the value judgment, the entire object of this judgment
being the existence of an interest in relation to an appropriate object. In order, then, to support the Interest Theory
we must first have some criterion for knowing that interests
exist which is distinct from our criterion for knowing that
objects of interest exist ; and we must then show that value
exists solely in this relation. But before considering these
matters we shall have to try to become clear about the
central concepts of the Interest Theory.

2. *The Concepts of Interest and Desire*

There are several terms which are closely related to
'interest' — 'desire', 'want', 'impulse', 'instinct', 'need'.
With respect to action the class to which all of these belong
is that of 'motive'. Of these terms I think 'desire' and
'want' best represent the value factor which the Interest
Theorists have in mind. But I shall consider the other
terms first.

'Instinct' and 'need' differ from these other concepts
in being much narrower in their reference, and in involving
limiting criteria. 'Instinct' is primarily a biological concept, referring to tendencies common to a biological class.
Only in a figurative sense would we use the term 'instincts'
to refer to tendencies which were peculiar to a single
individual ; while we might refer to some 'need' which
belonged to a person uniquely. 'Need', like 'instinct', is
in its standard use applied to a fairly small class of motives ;
but here the limiting criterion is not commonness to a
biological class but the nature of the particular individual.
Two human beings (having the same instincts) may have
different needs. Also, the limiting criterion seems to be
basically ethical. The things for which a person has a
'need' are things which will benefit him. Thus he may
have 'impulses' for things which he does not need, and
need things for which he has no 'impulses'.

In some uses 'want' has the same suggestion of way-
wardness or caprice that 'impulse' has. A person may ex-
plain an action by saying either, 'I simply $\begin{pmatrix} \text{had an impulse} \\ \text{wanted} \end{pmatrix}$

to do it'. However there is a difference. 'Had an impulse' suggests momentariness and perhaps inexplicability, while 'wanted' more often suggests something more like arbitrariness. One may refer to the impulse to indicate that he cannot explain what he did, while he refers to his want to indicate that he does not intend to try to explain it. However, 'want' is also used, though infrequently, as a noun, and here the term connotes the sort of stability connoted by 'need'. But a person's 'need' is, as we said, for something that will benefit him, while he may have a 'want' for something that will not do this.

The closest bond is that between want and desire. It would be paradoxical to say that a person desired something but did not want it, or wanted it but did not desire it. We might invoke such a contrast to indicate a real distinction in the features for which the thing were desired or wanted, but then this distinction could also be expressed by using a single one of the terms. One conceivably might say, 'Jones had a great desire for Smith's wife, but he didn't want her', meaning that he desired her in one way but not as a wife. But the sentence is unclear, and could be expressed clearly by using just one, and either, of the terms 'desire' or 'want'. However, there are some differences in their use. 'Want' is seldom used as a noun; 'desire' is used, I believe, about equally as a noun and a verb, or, if anything, more frequently as a noun. As a verb 'want' is more colloquial than 'desire' — 'I want it' (or 'He wants it') is more colloquial than 'I desire it'. But these differences are minor.

Of more importance are the relations of both of these terms to 'liking' and to 'interest'. Desire and liking are related to each other in a special way. To desire (or want) a thing is to like having it, at least under some circumstances. We speak of liking this object when we do possess it. The difference between desire and liking is just the difference between an attitude toward an object which is conceived as absent and that same sort of attitude toward the object when it is present. We would not speak of a person as desiring an activity in which he is presently engaged. Nor would we speak of a person liking the activity unless we were thinking of the attitude which he

F

has while engaging in that activity. We do utter sentences saying that a person likes a thing when at the moment of utterance the person does not have the thing (and may or may not be desiring the thing), but then what we mean is that the person does or would at least sometimes have the attitude of liking if the thing were present. Thus if a person does desire a thing, he would like having it; and if he likes having it, then it is conceivable that there could be a situation in which he would desire it.

However, there may seem to be negative instances of this. A person may say that he desires a thing; then he is given an ideal opportunity to have it, and after the experience he says that he does not like it. But here we would simply say that the person was wrong. He did not in fact desire it; or, if he did desire it at one time, then he ceased desiring it before he got it. He may have sincerely said he desired it, when in fact he only thought he did. On the other hand, it would seem that we can like things without ever desiring them. It does seem that we can experience new things, and like them, without ever again having a thought or desire of the thing. Let us suppose this does happen, just as it happens that we can desire things which we never obtain and hence which we never have an opportunity to like. The point is that if we did have toward the absent thing which we liked when present, an attitude that resembled the attitude of liking, this attitude would be one of desire.

There is another important difference between desire and liking which is associated with this contrast between the prospective character of desire and the consummatory character of liking. We speak of unconscious desire but not of unconscious liking. One can have a desire without ever being aware either that he has this desire or of its object, while a person cannot like something without sometimes being aware that he likes the thing and what it is that he likes. Liking involves being satisfied or enjoying or taking pleasure, and these are experiences or states of consciousness. Desire, on the other hand, may be regarded either as a conscious state or an action or a disposition to act. This difference has one other important aspect. Liking a thing entails experiencing pleasure from it, and experiencing pleasure from it entails liking it. Desiring a thing entails being able to conceive of some occasion on which one would like it, and hence on which it would provide pleasure. But desiring entails just the possibility of pleasure, while liking entails its realization.

It would seem that a conscious desire also involves a thought of the pleasure to be got from satisfying the desire. For desire involves a thought of the desired object, and it would seem to involve a thought that this object is desired ; finally, this thought that the object is desired would seem to involve the thought that the object will satisfy the desire and in satisfying give pleasure. What distinguishes the mere thought of possessing an object from the desire to possess that object would seem to be that the desire includes besides this thought the thought that the possession will bring pleasure.

This is not to propose (what Bishop Butler showed false) that every desire has as its object maximum pleasure. The object of desire is some specific sort of thing, and not just pleasure or satisfaction generally. But the thought of the desired object involves the thought that this object would give pleasure. It is primarily the thought of the object as desired which leads to the thought that the object would give pleasure ; it is not, as the Psychological Hedonist holds, the thought that the object would give pleasure which leads to the thought that the object is desired. It is because the object is desired that it does give pleasure ; it is not (in the first instance) because it gives pleasure that it is desired.

Coming now to the term 'interest', we see that this concept is related rather differently to 'liking' than is 'desire'. We may say that a person is interested in a thing without implying that there could be any occasion on which he would like having it. Being interested may mean only that the person would like to give it a try, in order to see whether he would like it. This meaning is close to the meaning of 'interest' as curiosity, which is just a desire to know. A very common way of saying that a person wants to know about a thing is to say that he is interested in it.

Likewise a person may say that he is interested in a thing to convey that he does not know whether he desires the thing but he desires to try it so that he can know whether he desires it. We might summarize this by saying that 'interest' connotes a desire to know, while 'desire' and 'want' do not; and associated with this, that when 'interest' is used in the sense of a desire to know about one's desire (and not simply in the sense of a desire to obtain knowledge about the thing itself) it connotes a less strong or definite desire for the thing than does a simple 'desire' for it. Now this brings out that there is something misleading in the name 'Interest Theory' and in this theory's concentration on the term 'interest'. For surely what the theory wants to hold, and the only view which it is plausible to hold, is that value exists in relation to a definite desire, and not merely in a relation to a desire to know whether one has a desire.

3. *Desire and Action*

The concept of 'desire' has in common with the concepts of 'intention' and 'choice' that it is applied both to phases of a person's experiences and to phases of his behaviour. To the question, 'What was his X' where for 'X' we substitute 'intention', 'choice', or 'desire', we can answer by mentioning either a particular act which he performed or a thought which he had about the act. By a person's 'desire' we may mean the thing the person did, which is often called the object of his desire. Let us call the use of 'desire' to refer to a personal experience its use in its 'experiential sense', and its use to refer to a publicly observable act its use in its 'behavioral sense'. I shall try to show that the experiential sense is primary, and that the behavioral sense is derived from this through (a) the behavioral sense's being generally correlated with the experiential sense, (b) the behavioral factor's being more easily observable, (c) the behavioral factor's serving in some cases to correct the report about a desire based on immediate experience.

One might propose using desire in a perfectly general way, as identical with 'cause of behavior'. Then all organic movements, including those of the internal organs, of which a person might never be directly aware, would be 'desired'. But this would be a drastic metaphysical extension of the ordinary concept of desire. There would be no apparent advantage, and much confusion, in saying that a person is at once satisfying as many desires as there are bodily movements (however 'movement' might be identified). If this extreme is rejected, let us ask about the other extreme in which 'desire' is confined to intentional actions only.

We do conceive of intentional action as always involving some desire to obtain or avoid something, either by the action itself or as a result of it. Acts are intended which are not themselves desired or not desired consciously, but there is no intention in which desire is not in some way involved.

(1) We would not allow that a person intentionally did something for which he had no desire of any sort. He might say that he felt no desire for it, and did not know why he did it. But we would insist that he must have had some desire. In Homer these apparently motiveless acts are attributed to divine beings. In our time they are attributed to unconscious desires. The difference is that we can bring unconscious desires into consciousness, while we cannot bring Ares and Athene before us. The psycho-analyst detects the patient's unconscious desires through the patient's reports of his thoughts and behavior, and partly also through observing a small segment of his behavior. But what gives credibility both to the notion that all intentional actions entail a desire, and to the associated notion of unconscious desire, is the fact that we do frequently discover in consciousness desires which have been previously motivating us unconsciously.

From this notion that there are unconscious desires we are apt to move to the notion that there is no real separation of desiring and acting — that just as a person cannot act without having a desire, so he cannot have a desire without acting upon it. We say that if a person really does desire a thing, then he will attempt to get it; and that if a person does earnestly pursue a thing then he must desire it. But though we do sometimes treat desire as if it entails action, and action as if it entails desire, on other occasions we regard these as separable. We may say that 'He desired very much to do it, but in the end he decided not to'. And we are aware of having desires which we believe we cannot satisfy, hence which we take no action to satisfy. Perhaps we should call these 'wishes'.

(2) Further, one may intend to do, and intentionally do, something which he does not desire to do, but which is only a means to something which he desires. One might say that still one does desire the means — that if he desires a thing he must logically desire whatever is a means to it. But this is false. The principle that 'To "will" the end is to "will" the means' is true if we substitute for 'will' the term 'intend' in the secondary sense of 'aim' or 'plan'; but it is false if we substitute the term 'desire'. It is only the intention of satisfying the desire, not the desire itself, which involves, or commits one to the intention to take, certain steps. And it commits one only to the intention to take these steps, not to a desiring to take them. The satisfying of a desire necessitates the bringing about of certain conditions, and may also involve the having or satisfying of other desires. But the having of a desire does not necessitate the having of a desire for the conditions necessary to satisfying it. Nor is there anything 'irrational' in desiring a thing and not desiring to do what is necessary to satisfying it. It is neither single desires nor combinations of desires that are rational or irrational, but only actions, judgments and intentions. It would be irrational to intend the end of satisfying the desire and not to intend the means to it. But one may have the desire and intend to satisfy it, while only intending, not desiring, to do the act of realizing the necessary means.

An important application of this principle is to the case in which one intends to do something which he does not want to do but which he thinks he ought to do. A person may want to do what he thinks he ought to do. He does not want to do the act considered simply (say, to fight a battle), but he does want to do the act in so far as it is, or is considered under the description of being, his duty. There is a difference between this desire to do one's duty and other desires. In the case of every other desire the description of the thing desired includes some characterization of the object besides its characterization as merely a potential satisfaction of one's desire. The object is desired as being something other than merely the satisfying of the desire; it is desired as an object of a specific sort. If, for example, a person wants to fight a battle in order to satisfy his desire to be brave, he will want to fight a battle conceived as dangerous. While if he wants to fight a battle in order to fulfill his duty, he will want to fight the battle just as satisfying this desire and not as being dangerous or anything else. Both the person who wants to feel brave, and the one who wants to do his duty, fight the battle, and each knows that what he is doing is dangerous. But the thought that it is dangerous is essential to the satisfaction of the man who wants to be brave, while it is not essential to that of the man who wants to do his duty. The conscientious person takes no pleasure in the thought that the act is of a particular sort, namely dangerous, but only in the thought that the act is his duty. One might say that the difference is only in the generality of the description of the act. But the crucial difference is that any other desire permits some more specific description of the sort of act which would provide satisfaction, while a desire to do one's duty permit no such more specific description. There is a peculiar sense, then, in which the conscientious act is not wanted in its concrete character but only in its general description.

But there is an extreme view, which we may call Behaviorism, which denies this distinction between desire and intentional action. Behaviorism may be taken to assert that the phrase 'desiring a thing' and 'pursuing or acting in pursuit of that thing' are two expressions for exactly the same state of affairs. But this view cannot be true, for it would make unintelligible a kind of statement which we do commonly make and understand, namely the statement that a person wants to do a thing but is not going to do it. Suppose a person says: 'I want to take a vacation this year, but I am not going to take it'. Now if desiring a thing and pursuing it are the same, then any statement of desire concerning the future is a statement of what the person will do. On this account the above statement is unintelligible. Properly translated it becomes: 'I am going to take a vacation, but I am not going to take a vacation'. If we interpret the second clause as a prediction, then the sentence is self-contradictory. And if we interpret it as a declaration of intention, it implies a self-contradiction, since a statement of intention to do a thing implies a prediction that one will do the thing.[1] Obviously, then, the person making such a statement of desire does not think he is making a prediction about his future action. He would say that he is giving a description of his present feelings.

Other interpretations of a statement of desire can be constructed, but they work no better. A second interpretation might be that the sentence ('I desire to do X but I will not do it'), though not expressing a prediction, is expressing the person's doubt about what he will do. He is in effect saying: 'Perhaps I will take a vacation, but probably I won't'. But this will not do; for the person may be quite positive in his assertion of both clauses. He is sure he does want to take a vacation, and he is sure that he will not take it.

One more interpretation is possible, namely that the meaning is: 'I want to take a vacation, but I want more not to take it', or: 'If I could take a vacation and do other things as well, then I would take it, but since I can't do all these things, I won't take a vacation'. On this account the person has several desires; when he refers to desire in the first clause he is referring to one of these desires, while in the last clause he is referring to another. But this interpretation still allows that there may be desires of some sort that one does not act upon. For it allows that a person may have several desires at a time when he can act, and can think he can act, upon only one of them. The account must then provide some way of distinguishing the desire on which the person acts from these other desires.

A principle which has been invoked is that of 'greatest desire'. What are we to understand by this? Evidently we must understand it to be the greatest desire at the par-

[1] See Chapter IX, Section 4.

ticular moment of action. The objective pursued is always something particular; hence if the objective of the greatest desire is the same as the objective pursued, it must likewise be particular. This fact makes it impossible for us to accept any of three possible interpretations of the doctrine that we always pursue the objective of our 'greatest desire'. (1) Someone might mean by the phrase a desire for that objective which a person pursues most often or most completely. But sometimes a person pursues the objectives of other desires, so it would not be true that he is always acting on his 'greatest desire'. (2) Likewise a person must sometimes pursue the objective of a desire which he does not prefer most or evaluate most highly in his moments of reflection. (3) A third interpretation might be that by 'greatest desire' we mean that desire which the person feels with the most intense emotion. But again there are cases when a person resists an intensely emotional desire in order to pursue something which he desires less intensely. Thus on none of the possible interpretations of 'greatest desire' is it true that one always acts according to this desire. And if one insists on asserting this principle it can only be that he wishes to stipulate how we are to talk and think. One individual who might want to do this would be a theorist who wanted to think that he could understand everything of importance about human beings by observing only how they behaved.

Still the principle, that one always pursues what he most greatly desires, does have a great deal of superficial plausibility. There does seem something odd in saying of anything a person did that, at the time he did it, it was not what he most desired. It seems to follow that, if he did a thing, say insult a friend, then when he did it he desired it more than anything else he might have done. 'Otherwise', we ask, 'why did he do it?' On the other hand, the person who insulted his friend might find it equally odd to have to say, 'Because at the moment I desired this more than anything else I might have done'. He might say that he did not desire it at all; he just did it. Or he might say that perhaps he did desire it to some extent, but he did not desire it more than anything else.

The reason for the great plausibility in the view that one does always attempt to realize his greatest desire is that ordinarily we apply a Behavioristic criterion of desire. It is, in fact, the easiest and often the most accurate criterion. We find that people often speak falsely of their desires, and often do not speak of them at all. Further, we find a high correlation between what people do and what they desire. Thus we come to take a person's repeated pursuit of a thing as a sign that he desires it. But then the principle has to be further complicated. For sometimes a situation provides an opportunity for a person to pursue several things which he has repeatedly pursued and so has shown himself to desire; moreover he shows himself now to have tendencies to pursue each of the different things, though he does finally pursue only one. Thus to continue to apply our criterion we invent a fiction, namely a notion of 'real desire' or 'greatest desire', which will always be identical with the desire on which he acts. If our criterion for what he desires is the fact of his pursuit, and yet we know by various signs that he has tendencies to pursue other possible objectives, our only recourse is to say that, though desiring them all, he must desire most the one he in fact pursues. This explanatory fiction is just a natural consequence of the effort to convert a useful general criterion of a thing into a universal condition of it.

We conclude that desire is not the same as intentional action; that, on the contrary, a person can do things he does not desire, and desire things he does not do.

4. *Does Value Exist in a Relation?*

Now that we have before us this concept of interest and its related concepts, we are in a position to assess the merits of the Interest Theory. The first problem is to get clear just what, according to this theory, is the mode in which value exists, and just what is the peculiar role of 'interest' or desire with respect to value. The usual account of the Interest Theory is not consistent in its description of value as a relation, nor is it clear as to just what is the specific character of this relation. We shall consider each problem in turn.

The Interest Theorist defines value as a certain relation of an object to interest, but he does not consistently adhere to this definition. Rather, he treats value as if it were solely a product of interest. The major expositor of the theory, Professor R. B. Perry, wrote as follows in his *General Theory of Value*: 'The view may be otherwise formulated in the equation : x is valuable = interest is taken in x. Value is thus a specific relation into which things possessing any ontological status whatsoever, whether real or imaginary, may enter with interested subjects' (Section 49). Perry speaks of interest sometimes as 'constituting' value and sometimes as 'creating' it. And he speaks of the object as 'acquiring' value: 'That which is an object of interest is *eo ipso* invested with value. Any object, whatever it be, acquires value when any interest, whatever it be, is taken in it; just as anything whatsoever becomes a target when anyone whatsoever aims at it' (Section 49). At another point he speaks of 'interest being constitutive of value in the basic sense' (Section 49).

But plainly it cannot be true that interest constitutes or creates or originates value, if (1) value is a relation into which interest enters and if (2) an interest can exist apart from this relation. (1) The Interest Theorist asserts that value is a relational property, and not a property of interest alone. Moreover, even if value were a property of interest, we would not express this by saying that interest creates value, but rather by saying that interest has value or perhaps is of value. (2) The Interest Theorist thinks, and it is obviously true, that interest can exist when its object (hence its relation to its object) does not exist. We distinguish desire from liking in that desire is an 'interest' whose object is absent and in whose absence the interest is unsatisfied or unfulfilled, while liking is an 'interest' whose object is present and in whose presence the interest is satisfied. Many desires exist prior to their satisfying objects, and many exist for which satisfying objects never exist.[1]

[1] In his book *What is Value?* the late Professor E. W. Hall offers an interesting criticism of Perry's view which coincides in some ways with the criticism here. In attempting to consider Perry's view as conceiving value

Perry's idea might be that interest generates its object in the sense, not of causing its existence, but of conferring on it the trait of 'interesting' and hence 'valuable'. Still, the object must exist in order for interest to confer value upon it. The proper object of a particular interest may be something which is merely imaginary, as perhaps in an aesthetic interest; but then, if value is to exist, this imaginary object must exist in the imagination. Let us distinguish the 'object of interest', which is the object as it is apart from the interest taken in it, from the 'object-of-interest', which is the object of interest as qualified by interest. Plainly there cannot be an object-of-interest unless there is an object of interest. If interest 'confers' value on an object, there must be an object on which it confers value. Thus the object, under one sort of description, though not under an ethical one, is a condition of value, just as much as is interest. If value exists in a relation of interest to object, then interest cannot bring value into existence. Only interest together with an object can do that.

Perry, though he says that value is a relation, puts almost exclusive stress on one term, the subject-term, of the relation. When he assembles arguments for the truth of his Interest Theory, the particular point which he describes as offering 'a certain positive plausibility' is 'the fact that in order to create values where they did not exist before it seems to be sufficient to introduce an interest. The silence of the desert is without value, until some wanderer finds it lonely and terrifying. . . .' But all that this 'fact' could possibly show is that interest is a necessary condition of value. It does not show that interest is the sufficient condition, or constitutes or originates value. The desert must exist in reality or imagination in order for an interest to 'confer' value upon it. Thus this object must be as essential a condition, 'as original a source and constant a feature' of value, as is interest.

as the referent of a semantical predicate, Hall admits that this may involve some distortion, and I believe this to be the case. However, what primarily leads Hall to the semantical interpretation is his puzzlement as to how, on any other view, Perry can hold (as he does) that value can be both a relation and yet exist when there exists only one term of the relation, the interest (pp. 69-70).

The reason the Interest Theorist so stresses the subject-term of the relation might be the notion that the most variable factor in the relation is the interested subject. That is, the idea here may be that changes in value occur more through changes in us than through changes in things. The factual properties of the object of our interest change, so goes the interpretation, less rapidly and drastically than our interests change. The main changes in value are then ascribable to the changes in us. If one has an interest in the desert, and later loses this interest, then the desert, according to the theory, loses its character of value; but with this loss of interest in the subject, and of value in the object, the object may remain otherwise the same. But this would not show that value is not dependent on these other properties of the object; it would show only that value is not wholly dependent upon them. Perry says that the desert 'is without value until some wanderer finds it lonely and terrifying'. But if value is a relation, then one must also say that the interest in the desert is without value until there is a desert — a real desert, if this is the object of the person's interest, or an imaginary one, if he is interested only in contemplating an object of imagination.

5. *What is the Relation of 'Interest' to its Object?*

The Interest Theory is also not clear as to the specific sort of relation of desire and its object which must exist in order that value exist. Evidently both the desire and its object must be 'real' or really exist. If this is so, then we can see how the Interest Theory would account for some cases of value (as in (1) below) and for some cases of its absence (as in (2) and (3) below); but it is not clear how it would interpret another crucial case (4). And when we attempt to get clear about this case we find ourselves led away from the Interest Theory and towards Hedonism.

(1) A value may exist in the relation of a real desire to an object which is purely imaginative as concerns physical existence, but then this imaginative object is the real object of the person's interest. A person may have a real desire to contemplate a merely imaginary object; then this merely imaginary object is sufficiently real for the purpose of his

interest. The imaginative figment does exist as an imaginative figment, and that is all that the person desires. Aesthetic desire would seem to be of this sort. (2) But if the person desires an object which he truly knows does not exist as he desires it, then surely there could (on the Interest Theory) be no value. (3) Likewise, it would seem that there could be no value if the person really desired the thing on the false belief that it exists — as if, for example, he were to desire to reunite with a lost relative who is in reality dead. But what of the cases that arise when we introduce the factor of possible possession? (4) Taking the same example, suppose that the person really desires reunion with the relative, and that the relative is alive but will die before the reunion can occur. Does value exist at the time when the desire and its object exist? If so, what sort of relation is this of desire and its object? It would seem to depend upon how we conceive the object of desire. If the object is just the relative, then the object is real and the value would evidently be real. But this does not in fact seem to be the object. This object is, rather, the reunion with the relative; and since this does not exist, the value does not exist.

This last suggests a much more general difficulty, namely that the actual goal of a desire is always the sort of relation with its object which we call the 'satisfaction' of desire. And the satisfaction of a desire is the replacing of desire with liking. Sir David Ross has implied this in a criticism of the Interest Theory. He argues in *The Right and the Good* that on the Interest Theory nothing of value could exist, for 'The object of desire is always something nonexistent' (p. 96), whereas 'actual goodness presupposes actual existence' (p. 98). He reasons: 'it is only a rough and ready description of my desire to say I desire a primrose. What I desire is to be seeing it or smelling it or possessing it. As soon as we describe definitely what it is that we desire, we see that it is something which does not yet exist. There are no doubt cases in which we desire to go on doing what we are doing, or being in the same sort of state that we are in. But even if I desire, for instance, to go on looking at a primrose, what I desire is not the looking

which is taking place at present, but the looking which I
wish to take place in the immediate future. The object
of desire is always something non-existent' (pp. 95-6).
Dr. A. C. Ewing answers in *A Definition of Good* (though
without mentioning Ross), that 'this objection could be
met, without fundamentally altering what the holders of
these theories maintain, by substituting "desired or liked"
for "desired". Desire and liking are, I think, fundamentally the same attitude except that desire has for its object
what is absent and liking what is present' (p. 63).

But this modification would not be inconsiderable. If
this modification were adopted, and the theory reformulated
to read : '*X* is valuable = *X* is an object of liking', the
theory would have come to approximate the Hedonist
Theory that the only thing that is good is pleasure or
satisfaction. Further, Perry evidently would not accept
the modification, for he holds that even pleasure involves
an object which does not fully exist. The paradoxes required in insisting that value is a relation of desire to its
object come out clearly in Perry's view of pleasure. He
maintains that pleasure has value not as an immediate feeling but only in so far as an interest is taken toward it ;
and that in fact enjoyment is partly future or prospective
(Sections 100, 127 and 97). He writes : 'In our analysis
of interested response we have emphasized its aspect of
futurity, or its determination by expectation. While this
analysis evidently fits the case of desire, where the object
of interest does not yet exist, it may be supposed by the
same token to be inapplicable to the case of liking, where
the object of interest already exists. We meet here with
one of the fundamental paradoxes in the theory of value.
It would be manifestly absurd to contrive a theory which
implied that existence is a disqualification for value. . . .
The difficulty is, however, by no means insuperable. It is
created by the false supposition that liking or enjoyment is
directed to the present instant of time, and thus disappears
when it is remarked that enjoyment is directed to the
immediate future. If enjoyment were directed to the
present instant of time then the passage of time would
dispel it, instead of fulfilling it, as is actually the case.

Suppose a situation a at time t^1. The enjoyment of this situation does not imply a disposition to hold the instant t^1 and suspend the flow of time, but a disposition to hold a through time. It is an interest not in a's occurrence at t^1, but in the prolongation or recurrence of a : an interest, therefore, which will be satisfied by a's occurrence at t^2, t^3 etc.' (Section 97).

This is very confused. The root confusion is the notion that enjoyment is 'directed toward' something, and in the resulting assumption that enjoyment must be directed toward either the present instant or a future instant. Enjoyment or pleasure is not 'directed toward' anything; rather enjoyment is 'of' a specific object. But it does not make sense to speak of our enjoying this object unless it is present. We enjoy or take pleasure only in what is presently given, although we do not enjoy the thing as being present, rather than as being past or future. We can enjoy the fact that a thing is present, as we can also enjoy the fact that a thing is in the past or the future. But then it is the present thought of this fact which is enjoyed. In many or most cases we enjoy things without any thought of or attitude towards the temporal dimension. Perry seems to think that we cannot take pleasure in a thing without an expectant attitude toward something yet to be given. This is simply false. Sometimes we are so completely satisfied that it does not occur to us that time is passing, or that the pleasure may end. Perhaps most experiences which we regard as mainly ones of enjoyment do contain some reference beyond themselves. But this is to say that enjoyment is seldom pure. When we do enjoy, and to the degree that we enjoy, we enjoy what we now have and not what we are going to enjoy in the immediate future. We can also agree that when desire is present along with enjoyment it is a desire for the continuance of the enjoyment; but such desire complicates and adulterates the enjoyment.

If, on the other hand, we accept Ewing's idea that value exists in the relation of a thing not to desire but to liking, then there would seem no reason for holding that value exists in this relation and not rather in the satisfaction, as a property of the satisfying experience. In fact any value belonging to a desire as a desire, and not at all to it as being a desire of a particular sort, would seem to be the extrinsic value of leading to the value of the pleasure experienced in its satisfaction. But then value exists not in a relation of liking or desire to its object, but as a property of an experience, which experience is dependent upon the existence of this relation.

Let us here sum up the difficulties which we have found in the Interest Theory during these last two sections. In its strictest formulation, the theory holds that value exists in a relation of an interest to its proper object. But the theory is not presented in terms which adhere to this strict formulation. Nor does the theory tell us clearly what is the specific sort of relation which obtains between an object and its interest when value is said to exist. Moreover, when the theory attempts to account for a particular sort of value, such as pleasure, it is forced, in trying to bring this sort of value into accord with its doctrine, to propose a highly implausible description of pleasure. Further, if we adopt a variant formulation of the theory such as Ewing's, holding that value also exists in relation to present interest or liking, the result appears to be that the value which so exists is just satisfaction or pleasure. One may still hold that the value of the satisfaction depends upon the present interest which is being satisfied, but the facts here would seem sufficiently accounted for by the principle that this interest is a causal condition of this value rather than a logical ingredient in it. As we shall see in Chapter III, Section 1, there appears less reason for taking the liking to be a basic element in the analysis of pleasure, than for taking pleasure to be a basic element in the analysis of liking. Thus if it is held that value exists only in relation to liking, we are led away from the Interest Theory into Hedonism.

We may now pass to another difficulty which confronts the Interest Theory, namely that of accounting for our knowledge of interest and of value.

6. *Knowledge of Value and Interest*

The existence of desire in two modes — experiential and behavioral — has implications for our knowledge of

G

desire, and consequently for the way in which the Interest Theory would give us knowledge of value in concrete cases. If value exists in a relation of an object to a desire, then to judge that value exists one must judge that desire exists. Now if desire were knowable either solely in experiential or in behavioral terms, then the knowledge of value would in the first case be very easy or in the second very scientific. Either would give the Interest Theory an advantage over most other theories. But if the Interest Theory were construed along either of these lines, it would not have the other advantages which the theory claims to have, namely of combining in a particular way value relativism and objectivism. And in fact the Interest Theorist thinks that desire is of both sorts. The consequence is that the Interest Theory does not have any particular advantage in the knowledge of value. It cannot provide a scientific knowledge of value, for desire cannot be entirely known by scientifically observational methods.

Since interests are modes of behavior and modes of experience, they can be known both by the experiencer and by the observer. Both sources of knowledge have certain limitations. The experiencer is subject to self-deception; he may have a desire which he has a desire not to recognize and which prevents his recognition. On the other hand, he has a direct access to his desires which no outside observer of his behavior can have. Further, he is both an observer of his behavior, as well as an experiencer of his feelings. Though he can never completely overcome a desire to deceive himself about his guilty desires, the outside observer is likewise subject to temptations, though usually less severe ones, to deceive himself about the desires of others. But the temptations to error can in principle be overcome — a person can become a rational observer of himself. While the limitation of the outside observer cannot be overcome.

The nature of these limitations is clearest in the case of an activity that satisfies several of a person's desires. For example, a person may play golf because he likes (a) hitting the balls, (b) the exercise, (c) winning, (d) being with his playing companions, (e) contemplating the course's vistas, and because of still other things. On particular occasions he may want some of these things more than others, or he may want only one of them. Now an observer could not say what he wanted on a given occasion so well as the person himself. An observer could know that at some times, whether simultaneously or not, the person desires all of these things, for he sees that on different occasions the person plays when only one of the elements is present. For example, he may play when he is tired, certain to lose, his companions distasteful, the course uninteresting. The conclusion is that he just likes to hit golf balls toward and into golf holes. Likewise one might observe variations in the other elements. But this method would provide knowledge only either of what the person liked generally, or what he wanted on an occasion on which only one of the elements was present. On an occasion when all of the factors liked were present, and when the person did not by some marked focussing of attention show that he was interested in just one of these factors, the observer could not say what it was that the person chiefly desired. But the experiencer might be able to tell him.

Perry himself recognizes this. He distinguishes two elements in interest, a 'governing propensity' and an 'accompanying expectation' of 'an object of reference'. And he asserts that the 'governing propensity' can be better known by someone other than the interested agent, while the interested agent is better able to know the 'object at any given time'. 'Whether a given child does or does not like olives may perhaps best be judged by the watchful parent in the light of the child's total behavior. . . . But of the fact that he likes *this taste* (assuming it to be of olives or waiving the question of its external origin) the child is the best judge.' Again : 'If the agent does not know the object of his interest, no one does. No one can know the object of the agent's interest better than he does himself, for the object of the agent's interest is *what he judges*, whether he judges truly or falsely' (Section 147). Nor does Perry question that an agent may have an interest which is 'at any given time' or merely momentary. He quotes from Santayana : 'No doubt any desire, however capricious, represents some momentary and partial interest, which lends to its objects a certain real and inalienable value . . .' (Section 56). A momentary interest could not be known in its governing propensity by an outside observer, for the observer knows this propensity through repetitions of the act of pursuit. Thus the observer cannot estimate what a person's interest is in any particular case; and he cannot judge what action will maximize his interest in a given case. He can know what a person is interested in generally, and he can judge what action will maximize his general interests. Moreover, if it is true that a person should always act to satisfy the greatest number of his interests, then that action will be right in the particular case which satisfies these interests, rather than those of the moment. Thus the observer can judge which action is right in the particular case when the action affects the person's general interests. But when the action does not affect these interests, the observer cannot judge. In this respect the limitation of the Interest Theory is no greater than that of the other objective theories, but neither is it any less.

7. *Final Objections to the Interest Theory*

We have seen various shortcomings of the Interest Theory, but we have not yet stated the most obvious and fatal objections. I shall state two such objections, then conclude by mentioning two truths which can be extracted from the Interest Theory and which may account for its wide acceptance.

(1) Some desires and some activities are good or bad in themselves independent of their relation to a desire. The value of the desire does not depend upon its existing in relation to an object or to another desire, nor does the value of the activity depend upon its existing in relation to a desire. According to the Interest Theory, any desire can be good or bad only extrinsically, by leading to the satisfaction or frustration of other desires. It is obviously true that desires are good and bad in this way. But we also think they are good and bad in themselves. Benevolence is generally thought to be good in both ways, and malevolence bad in both ways. We think it bad that a person desires to

hurt another person, even if there is no possibility of hi[
realizing that desire. And we think it bad that he is impelled to construct fantasies in which he does hurt another
person, even when this imaginative sort of success gives
him satisfaction and hurts no one else. We think that he
would be in a better state if he were unable to indulge in
such satisfactions.

(2) It cannot be true that desire is the source of all
value, for in many cases it is a belief in the value of a
thing which is the source of our interest in it. If Perry's
formula is right, that a thing's value consists in its being
an object of desire, then we could not desire it as being of
value. For this would be to desire it as being an object of
desire. Plainly we do not desire things for this feature.
But we do desire things as having value. The belief that a
thing has value or is good is usually sufficient to arouse some
desire for it. And this belief often arouses a desire sufficient
to lead us to suppress the satisfaction of other desires.

We can conclude by noticing two truths about value
and desire which can be extracted from the Interest Theory.
It is possible that the Interest Theory has its basis in a
misconstruing of these facts.

(1) Desire is often a source of our *belief* that things
have value. But the belief so caused may be false ; a strong
desire for a thing may cause us to exaggerate its value. In
this case, then, desire is a source of neither value nor of
truth about value.

(2) However, desire is often a source of things which
have value. We often engage in valuable activities only
because we have a strong desire for the activity. Or when
we engage in an activity with desire it may acquire new
properties which give it value, and which it lacks when it
is done without desire. For example, if a person plays a
game with desire his playing may have a spirit and grace
which give the activity a value which it lacks when he plays
without desire. But it is plain that desire is in these cases
only an indirect source of value. Desire is a source of
activities and of particular properties of these activities.
The value resides in the activities, not in the relation of
these activities to desire.

CHAPTER III

PLEASURE

would seem to be something whose value is un-
. Experiencing pleasure seems to be the experi-
t of a thing which is good but of good itself.
e of other things may require discernment and
the value of pleasure appears as an immediate
of the pleasure, no more capable of being overlooked
e extendedness of color. However, there is another
hich seems to conflict with this. This fact is that we
d some pleasures as bad. There are several possible
of attempting to reconcile these two facts. One,
h is that of the Hedonist, is to say that pleasure is the
good, but that we call particular pleasures bad when
y lead to future pain or to a reduction of future pleasures.
second, which I shall label Kantianism, asserts that any
ppearance pleasure has of being good is a deception; for
leasure is not good by itself, but only when joined with
virtue. Finally one can hold, as I shall, that pleasure is one
of the things which are good, but not the only one; and
that when we call certain pleasures bad we mean that
though the experience has a good feeling it involves a bad
act or character or life. This last view is a compromise
between the Hedonistic doctrine that nothing is good
except pleasure and the Kantian doctrine that pleasure is
not good at all.

1. *Pleasure and Feeling*

The concept of pleasure is linked to biological, psychological and ethical concepts, and the role of the concept in
the biological and psychological realms throws some light
on its ethical role. Our main way of thinking of pleasure
is as a psychological phenomenon, and I shall be mainly
concerned with pleasure in this aspect — in relation to the
concepts of experience, feeling, attention and desire. But

I shall first briefly comment on pleasure as a biological concept.

It is plain that pleasure is closely related to the preservation of the living organism. A thing's pleasantness may be a sign that it will promote the health of the organism, and the feeling of pleasure is generally a sign of health. These facts have led such writers as Hobbes and Spinoza, who believed self-preservation to be the chief good, to conceive pleasure just as the mental representative of the healthy condition of the organism. But this is not adequate. Pleasantness and pleasure are not always signs of healthfulness or health. As Aristotle observed, some pleasures are signs of disease. Aristotle's more cautious account is that pleasure is a completion of the *activity* (not of the entire self) which it accompanies. Pleasure tends to increase whatever activity it accompanies, and tends to inhibit contrary activities. But there are activities and pleasures which are inimical to the self.

Most often we regard pleasure as a psychological phenomenon, as a feeling or experience. Pleasure is something which belongs to us as having experiences, not either to external objects or to our bodies. We do say that certain objects are pleasant; but what we mean is that they cause pleasure or enter into our pleasant experiences. And we do not say that a certain part of our body feels pain (or pleasure) but that we feel pain in a certain part of the body. Pleasure (and pain) are concepts which require the concept of experience. However, certain objections may be made to this.

Professor Ryle has pointed out that pain is not an exact counterpart of pleasure. He says first that 'We can tell the doctor where it [a pain] hurts . . . but we cannot tell him, nor does he ask, where it [a pleasure] pleases us'.[1] Let us express this as the view that pains seem to have bodily

---

[1] 'Pleasure', *Dilemmas*, Cambridge University Press, 1954, p. 58. Ryle's main concern in the above section is to show that pleasure is not the sort of causal force that Psychological Hedonists have supposed; and I believe he does show this. See also Ryle's article 'Pleasure' in *Proceedings of the Aristotelian Society*, Supplementary Volume xxviii: and in the same volume W. B. Gallie's comments on Ryle's essay. See also T. Penelhum's 'The Logic of Pleasure', *Philosophy and Phenomenological Research*, 1957.

locations but that pleasures do not. Doubtless it is true and worth noting that pleasures and pains generally differ in this way. But as Ryle himself indicates, the distinction is not a universal one. Some pleasures seem to have a bodily location, and some pains do not. We can tell a masseur that 'it feels good' when he rubs a particular muscle, and we cannot say of a pain of bereavement that it feels bad in any particular place. Further, when we say that 'it hurts here' or 'it feels pleasant there' we are, I think, either concerned with directing someone about what to do to give us pleasure or to remove a pain, or with describing to him the nature or quality of the pleasure or pain. And surely we suppose that the pleasure or pain (when we locate it) is something that we experience, and not just a state of our body or a feature of our behavior. To say 'My toe hurts' is to assert or imply that 'I *feel* my toe hurting'. It would be absurd to say, 'My toe is hurting but I can't feel it'. Reference to the source of the hurt is, then, a way of telling someone where to look for the cause of the trouble or of telling him what sort of hurt it is. It does not indicate that pain belongs primarily or exclusively to the body. What does emerge from Ryle's observation is that the source and description of pains more often involves a specific bodily location than does the source and description of pleasures.

But against the notion that pleasure is a feeling Ryle asserts in his paper for The Aristotelian Society that, while various sorts of feeling are processes which can be 'clocked', pleasure cannot be clocked. He writes : 'Sensations, emotional states and moods can, in principle, all be clocked. We can often say roughly how long a tingle or a headache lasted, very roughly how long a fit of rage or amusement lasted, and extremely roughly how long a mood of depression or cheerfulness lasted. But pleasure does not lend itself to such clockings. The walker can, indeed, say that he enjoyed his walk until it began to rain, two hours after he started out ; or the diner can say that he enjoyed, though decreasingly, every bite of Stilton Cheese that he took until satiety set in with the penultimate bite, and that this series of bites took six minutes. But he cannot clock the duration of his enjoyment *against* the duration of the thing he enjoyed. He can, at best, divide the duration of the walk or meal into the parts which he enjoyed and the parts which he did not enjoy. The enjoyment of a walk is not a concomitant, e.g. an introspectible effect of the walking, such that there might be two histories, one the history of the walk, the other the history of its agreeableness to the walker' (p. 138). But as Ryle here and later develops the point that pleasure cannot be clocked, what he seems to stress is just (a) that there is no pleasure which is distinct from the activity in which pleasure is taken, and (b) that the pleasure involves an attending to the thing which is pleasant. But plainly neither of these facts (a) or (b) would show that pleasure is not a feeling-episode. It would only show that pleasure is at most a feature of a complex episode which involves some content other than pleasure as well as attention to this content.

Both Ryle and commentators on his view (Professors Gallie and Penelhum) regard pleasure as a variety of attention or 'heed'. But, as all these writers observe, taking pleasure in a thing cannot be just attending to or heeding it. We can also give attention to things which give no pleasure; and we give very sharp attention to things which give pain. So pleasure is not to be distinctively described, in the manner of Penelhum, as an 'effortless form of attention'; pain also involves an effortless attention.

More complex considerations are required to evaluate Gallie's notion that pleasure is the sort of attention which he calls 'appraisive' — i.e. 'such as either to contain or to be suited to develop into an evaluation or appraisal of it [the thing to which attention is being given]' (p. 158). Gallie further specifies the appraisive attention in enjoyment as '(i) positive (pro-), (ii) simple, i.e. non-comparative, (iii) direct, i.e. directed on to an object or activity regarded as a unit *per se*, and not in virtue of its consequences' (pp. 160-1). Both these general and specific descriptions of pleasure seem accurate. Pleasure is positive, simple and direct; it either contains or could develop into an evaluation; and it involves attention. That pleasure is appraisive seems very like the account which I shall later recommend, namely Sidgwick's view that pleasure is a feeling apprehended as implicitly desirable. But whether the genus of pleasure is attention is very hard to assess until we are provided with some systematic and detailed account of attention. It would appear that the advantage which might be thought to follow from this account of pleasure as a form of attention is that attention, and thence pleasure, might be describable in purely behavioral terms. However, Gallie suggests that perhaps the three varieties of attention ('inquisitive', 'practical' and 'appraisive') are introspectively distinguishable. And if this is so (as I think it is) then it seems safer at this stage of inquiry to treat pleasure just under the very broad genus of immediate apprehension, or experience, or — in one of its uses — 'feeling'.

Perhaps Ryle, as well as Gallie and Penelhum, have been partly led to the notion that pleasure is a sort of attention by their tendency to speak of 'enjoyment' rather than of 'pleasure'. 'Enjoyment' might not so naturally be classed as a kind of feeling as a kind of attention ; while 'pleasure' is more naturally taken as the name for a feeling than for a sort of attention. Objective reference is built into the grammar of 'to enjoy' ; it is not similarly built into the grammar of 'to be pleased' or 'to take pleasure in'. 'To enjoy' is a transitive verb, requiring an object which the enjoyment is 'of'. While to say that a person 'was pleased' or 'felt pleasure' is a complete expression. Again, we naturally speak of an 'object' of 'enjoyment', as we also speak of an 'object' of 'attention' ; while we speak not of an 'object' but of a 'source' or 'kind' of 'pleasure'. Thus if we treat pleasure in the same way as enjoyment we are more likely to regard attention as its genus than if we examine the word 'pleasure' without making this identification.

As Gallie notes, Ryle's account of pleasure in terms of enjoyment and liking somewhat resembles Professor C. D. Broad's tentative analysis of pleasure as a liking of an experience for its emotional qualities. Broad writes in *Five Types of Ethical Theory* : 'Is it not possible that what we have called "hedonic *quality*" is really a "*relational property*" and not a quality at all ? Is it not possible that the statement : "This experience of mine is pleasant" just means: "I like this experience for its non-hedonic qualities"? I may dislike the experience as a whole, because it will have causal and non-causal relational properties in addition to its emotional quality; but I cannot confine my attention to this. I have to consider also its relational property of having for its object the undeserved misfortunes of another; and my dislike for the combination of this emotional quality with this relational property overbalances my liking for the experience regarded simply as having the emotional quality. On this view we would no longer divide the qualities of an experience into hedonic and non-hedonic. All its qualities would be non-hedonic. But if its qualities were such that I disliked it *for them* it would be painful. And it would remain pleasant in the first case even though I disliked it *on the whole*. I think it is worth while to throw out this suggestion; but I do not wish to attach much weight to it. My argument against pure quantitative hedonism is independent of its truth or falsity. I am inclined to think that Sidgwick is taking a somewhat similar view in the very difficult discussion in *Book II, Chap. II, Sect. 2*, and in *Book II, Chap. XIV, Sect. 4'* (pp. 237-8).

The obvious truth here is that liking the emotional qualities of an experience involves getting satisfaction and pleasure from these qualities. And what one likes in the experience, as distinct from the object which may be liked for other features, is its pleasure. But there is no ground for regarding the liking as more elementary than the pleasure. Why not describe the liking of the quality as a taking pleasure in it, instead of describing the pleasure as a liking of the quality? In fact pleasure seems to be the more primary fact. We seem to be aware of the pleasure of the experience we feel before we are aware of our liking for the experience. Thus pleasure in an experience seems to explain the liking of the experience in a way that a liking of the experience does not explain one's pleasure in it. It would be intelligible, even if it were tautological, to say 'I like the experience of malice because it gives me pleasure'; while it would not be intelligible to say 'I get pleasure from the experience of malice because I like it'. We would offer as an explanation of our pleasure in an experience a liking for the activity or object which gave pleasure. A person might say 'I get pleasure from the experience of malice because I like to hurt people'. But he would not account for his pleasure in the experience by a liking for the experience.[1]

The hardest question about the psychological features of pleasure is how the experience of pleasure involves knowing. We have said that to have an experience of pleasure is to feel in a certain way; it is not merely to know certain things. This feature of experience is sometimes called its 'immediacy'. Whether there are experiences which are purely immediate — which contain no knowing at all — is a difficult problem. It is also relevant to the nature of pleasure. For we want to know whether pleasure contains an element of knowledge. I cannot deal with the general problem but I shall suggest that pleasure does contain a kind of knowing, namely a knowing that the experience is good.

I believe Sidgwick's view on this is approximately correct. Sidgwick described pleasure as a feeling which contains an apprehension, or 'implicit apprehension', of desirability or good. Pleasure, he said, is 'feeling apprehended as desirable by the sentient individual at the time of feeling it' (*The Methods of Ethics*, fifth edition, p. xxi). Later he writes more fully: 'When I reflect on the notion of pleasure . . . the only common quality that I can find . . . seems to be that expressed by the general term "good" or "desirable". . . . Hence, while I cannot define Pleasure . . . as the kind of feeling which we actually desire and aim at, I still recognize as its essential quality some relation to desire or volition. I propose therefore to define it as feeling which, when experienced by intelligent

[1] Professor C. I. Lewis in his *Analysis of Knowledge and Valuation* suggests that 'pleasure' does not so clearly indicate what is 'immediately valuable' (what is 'found good' in experience) as does the notion of liking. The connotation of pleasure is, he thinks, too narrow. He proposes that 'the immediately good is what you like and may want in the way of experience' (p. 404). Though Lewis evidently is not proposing to define pleasure, he does think that the value of those things we call pleasure is best understood in terms of the concept of 'liking' and this is, if I am right in the above, a mistake.

beings, is at least implicitly apprehended as desirable or —
in cases of comparison — preferable' (Bk. II, ch. ii, Sec. 2).
Evidently Sidgwick does not wish to say that this desirability (and good) can be merely felt. He says, then, that
this desirability and good are apprehended in pleasure, but
perhaps only 'implicitly'. Sidgwick does not explain this
notion of 'implicit apprehension' but I think we can see
what he wanted to get at. In feeling pleasure we are aware
of value but we do not identify the experience as containing
value. Pleasure is primarily a feeling, not a knowing;
hence the elements in the feeling will not be present in the
explicit form in which they are present in cognition. The
same phenomenon appears in other feelings. In fear we
are in some sense aware that the feared object is dangerous,
but we do not explicitly identify it as such. And in love
we are aware that the object is good, although we do not
frame a proposition to this effect. There is this difference,
that in love we are aware that the object is good while in
pleasure we are aware that the feeling itself is good. But
there is also an analogy to the case of a loving act. In this
act we may be implicitly aware that the particular event in
which we are engaged is good, in the same way that we are
aware that the feeling in which we are absorbed is good.
Indeed in the loving act we may in some implicit way be
aware of all of these : that the object is good, that the act
is good, and that the feeling of pleasure we get from the
object and the act is good.

2. *Pleasure and Desire*

Several views have described pleasure by reference to
desire. The oldest and most obviously mistaken view is
that of the so-called Psychological Hedonist, who asserts
that pleasure is the sole object of desire. J. S. Mill seems
to have taken this view in his *Utilitarianism*. As a kind of
proof of his Universalistic Hedonism, he evidently wished
to construct the following sort of argument : if only one
thing is desired by everyone, then that thing is desirable,
and if desirable then good ; and it is a fact that everyone
does desire nothing but pleasure. Mill's actual statement
of the relation of pleasure and desire is ambiguous. He

writes: 'And now to decide whether . . . mankind do desire nothing for itself but that which is a pleasure for them, or of which the absence is a pain. . . .' He answers: 'Desiring a thing and finding it pleasant, aversion to it and thinking of it as painful, are phenomena absolutely inseparable, or rather two parts of the same phenomenon; in strictness of language, two different modes of naming the same psychological fact . . . to desire anything, except in proportion as the idea of it is pleasant, is a physical and metaphysical impossibility' (*Utilitarianism*, Section IV). This statement could be interpreted to mean only what we asserted in the preceding chapter, (a) that desiring a thing involves a thought that satisfying the desire would be pleasant, and not (b) that this pleasure or some other pleasure is the only feature for which a thing is desired. But Mill needs this latter principle for the above argument that pleasure is the only thing which is good.

This principle is clearly false. Pleasure is not the only thing we desire, or the only feature of things for which we desire them. As G. E. Moore says in *Principia Ethica*: '. . . Plainly we are not always conscious of expecting pleasure, when we desire a thing. We may be only conscious of the thing which we desire, and may be impelled to make for it at once, without any calculation as to whether it will bring pleasure or pain' (Section 42).[1] This is just a fact about the way we do desire things. Often we are so occupied with a thought of the thing we want that we have almost no thought of the pleasure it will give us.

However, writers have also argued that we could not conceivably desire things for their pleasure unless we desired them in some other way. But there is no reason in the nature of pleasure and desire why we could not desire things solely for their pleasure. It just happens that we do not. What is true is that we could not desire pleasure in the abstract; we can only desire pleasure of particular sorts. Desire must be for something which will exist, and the only pleasures which exist are pleasures of particular sorts. It is also true that a desire for pleasure involves a

[1] For the most clear and complete development of this point see H. Sidgwick's *Methods of Ethics*, ch. iv, Sect. 2 and 3.

thought of the particular thing — the activity or object —
which provides pleasure. For any desire involves a thought
of the source of its satisfaction. But it does not involve a
desire for this source in its entirety. The 'source of satisfaction' is always complex; it is an event or object which
has many features, and the thing may be desired for only
one or several of these. Let us distinguish the 'objective'
of desire, or the feature of a thing which is desired, from
the 'object' of desire, or the total thing to which this
feature belongs. Now one cannot desire any objective
without having a *thought* of some object, either of some
particular object or of an object of some general sort. And
perhaps one may sometimes desire (as well as have a thought
of) this total object. But one may also merely have a
thought of this object as the source of what one desires
while desiring just a particular feature of it. Writers have
confused these in the case of pleasure — they have confused
the *desire* for the pleasure (the objective) with the *thought*
of its source (the object), and have consequently confused
the thought of this object with a desire for it. Moore
commits the confusion in a second argument purporting
to show that pleasure is not the only thing which we desire.
He writes: 'And, in the second place, even when we do
expect pleasure, it can certainly be very rarely pleasure *only*
which we desire. For granted that, when I desire my glass
of port wine, I have an idea of the pleasure I expect from
it, plainly that pleasure cannot be the only object of my
desire; the port wine must be included in my object, else
I might be led by my desire to take wormwood instead. If
the desire were directed *solely* to the pleasure, it could not
lead me to take the wine; if it is to take a definite direction,
it is absolutely necessary that the idea of the object, from
which the pleasure is expected, should also be present and
should control my activity' (Section 42). Moore is certainly right in saying that the idea of the object must be
present and control the person's activity, but its being
present as a controlling idea in the desire does not entail
its being present as an object we desire. One can desire a
particular feature of an object without desiring the entire
object, although one cannot desire the object for a particular

feature without having a thought of the object which has this feature. Thus it might be that one desired objects only for their pleasure. There is nothing in the nature of desire and pleasure which excludes this. It just happens not to be the case. We also desire things for quite different sorts of features, such as a thing's goodness or rightness.

We can now briefly state the relations of desire and pleasure. It is plain that these relations are close, as well as that both are closely related to value. (1) A desire can lead to pleasure, namely to the pleasure of satisfying it. (2) A desire can be part of an experience which is pleasant. A desire involves a thought of an object which will give pleasure, and the thought of pleasant things may itself be pleasant. Whether this experience is pleasant, and what degree of pleasure it has, depends upon several things — the degrees of the intensity of the desire, of the certainty of the belief that the desire can be fulfilled, of the intensity of the pleasure foreseen in satisfying the desire, and perhaps upon still other factors. In particular, if the desire is very intense and one is certain he cannot satisfy the desire, then the experience of desiring will be painful. The experience may also be painful if the desire is very intense and one is certain he will satisfy the desire, but the satisfaction is at some distance. On the other hand, if the desire is very weak, the knowledge that one cannot satisfy it may not prevent a person's desiring the thing with pleasure. This sort of desire is called 'wish'. (3) Likewise a pleasure can lead to a desire. A pleasure can arouse a later thought of itself, and this thought can arouse a desire for the thing which gives pleasure. (4) Finally, an experience of pleasure can contain a desire for the continuation of the pleasure.

It appears that all of these relations exist in many or even most instances of desire and pleasure. But none of them is necessary. (1) A desire may never lead to fulfillment, or to the pleasure of this. (2) A desire may be neither sufficiently strong nor sufficiently certain or uncertain of satisfaction to give an experience a positive or negative hedonic quality. (3) and (4) A pleasure may arise suddenly and unexpectedly, last briefly, and pass without regret, evoking no desire for its continuance and no later

desire for its recurrence. However these latter cases seem
most rare, and perhaps they do not exist; perhaps any
experience of pleasure arouses some desire to continue or
repeat the pleasure. But it does seem clear that such
experiences do not always arouse a conscious desire.

3. 'Good' and 'Bad' Pleasures

We have said that pleasure is a feeling or an experience
which contains an apprehension of good. It is a feeling
which includes the implicit knowledge that it is good.
Pleasure, then, is the good of feeling or experience. The
most obvious evidence that we do think pleasure a good
thing is that we reward persons by giving them pleasure
(and punish by giving them pain). For we reward people
with things which we think good, and punish them with
the opposite. But there is also contrary evidence in that
we think some pleasures are bad — for example, revenge,
rage, lust. The Hedonist's answer to this, which I shall
defend, is that what is thought bad is never the pleasure
itself but something associated with it. However the
Hedonist conceives these associated things to be just the
causes or effects of the pleasure, while I shall argue that
an event which is pleasant in its experiencing might be bad,
not merely in its causes and effects, but as the expression
of a bad personal disposition.

Of some feelings it is paradoxical to say that they are
good, however pleasant they may be. But this is because
the phrase 'good feeling' (or 'having a good feeling') is
used in two quite distinct ways. By it we sometimes mean
'a feeling about a good thing'; and it is with this sense
that it is paradoxical to speak of, for example, a 'good
feeling of malice'. But the phrase is also used to mean
'feeling good' or 'having pleasure'. And there is no
paradox in speaking of having a good feeling (in this sense
of 'feeling good') while doing a bad thing, such as an act
of malice. The general source of the confusion is in the
fact that pleasure is a quality of feeling, and that feeling
always involves some specific object or activity. What we
think bad are the specific objects or activities in which we
take pleasure, as well as our capacity to take pleasure in

H

them and our desire for them. When one takes pleasure in revenge what is bad is the revenge, and his desire for it. There is nothing bad in the feeling of pleasure he gets.

One may object that if this were so, then, since the pleasure one gets from revenge would be good, this good would somewhat reduce the total badness of the revengeful act, while on the contrary it aggravates its badness. It may be said that pleasure makes a good activity better — Aristotle compared it to the bloom on the cheek of youth — and makes a bad activity worse. This suggests that pleasure is only a sort of dependent good or bad, and neither good nor bad in itself. But we can explain this by the particular relation which exists between pleasure and desire. To take pleasure in a thing is generally a sign that one desires it. It is the desire which we think bad. One who thinks that taking pleasure in revenge is bad would agree that the desire for revenge is bad. Further, a general desire for revenge would be thought worse than taking pleasure in revenge on a particular occasion. For the occasion might be exceptional, and one might excuse the person for an occasional lapse of this sort. While if we thought the person were animated by a general desire for revenge we would consider the badness involved to be very serious. But taking any pleasure in a thing is generally a sign that one does like and desire the thing ; and if a person does, even on a single occasion, feel pleasure in an act of revenge, this is some evidence that he is a vengeful person. It is this inference to a desire which leads us to call the revenge bad. It is a confusion of the pleasure in the act with the act as the expression of a personal desire which causes us to call the pleasure itself bad.

One may say that if the desire is bad because it reflects a bad personal character, then the feeling is bad in the same way, for the person possesses the feeling no less than the desire. But this is not so. The desire is more closely connected with the person. The feeling of pleasure belongs more to the present moment, and is closely related to the person only by way of desire. What we chiefly judge bad is that the person *could* take pleasure in revenge or deception, and this is to judge not that the person's present feeling is bad, but that it is bad that he is the sort of person who could have this sort of feeling. We are inclined to say, 'How awful that he could feel that way!', not 'How awful was his feeling!'

The same principle causes us to regard a feeling of pain as mitigating an act's badness. Suppose a person deceives a friend, and suppose both we and the deceiver think that deception in general is bad but that it is the right thing to do in this instance. We think it better if the person feel some pain in committing the deception than if he enjoys his cleverness in doing it skillfully. We do not think his pain is in itself a good, but rather that his pain in the act attests a general tendency we think good.

There are other sorts of cases which show that what we admire in the so-called 'good pleasures', and what we deplore in the 'bad' ones, are not these as states of feeling but as the expression of states of character. Consider our attitude toward acts and feelings which are apparently out of keeping with the person's character. Suppose an habitually self-centered person feels evident pleasure in the stroke of good fortune of an acquaintance. Is our reaction to admire the momentary feeling? Do we think that though his character is not good, this particular feeling is both good and not in character? Our attitude is rather that the person may not be so bad after all, or that this may signify a change for the better. Further, instead of admiring, we detest the condition of one who is able to feel the pleasure of acting virtuously through deceiving himself into thinking he is acting virtuously. Such a person does have a generous feeling, but he is not in fact generous. Our attitude toward his generous feeling shows that what we are judging when we judge it bad is neither its specific character of generosity nor its hedonic quality but the state of character it exhibits.

4. *The Factors in the Value of Pleasure*

If pleasure is good, the question arises as to whether there are several factors in its value, and if so, what they are. Jeremy Bentham distinguished four factors affecting the 'value of a pleasure considered by itself' — intensity, duration, certainty and propinquity. His idea seems to have been that the greater the pleasure in each of these dimensions, the better a pleasure it was. But it is clear that of these four factors only intensity and duration are properties of the pleasure itself. Certainty and propinquity concern the relation of the pleasure to a prior moment. They are like intensity and duration in being relevant to a decision to obtain a given pleasure. If pleasure is good, one ought to pursue pleasures which are not only intense and long but which one is most likely to obtain.[1] But certainty and propinquity are like 'fecundity' and 'purity', or a pleasure's tendency to cause future pleasures and pains, in that they belong not to the pleasure itself but to a relation of the pleasure to some other event. A pleasure itself does not become better by being nearer and more certain, for if it is at any distance in the future it does not yet exist. But a present act in pursuit of a future pleasure is better in virtue of these relations. Thus certainty and propinquity do not affect the value of the pleasure itself but only the value of the choice and pursuit of pleasure.

The difficult question here, however, is whether pleasures possess a third property and dimension called 'height'. To meet the criticism that Hedonism is a 'base doctrine worthy only of swine', Mill asserted that pleasures possess not merely certain degrees of strength and duration, but also degrees of 'height' or 'quality'. If some pleasures are swinishly low, others — the pleasures 'of the intellect, of the feelings and imagination, and of the moral sentiments' — are as 'high' as the most elevated ethical doctrine could demand. Nearly everyone has criticized Mill for this contention, and there is much to criticize in his account. First, it is very vague. Moreover, Mill does not succeed in discovering a factor of pleasure which enables him to show that pleasure can provide for all the distinctions which we make among good things. Still, I think Mill is right in insisting that there is this dimension of height, and I shall

---

[1] There is also a minor point. Propinquity would seem to be relevant only so far as it contributed to certainty. In general the nearer the occasion on which one has an opportunity to obtain a pleasure, the more certain one will be of obtaining it, for the fewer changes there will be in the interval which might prevent it.

try to show that the charges of one of his most able critics,
G. E. Moore, are ineffectual.

In *Principia Ethica* Moore presents a detailed criticism
of Mill's view. He argues that Mill's doctrine 'means, that
a pleasure is something complex, something composed, in
fact, of pleasure *in addition to* that which produces pleasure.
For instance, Mill speaks of "sensual indulgences" as
"lower pleasures". But what is a sensual indulgence? It
is surely a certain excitement of some sense *together with*
the pleasure caused by such excitement. Mill, therefore,
in admitting that a sensual indulgence can be directly
judged to be lower than another pleasure, in which the
degree of pleasure involved may be the same, is admitting
that other things may be good, or bad, quite independently
of the pleasure which accompanies them' (Section 18). But
Mill would not have admitted (or should not) that the
sensual indulgence and the other pleasure are of the same
degree in every respect. They cannot be of the same degree
of height. The crucial question is whether the fact that
the height of the pleasure is associated with a specific
content, as sensual indulgence, implies that any value here
besides intensity and duration of pleasure must belong not
to the pleasure but to the content of the activity. Moore
seems to assume this. But the Hedonist could say that
sensual indulgence is neither good nor bad in itself, but
only in its pleasure. Further he can say that these pleasures
are *felt* as lower. It is not that we think sensual indulgence
in itself low and so think the feeling accompanying it low.
Rather we feel a baseness in the pleasure itself, and so far
as we speak of sensual indulgence as base we must be
understood to mean that its pleasures are so. (Of course,
he would add that we may also estimate sensual pleasures
low for the quite distinct reason that they tend not to lead
to other pleasures but often to pains.)

To show that pleasures cannot differ in height Moore
compares pleasure to color. 'It is plain that if you say
"Colour alone is good as an end", then you can give no
possible reason for preferring one colour to another. Your
only standard of good and bad will then be "colour"; and
since red and blue both conform equally to this, the only

standard, you can have no other whereby to judge whether red is better than blue. . . . Just so with pleasure : If we do really mean "Pleasure alone is good as an end", then we must agree with Bentham that "Quantity of pleasure being equal, pushpin is as good as poetry"' (Section 48). The argument assumes that color is perfectly simple in the sense that we can discriminate no elements essential to it. But plainly we can discriminate such elements. Any color must possess hue, saturation and brilliance, and each in particular degrees. Thus Moore's model of something simple is complex in the only sense in which it is required that pleasure be complex. A pleasure, though simple like yellow, might also be complex like yellow. Further, Moore apparently recognizes that pleasure has two attributes, intensity and duration, and that therefore it is complex. So there is nothing about pleasure to preclude its having a third attribute of height.

At another point Moore argues : 'And if colour is our only possible end, as Mill says pleasure is, then there can be no possible reason for preferring one colour to another, red, for instance, to blue, except that the one is more of a colour than the other' (Section 48). Now clearly no color can be more 'of a color' than another, if this means that one color is a color but another color is not. Yet we do sensibly, if loosely, speak of one color as more colorful, meaning that one has more of one of the attributes of color, just as we speak of one man as being more 'of a man'. Likewise we might loosely speak of one pleasure as being 'better' than another, meaning that it has more of one of the good-making attributes of pleasure. The statement is loose but intelligible.

The fact is that some experiences of pleasure do feel 'higher' than others. But it also seems that this is a result of our judging that the experience is associated with an activity or object which is better independently of the pleasure it gives. Our judgments color our feelings ; and it would be unnatural if our judgments of the value of an activity did not affect the character of our feeling of pleasure in that activity. That pleasure's height originates in this way does not alter the fact that pleasure contains height as one of its dimensions. It does, however, distinguish this dimension from the dimensions of intensity and duration. For the latter do not equally depend upon an estimate of the independent value of the content or activity which gives pleasure. Further — and this may have been Moore's only real concern — it shows the inadequacy of height to serve Mill's argument that pleasure itself contains the distinctions of height which have been attributed to other things. For it would seem that pleasure contains these distinctions only because these other things contain them. If nothing were good except pleasure, then pleasures could not differ in 'nobility' or 'height'. The sense of a pleasure's being of the noble sort is a sense of its being associated with something noble. This nobility is felt to belong to the content which gives pleasure, as well as to the pleasure itself.

This gap in Mill's doctrine comes out in particular difficulties in his account of the attribute of height. The hedonic calculus requires that the several dimensions be comparable with one another, but Mill sometimes seems to deny that height is commensurable with the other dimensions. He sometimes speaks as if no degree of the other pleasure-dimensions could equal the smallest degree of the dimension of height; so that a person would rightly choose to sacrifice the greatest quantities of intense and enduring pleasures for the smallest quantity of a high pleasure. Such statements might be construed to mean that height can be compared with the other dimensions, but in this comparison the others always come out second. However, if one attribute of pleasure is infinitely superior in value to the others, this should make us wonder whether the things compared are both attributes of the same thing. If the very smallest amount of elevated (or 'virtuous') pleasure is superior to the very greatest amount of base (or 'vicious') pleasure, it would seem that what is being compared are really not two forms of the one good, pleasure, not high pleasure and low pleasure, but two different sorts of goods, virtue and pleasure. Further, the critics of hedonism are right in saying that when we consider whether to choose an act of fulfilling obligation or an act of obtaining an intense sensual pleasure, what we consider is not the value of the pleasure we shall get from the virtuous act of duty as against the intense pleasure of satisfying some sensual desire, but the values of virtue itself as against pleasure. But we shall take up the relation of virtue to pleasure in a later section.

5. *Pleasure and Happiness*

Most discussions of pleasure, and most Hedonistic theories, either draw no distinction between pleasure and happiness or show considerable confusion on the matter. Mill says flatly: 'By happiness is intended pleasure, and the absence of pain; and by unhappiness pain, and the privation of pleasure' (*Utilitarianism*, ch. ii). But somewhat later, attempting to counter a charge against his theory to the effect that no happiness is to be had by human beings, he alleges that, 'the happiness which they (the Hedonists) meant was not a life of rapture; but moments of such, in an existence made up of few and transitory pains, many and various pleasures, with a decided predominance of the active over the passive, and having as the foundation of the whole not to expect more from life than it is capable of bestowing' (*op. cit.*). Whatever the merits of this second notion of happiness, it is certainly not just the equivalent of what we mean by pleasure! This sort of unconscious equivocation is indeed deplorable in a treatise of philosophical pretensions. Still, Mill once again is struggling to come into contact with our actual concepts of pleasure and happiness. For these relate to each other in various and intricate ways.

In some uses 'pleasure' and 'happiness' are much alike, but in others they are plainly different. On some occasions when one says that he had a 'feeling of pleasure' he might be willing to substitute 'feeling of happiness'. On other occasions he might reject this. He might explain that what he feels is something that goes beyond 'mere' pleasure. Nor is the difference one in the degree of some quantitative dimension of the pleasure, such as intensity or duration or height. We would not mean by 'a feeling of happiness' a 'feeling of intense pleasure' or a 'long sustained feeling of pleasure' or an 'elevated pleasure'. Some feelings of happiness are more intense and longer than some feelings of pleasure, and some feelings of pleasure are longer than some feelings of happiness. The difference is of another sort. We would speak of a 'deep feeling of happiness' but not ordinarily of a 'deep feeling of pleasure'. This adjective 'deep' suggests a special dimension which belongs only to happiness.

This difference comes out most sharply when we consider the possibility of mistake about the two. It is either impossible or odd to speak of being mistaken or doubtful about whether one is feeling pleasure, but it is less odd to speak of being mistaken or doubtful as to whether one is feeling happy.

The explanation is that happiness is not merely a feeling. It is also an enduring state. Thus it is meaningful to say: 'He may have felt happy, but was he really happy?' while we can say nothing comparable about pleasure. The 'depth' in some feelings of happiness, and the doubt and mistake which are possible in happiness, depend on the presence in the happy feeling or experience of a judgment about the happy state. One who 'feels happy' (in the sense distinct from 'feeling pleasant' or 'feeling satisfied') 'feels' something about his state which goes beyond the present moment of experience. The 'feeling of happiness' is partly a feeling about one's happiness as a person or about one's happy life. By contrast, the feeling of pleasure may exist without any thought that one is a person of pleasure or that one has a pleasant life. The feeling of pleasure is isolated in a way in which the feeling of happiness is not. Thus we can say that a person may feel happy but not be happy; his feeling or experience contains a mistaken judgment.

But how are we to characterize 'happiness'? Consider the feeling first. The feeling of happiness contains a reference to the state of happiness; but obviously there is more to the feeling than this reference. To feel happy is something more than recognizing that one is a happy person or has a happy life. This recognition may produce the feeling, but the feeling is more than the recognition. Besides the recognition, there is a feeling of *pleasure* in this recognition. My suggestion is that so far as happiness is merely a feeling or a feeling component, happiness is just pleasure. We noticed that there are occasions in which we use 'pleasant feeling' and 'happy feeling' as equivalent. This happens, I think, by a contraction of the notion of 'happy', rather than by an expansion of the notion of 'pleasant'. It is effected by 'happy' being attached here to 'feeling', and is possible because the feeling which is present in happiness is thought to be just a feeling of pleasure. The feeling of happiness is a feeling of pleasure in the recognition of one's state or condition of happiness (either as belonging to the enduring object called a 'person' or to the pattern of moments called a 'life').

This accomplishes a partial reduction of the feeling of happiness to pleasure. But it leaves us with the 'state of happiness'. To what primarily does this state belong — to the person or to his life? We speak both of a 'happy man' and a 'happy life'; is one primary or are they independent? Could a man be happy yet have an unhappy life? Could a man have a happy life but be an unhappy man?

The primary concept is 'happy life'. As Aristotle says in the *Poetics*, 'Character gives us qualities, but it is in our actions — what we do — that we are happy or the reverse'. Happiness belongs primarily to the moments of our experience, and secondarily to us as a set of dispositions which participate in these moments. It is true that the two — 'happy man' and 'happy life' — entail each other. First, it would be odd to say that a man had a happy life yet was not a happy man. We would think that his being an unhappy man would prevent his having a happy life. But though we judge a man to be happy prior to knowing about his life, the judgment appears to be an hypothesis which is to be confirmed by knowing about his life. If we do not know about his life, the strictly correct thing to say is that he *seems* to be a happy man. For if we found that his life were unhappy, we would withdraw the judgment that he was a happy man.

This raises a minor question: can happiness belong only to the whole life or to some smaller periods of life, such that a person could be happy in one period and unhappy in another? Plainly we would say that a person may have been 'really' happy during one period (as his youth)

though he did not have a happy life. One might conceivably argue that what alone counts for happiness (and
hence makes for a happy life) is just one period, namely old
age. If a man 'dies happy', then his life was happy. But
it would seem clearer to say in this case that the person's
life 'ended happily, but was not happy on the whole'.
These differences are relatively minor, involving, as they
all do, the recognition that happiness belongs not merely to
an experience but to a stretch of time.

Happiness is, then, primarily a condition of a certain
period in a life, and may include the whole of life. A
happy person is one whose life is in such a condition. But
we still lack a characterization of the condition of life that
makes it happy. It is a condition of a pattern of moments,
but what is the condition of these moments? Specifically,
is it one of pleasure or virtue or both? These have, at any
rate, been the chief alternatives which writers have considered. To be happy must one have pleasant experiences,
or perform virtuous acts, or take pleasure in performing
virtuous acts?

Aristotle's answer was the last, but surely this is at most
plausible only as an account of consummate happiness.
The ordinary understanding employs the Hedonistic account: A person is happy if he has a certain balance of
pleasures in the moments of his life. And even with the
ideal realization of both virtue and pleasure we can still
ask whether happiness means chiefly the pleasure which
virtue gives or the virtue which gives pleasure. Aristotle
does give the right clue here. He implies that virtue is the
chief factor in happiness, because it is the chief source of
pleasure. Virtue, he says, does not ensure happiness ; a
man may fall on great misfortunes, and these external ills —
sickness, poverty, friendlessness, dishonor — maim happiness. External goods are necessary for complete happiness.
Well, if they are necessary, surely they are so as sources of
pleasant experiences. And if so, virtue also would seem to
contribute to happiness by contributing to pleasure. Aristotle's view seems to be that happiness requires pleasures
from various sources, chiefly from a sense of virtue but
also from sources independent of one's action. This is also

the view of common sense. We may most admire the hero who suffers great or frequent torment for the sake of virtue, but we would not cite him as a model of happiness. Finally, it makes sense to ask whether it would be better to be exceptionally virtuous or exceptionally happy, as it would not if happiness consisted merely in the pleasure given by virtue. Virtue is necessary to happiness because it is necessary to pleasure; but what a person contemplates when he contemplates and feels his happiness is not his virtuous actions but his pleasant experiences. The 'feeling' of happiness is a pleasant awareness of a state of life with regard to pleasures; the 'state' or condition of happiness is the fact corresponding to this belief.

We can raise one more general question without broaching the detailed problem concerning the specific content and ordering of pleasures which make for happiness. Does the feeling of happiness depend chiefly on an awareness of past or future pleasures, or on both? Both are important for our state of happiness; but evidently both are not equally central to our feeling of happiness. A person is best acquainted with his past pleasures, but he is most interested in his future ones. Our sense of happiness chiefly depends on what we look forward to. The suggestion that a man is not happy until his life ends could only come from giving undue weight to verification. We have better knowledge of our past experiences; but our concern with them is as a guide to the future or a refuge from the present. One who is unhappy in the present may dwell on a happy past. Or one who has been unhappy in the past may ask how he can prevent the same thing in the future. But when he contemplates and feels his happiness, what affects him most are the events which he anticipates.

6. *Criticisms of Hedonism*

It is already clear that pleasure cannot be, as the Hedonist holds, the only thing which is good. For pleasure is not the same as happiness, yet happiness is also good. The feeling of happiness is a pleasure, but it also includes a recognition of a state of happiness. This state is a certain relation of pleasures; and a relation of pleasures is not just a pleasure. Pleasure itself exists only in the particular moments of experience which are thus related. If what is good is not just that pleasures exist at these particular moments, but that the pleasures exist in this relation, then we think that something is good besides pleasure. Further, though the knowledge of this relation gives a pleasure, this single pleasure also exists at a particular moment, and is distinct from the relation of pleasures which is known. Thus the state of happiness to which the pleasurable feeling of happiness refers is a good of a different kind from pleasure.

The point can be put in another way. The good of pleasure is the good of an experience. We speak of a 'good experience' but also of a 'good life' (as well as of a 'good person' and a 'good act'). And we do not think that the good of an experience is the same as the good of a life. For an experience could not be the same as a life. It is doubtful whether there is nothing in life but experiences; but let us not question that. Still a life is not just one long experience; it is, at least, a certain relation of experiences. Experiences have longer and shorter duration, but no experience could be life-long. Thus any value which a life had would be of a different sort from the value of a single experience.

Because an experience is one kind of thing, and a life another, their values also are of different kinds. The two have some similar traits : both involve temporal movement, and both may be more or less orderly, progressive and intense. Further, these same traits may be valuable in both an experience and a life. Finally, it might be that these traits could occur in one of these (an experience or a life) only if they occurred in the other. Still the values of the two are not the same. The value of an orderly and progressive life is one kind of thing and the value of an orderly and progressive experience is another. The only way in which the value of one could be reduced to the value of the other would be if one of these things could be reduced to the other — only if we could have 'experience of a life'. But in this phrase 'experience' cannot be taken strictly. We can conceive or imagine or know a life, and we can have experiences in a life; but we cannot 'experience' a life. To experience a thing is to have a single experience, with some rough boundaries and some degree of internal unity of which we are immediately aware. We do not experience our lives in this way. Professor C. I. Lewis makes a similar point in his *Analysis of Knowledge and Valuation*; but it is not entirely clear in his account that the value of a life is not itself the value of an experience. The important difference between the value of a life and that of an experience is that an experience is known as good at the moment in which it occurs, while the value of a life is not known in this way. Lewis seems to confuse these. He says on the one hand that nothing has 'intrinsic' value except experience; on the other hand he says that a life has a value which is not just the value of its separate experiences. He declares that 'the only thing intrinsically valuable — valuable for its own sake — is a goodness immediately found or findable and unmistakable when disclosed' (p. 387). And about the value of a life, he says: 'This value characterizing a whole life is also intrinsic; there can be no goodness or badness of it except a value or disvalue to be realized in the living of it' (p. 486). But later he also writes: 'The value-assessment of experiential wholes (such as a life) can neither be directly certain nor capable of any decisive and final verification. Because what is to be assessed is a whole of experience *as experienced*, and there is no moment in which this whole can be presented in the actuality of it' (p. 507). Thus there is a sharp incompatibility between Lewis' statement that all intrinsic value belongs in experience and is thereby 'unmistakable', and his statement that a life has intrinsic value and yet that a life is not at any moment of experience presented in its actuality.

The source of Lewis' difficulty seems to be a confusion of the 'experience' in which a value is possessed with the experience in which it is known. The peculiarity of pleasure is that in pleasure the experiencer possesses value in the experience and knows that he possesses value. But in any apprehension of a life, the value which is apprehended belongs to something outside the moment of experience in which the apprehension occurs. Lewis seems to confuse these in his notion of an experience which is also a 'synthetic apprehension'. He asserts that we are familiar with the sort of experience to which he is referring, the only difficulty being in finding a name for it. But all he does to explain the notion is to mention the following very different sorts of examples. He writes : 'If it be objected that there is no such thing as synthetic intuition, then let us reply by reference to such envisagement as that by which we hear a symphony, or discover that a journey is comfortable or uncomfortable, or decide that a lengthy undertaking goes smoothly and is a rewarding experience or proves difficult and tedious' (p. 506). Plainly these things are very different. Perhaps we may have a single experience of the symphony, but we cannot have a single experience of a journey which takes more than a few hours and even less of a long undertaking or a life. Perhaps Lewis regards both as 'synthetic' because he thinks both involve memory. But if they do both involve memory, plainly the memory involved in a single developing experience and the memory of events explicitly referred to the past are of different sorts. We would say that the earlier parts of the aesthetic experience of the symphony are parts of a single experience which is going on at the moment and which includes the earlier and the later parts, while we would not say that the 'synthetic apprehension' of a life is a single experience which includes the remembered events as its parts.

Lewis' chief point seems to be that the value of an 'experiential whole', such as a life, does not equal the sum of the values of the particular experiences it contains. But this does not at all depend upon the notion that a life is just a single large experience.[1] We may be able to add up

---

[1] In an interesting essay on 'The Good as Form and Quality' (*Ethics*, January 1946) Professor A. Campbell Garnett similarly recognizes two sorts of goods — 'form' and 'quality' — which are distinct and may conflict in particular cases. But he seems to commit the same confusion as Lewis, in regarding both of these goods as belonging to something called 'experience' and not, in one case, to an experience and, in another, to a life. He says that 'intrinsic good . . . is always content of experience'. Then he says that a single intense experience which lasted a whole life would be 'a very small good compared to a life in which there was change and complexity in the *form* of experience while still retaining the same degree of positive quality'.

the value of units of separate things which we cannot combine into a larger thing of the same kind; as we can add up the weight or value of horses when we cannot combine them to form a single horse. And we may be unable to add up the value of units of things which we can combine into a thing of the same kind; as we cannot add up simply the values of the experiences which go into the seeing of a play to yield the total value of the experience of seeing the play. The point to reject in the Benthamite calculus is the doctrine that experiences or feelings are the only kind of thing which has value. So long as we are clear that the value of a life is of a different sort from the value of an experience, we can allow that it may be possible to compute the aggregate value of several experiences. We can also allow that we may be able to add up the value of the synthetic experiences contained in a life, and that we may be able also to compare and combine in calculation this total value with the total value of a life. But we allow this while we still insist, as Lewis does, that the value of the life is not just the value of its component experiences. For the total value of one man's experiences combined with the value of his life may exceed that of a second man even when the total value of the first man's experiences considered alone exceeds that of the second man's.

It is important to distinguish the criticism of Hedonism which I have been making from the contention just that pleasures, or good experiences, cannot be aggregated. F. H. Bradley has offered the latter as a criticism of Hedonism in his essay 'Pleasure for Pleasure's Sake' (and it was offered before him by T. H. Green). But this charge can be met by a fairly simple revision of the Hedonistic formula. Bradley argues that a sum of pleasures is not itself a pleasure. For the sum cannot, like the single pleasure, be experienced at a single moment. Pleasures perish with the moment; they

Clearly what he called 'form of experience' is in fact the form of a life. Let us agree that a life composed of a single experience, however good, would be worse than a life composed of a variety of experiences. But this judgment must be made from the standpoint not of good experience but of good life. If we were to take as the sole kind of 'intrinsic good . . . content of experience', we could not make this judgment that the best experience could ever be bad.

cannot be retained and accumulated into a sum. Thus if pleasure is the only value, a sum of pleasures, since it cannot be experienced as a pleasure, is not good. A consistent Hedonist (though Bradley does not say this) would have to be a 'Momentary' Hedonist; he could not advocate, after the fashion of the Utilitarians, a maximization of pleasures either on a personal or a social scale.

But to meet this criticism the Hedonist needs only to substitute for the notion of a sum of pleasures the notion of a repetition of pleasure. He can admit that the only good thing is the single experience of pleasure, but insist that, because this is the only good, it is good to have it whenever possible. This is just to say that if a thing, as pleasure, is good, then it is good that it exist, and it does exist only when it recurs. The temporality of pleasure is a condition of its existence, and this temporality does make impossible the accumulation of pleasures in space. But it also makes possible the recurrence of pleasure in time.

On the other hand, to the point which I have been arguing, that we think something good which is not merely a pleasure but rather a relation of pleasures, the Hedonist's only recourse is to deny either that we do think good such things as happiness and a good or successful life, or that though we do think this we are mistaken.

7. *Pleasure and Virtue*

Judicious Hedonists, such as Sidgwick, recognize that Hedonism does conflict with certain common opinions, but they think that these opinions are superficial and that when we carefully consider the matter we do not think anything good other than pleasure. I have first considered the value of happiness and a successful life, because pleasure and happiness relate so closely and because the advocate of pleasure's value has also advocated the value of happiness no less than of pleasure. However, there is another sort of value, virtue or the good of character, which has always been sharply distinguished from pleasure. Indeed it has seemed often to occur to ethical theorists and to ordinary men that it was between these two, as candidates for the title of sole good, that they had to choose. Those who

I

have chosen pleasure have argued that virtue is but an instrumental good — it is good so far as it leads to pleasure. While the advocate of virtue as the sole good has had to argue that pleasure is only a conditional or dependent sort of good. It is not good in the way things are good which determine an obligation to pursue them. I shall take up in turn these Hedonistic and anti-Hedonistic treatments of virtue.

The major views of the relation of pleasure to virtue are as follows : (1) pleasure alone is good, virtue being a means to pleasure ; (2) virtue alone is truly good ; (3) both are good. But it has also been held that (4) virtue is a pleasure in its exercise and (5) virtue is pleasant to contemplate.[1] I shall argue (3) that virtue, as well as pleasure, is good in itself. If virtue is good in itself, this will explain why it is (4) pleasant to exercise and (5) pleasant to contemplate. For in general we take pleasure in doing and in contemplating what is good. Also, in general we desire what is good ; and the fulfilling of this desire gives pleasure.

It is obvious that virtue is a cause of pleasure, both in oneself and in others. And it is certainly true that virtue has been recommended by all sorts of persons for the pleasure it gives. But we do not think character is of value only for its hedonic products, or for any other of its products. We think certain persons are good as persons. We prize this sort of goodness just as we prize the goodness of pleasant experiences. Indeed we get pleasure from contemplating a good person. And what we thus contemplate is not just the pleasures he causes but the sort of person he is.

Consider a person whom one thinks outstandingly good— an historical figure such as Socrates, or a close friend. When we say that the person is good or that his character is good, surely we do not mean by this just that his experiences and acts are good. We not only esteem and admire persons for their goodness, but we love them for this. And we believe

---

[1] Shaftesbury forcibly argues (3), Hutcheson (4). Hume strongly adopts the point of Shaftesbury and weakly adopts the point of Hutcheson, though his stress is upon virtue's utility (but see *The Principles of Morals*, Section VIII, note 1). Mill likewise stresses virtue's mere utility, but says that it may come to be pleasant in its exercise.

that the good object which we love is not just the person's particular acts and feelings, but the person himself, who is the general source of these. His acts and feelings arouse our love, and show that he is lovable; and we love him 'for' these things. What we love, and what we want to be with and possess, is the person.

But both Sidgwick and Moore argue that a 'good character', since it is not immediately experienceable, cannot be really good. Sidgwick writes in *The Methods of Ethics*: 'From a practical point of view, indeed, I clearly recognize the importance of urging that men should aim at an ideal of character, and consider actions in its effects on character. But I cannot infer from this that character and its elements — faculties, habits, or dispositions of any kind — are the constituents of Ultimate Good. It seems to me that the opposite is implied in the very conception of a faculty or disposition; it can only be defined as a tendency to act or feel in a certain way under certain conditions; and such a tendency appears to me clearly not valuable in itself but for the acts and feelings in which it takes effect, or for the ulterior consequences of these — which consequences, again, cannot be regarded as Ultimate Good, so long as they are merely conceived as modifications of faculties, dispositions, etc.' (Bk. III, Ch. 14, Sec. 1). But it is hard to see why Sidgwick thinks that the facts he cites or suggests yield his conclusion that virtuous states of character are not intrinsically good. Let us enumerate these facts. (1) Virtues are extrinsically good; they produce good results. (2) We can only know that someone has a virtue by the way he acts and feels — by the particular moments of action and feeling in which these dispositions are manifested. (3) A particular experience of feeling and acting virtuously may be intrinsically good. Now none of these propositions implies that the virtuous character is not itself intrinsically good. Sidgwick says that this conclusion is implied in the very conception of a faculty as a tendency to act and feel in a certain way. But it is not clear how it is implied in this. Is the point that a disposition is an extrinsic good? But this does not prevent its also being an intrinsic good. One might espouse a metaphysics according

to which dispositions do not really exist, hence could not
be good or anything else. But Sidgwick evidently does
not conceive his doctrine as resting on any such remote or
metaphysical considerations. Thus his contention remains
without any support ; and it is directly at odds with what
we ordinarily think. We think that virtuous persons, and
not merely the experiences they have and cause, are intrinsically good.

Moore takes a view similar to Sidgwick's, and it likewise
is but feebly supported. He writes in *Philosophical Studies* :
'One thing, I think, is clear about intrinsic value . . .
namely that it is only actual occurrences, actual states of
things over a certain period of time — not such things as
men, or character, or material things, that can have any
intrinsic value at all' (p. 327). But all that one finds by
way of argument is the following : 'For, as Aristotle says,
a good man may exist, and have a good character, even
when he is fast asleep ; and yet if there were nothing in
the Universe but good men, with good characters, all fast
asleep, there would be nothing in it which was "good"
in the fundamental sense with which we are concerned'
(p. 326). Moore's point is that a thing which is intrinsically good will be good if it exists quite alone ; and that
a virtuous character, when it exists apart from the acts and
feelings in which it is ordinarily manifested, is not good.
But the reply is just that the man of good character is intrinsically good, awake or asleep. The difficulty here is, I
think, not that of associating intrinsic goodness with a man's
character when it is considered quite alone, but in associating his character with him while he is asleep. The reason
this is difficult is that we think of a man's character as a
potentiality for responding in particular ways to particular
sorts of situations ; but a man who is asleep or unconscious
cannot respond in the appropriate ways. Character constitutes a set of dispositions for *intentional* action (as well
as for non-voluntary feelings), and in order that these dispositions come into play the conditions of intentional action
must exist — as they do not in sleep or unconsciousness.
However, we do say that the man is the same man asleep
or awake, and has the same character ; because he has the

potentiality of waking and hence of fulfilling the first condition for the manifestation of the other potentialities which are his character. If he had lost this potentiality of waking, then we should think it proper to say that he had lost his humanity and his character (and thus the goodness of his character), no less than one who was dead. Once this is clear, I think we will be ready to say that a man who has a virtuous character, and who is asleep, is intrinsically good. It helps to see this if we take Moore's bizarre example with a slight modification. Suppose that we imagine that the men all fast asleep are persons of unalterably bad character. Would we not think it somewhat bad that these men did exist, and somewhat worse that they existed than that the same number of men of good character existed ? One reason Moore's example may initially seem somewhat convincing is, I think, that we are so aware of the great loss in value that would come from the persons' being asleep. But that their value does not consist wholly in what they do and feel is apparent in our judgment that these good men even 'fast asleep' would be somewhat better than the same number of bad men all fast asleep !

At the opposite extreme to the writers who say that nothing, not even virtue, is good except experience, are those who say that pleasant experience is in itself not good at all. Kant describes pleasure as a kind of good which is dependent on virtue ; Sir David Ross describes it as a special and inferior sort of good. I shall criticize each in turn.

Kant maintains in the first section of the *Fundamental Principles of the Metaphysics of Morals,* that just one thing is good in itself, namely the 'good will'. But he implies that, given a good will, happiness will increase the amount of good which exists. His idea seems to be not that happiness is a means to 'intrinsic good', but rather that the presence of a good will is necessary to happiness having the attribute of goodness. The Good Will is good if existing by itself, but it is not the complete good ; happiness is not good if existing by itself, but only when combined with the Good Will. Happiness is not at all a cause of the existence or of the goodness of the Good Will ; but the Good Will is a cause of the goodness, though not of the existence, of happiness. The view must be, then, that a pleasure is either bad or contributes to a bad whole when combined with a bad will, but is good or contributes to a good whole when combined with a good will. It follows that if a pleasure is not joined to a will either bad or good, there is nothing intrinsically bad or good involved.

But this is surely implausible. It is true that we are offended by the idea of a wicked person's being happy, and we want to say that his happiness cannot be good. But it is surely perverse to think that harmless pleasures, which are joined with acts that are neutral with regard to moral virtue or vice, are of no value at all. We could account for both of these facts if we revised Kant's principle to state that a good thing such as pleasure could, in conjunction with a bad thing, contribute to a whole greater in evil than one from which this good thing were absent. This would allow that pleasure is good even when existing alone, while allowing that its good or the good to which it contributes will alter with the relations into which it enters.

But on Kant's view pleasure is of no value at all in itself. And then there is the puzzle of why, if pleasure is of no value, it should increase the value of a whole into which it enters. It might occur to us to analogize the relation of pleasure to a Good Will in a good whole, to the relation of the taste of a spice to the taste of a meat in a dish. The taste of the spice is not good alone, while the taste of the meat is good alone, but not so good as when seasoned with the spice. But the analogy breaks down at a crucial point; for the taste of the spice improves the taste of the meat and not merely the taste of the 'whole', while on Kant's account the pleasure is not supposed to improve the Good Will (nor is it reasonable to think it does) but only the good of the 'whole' in which it partici-pates. But if the pleasure cannot improve or alter the Good Will itself, it would appear that the relation involved is not at all organic or chemical but simply additive; hence that pleasure can increase the value of such a whole simply by adding to the whole whatever value it has prior to this relation.

This is not to suggest that the experience of pleasure cannot enter into an organic relation to virtue such that the pleasure's own value is changed. Certainly it can. But then the experience of pleasure itself is changed. It is not that the value of the old pleasure changes, but that a new pleasure with a new value comes into existence as a result of the conjunction of the old experience of pleasure and a new sort of virtuous act. For example, acquiring the pleasures of health may change a person's virtue, and being virtuous may in turn change his health. But then the relation is chemical; the experiences of pleasure and the acts of virtue are themselves changed, and thus their value is changed. But this is not the sort of change Kant envisaged. He seemed to suppose that pleasure which was a bad thing when combined with a bad will became a good thing when combined with a good will. And this is not plausible. The pleasures of health are a good to the bad man as well as to the good one. It is just the fact that the person has a good which we think he does not deserve that offends us.

Sir David Ross, in his *Foundations of Ethics*, takes a view of pleasure's value which is somewhat like that of Kant's. He holds that pleasure is good 'in a secondary sense'. The sense turns out to be very secondary indeed. For he holds that the value of pleasure is actually incapable of comparison with the value of virtue. 'If virtue were really on the same scale of goodness as pleasure, then pleasure of a certain intensity, if enjoyed by a sufficiently large number of persons or for a sufficient time, would counterbalance virtue possessed or manifested only by a small number for only for a short time. But I find myself quite unable to think this to be the case; and if I am right in this, it follows that pleasures, if ever good, must be good in a different sense from that in which good activities are so' (p. 275). Ross believes that this difference between pleasure and other good things appears in several ways. (1) What is good is usually admirable or commendable, while pleasant experience is not. (2) The good in good activities is reflected on to its possessor so as to make him in some sense good, but this is not true of pleasure.

(3) Evidently most important, 'we feel ourselves under no obligation to produce even innocent pleasures for ourselves' (p. 272). Ross believes this last is so clear as to need no argument.

On the other hand, he recognizes two 'facts which point to pleasure being under certain limitations a good thing. We do consider the state of pleasure, when the pleasure is not a morally bad pleasure, to be in some sense a better state of affairs than the state of pain ; and we feel ourselves under a certain obligation to produce it for other people, when it is not a morally bad pleasure . . .' (p. 275). In the face of this, Ross defines the value of pleasure in terms of a relation to rightness : 'the sense in which from the point of view of any man the innocent pleasures of another are good is that it is right for him to feel satisfaction in them' (p. 279). While in admiration we think that the thing admired is good in itself, 'satisfaction at another's pleasure is simply a feeling, not involving the thought that the other's pleasure is good in itself, but only the thought that he is being pleased . . .' (p. 282).

First, it is not evident why Ross wants to say that pleasure is good at all. He has said nothing to show that pleasure is anything more than an object of obligation. He might have said that just one kind of pleasure is good, namely pleasure taken in another person's pleasure. But he does not say this. He asserts, rather, that the pleasures of others are good in that it is *right* to pursue them. Now if everything that we ought to pursue were in some respect good, then this particular class of pleasures, the pleasures of others, would be good. Their goodness would derive from their rightness. But in fact Ross holds that we may have obligations which are not obligations to produce the good. So it is not clear why pleasure's being in one case obligatory should indicate that this pleasure is good.

The more important objection is that the three arguments Ross offers to show that pleasure is not good in a primary sense are faulty. (1) He says that pleasure does not reflect good upon its possessor. But (a) we do sometimes think that a person is to be commended for taking pleasure in something. Taking pleasure may be a sign of mental or physical health, and may be a sign of a developed capacity pertaining to the thing in which pleasure is taken. However, what is good here is the capacity, the pleasure being just an evidence of the capacity. (b) The main point is that although we do not think that having a pleasure makes a person a good person, we do think that it gives him a good experience. (2) Thus though we do not commend or admire a person for his pleasures, we do congratulate and envy him for them. And these latter attitudes are as much as the former ones an indication of our estimation of the goodness of their objects. (3) It is true that we do not ordinarily say to a person that it is his obligation to pursue his own pleasure ; but we do sometimes say this. In general we conceive of duties as being directed to other persons. But we also admit that a person has an obligation to develop his talents. And we sometimes say that a person 'owes it to himself' to get more pleasure out of life.

A possible source of the mistake of thinking that we are not obligated to pursue our own pleasure is a confusion of the technical or instrumental sense of 'ought' with its ethical sense. It is commonly recognized that pleasure is not best attained by being directly pursued. Thus even if a person 'ought' ('ethically') to pursue pleasure he 'ought' not ('instrumentally') to pursue it directly. The person who gets pleasure from music does so not by concentrating on the use of music for pleasure but by concentrating on music. This judgment is causal and psychological, not ethical ; it concerns not whether pleasure ought to be chosen, but how pleasure can be most effectively obtained.

The truth which we can extract from Ross' view is that we think that there is a duty to produce pleasure, but it is a 'secondary' duty, because pleasure is not as great a good as virtue. The best things are enduring objects and not momentary feelings. We think that it is less important what a person feels than what he is. Of course these are connected ; generally, his feelings will mirror his nature. But his feeling is momentary, therefore its good or bad is momentary ; while his nature is relatively enduring, and its good likewise. Thus we think our primary obligation, both towards others and towards ourselves, is to promote

virtue. Ross holds that we are morally obligated to promote the pleasure of others but not of ourselves, and he
finds it puzzling that giving others pleasure is an obligation
while giving ourselves pleasure is not. But in fact we think
our obligation to promote others' pleasures is less of an
obligation than our obligation to promote certain basic
conditions by which they can promote for themselves certain goods, including pleasure. We think our primary
obligation is to promote, both for others and for ourselves,
such things as health, material security, emotional maturity,
freedom and opportunity to develop personal talents. And
we think that promoting these is the best we can do toward
providing for both virtue and pleasure.

8. *The Appeal of Hedonism*

It is for good reasons that Hedonism is one of the
perennial and popular ethical doctrines, and it is worth
considering these before leaving the subject.

In its general appeal as an ethical theory Hedonism is
rivaled only by the Interest Theory. Kantianism, or the
view that virtue is the sole good, strikes the ordinary person
as very noble and 'idealistic' but as also romantic and
perverse. Once the ordinary person has had the leisure
or the compulsion to look for a most general account of
value, he is apt to end by espousing a Hedonism or an
Interest Theory, or both — for in an elementary stage he
is unable to distinguish the two. Hedonism, like the Interest Theory, allows for a 'relativity' of value with respect
to concrete objects. On the Hedonistic view there is nothing
odd in the fact that we evaluate material things so differently
nor is there any reason to attempt to correct or remove the
difference. For if the only good thing is pleasant feeling,
then external objects are 'good' only as stimuli of this
feeling, and there is no contradiction in different persons'
saying that the same object gives them contrary feelings.
This 'relativity' is one of the features which gives Hedonism
a wide appeal.

But I believe the primary source of Hedonism's appeal
is that the value of pleasure is so *universal*, so *obvious*, and
so *certain*. Pleasure accompanies other sorts of value, and

the value of pleasure cannot be overlooked when these other values are overlooked. Further, the value of pleasure seems more certain than the value of other things. The value of pleasure is known 'immediately' — it is included in the experience of pleasure. The value of other things, as happiness and virtue, are not presented with the same immediacy. If a person says that he has a pleasure, and that he feels its value, there is hardly any arguing him out of it. We have more to argue about if he asserts that a particular quality of character or pattern of life is good. In these the value attaches to various elements and relations, which can be analyzed, while the value of the pleasure seems to belong to a simple feeling.

All of these are genuine features of the value of pleasure, but they do not show that it is the only thing that is good. Nor do they entail another advantage which the philosophical Utilitarian thought he had found in pleasure. Pleasure's qualitative simplicity does not suit it to provide the basis of a systematic and precise ethical system, such as Bentham envisaged. Decision is no less difficult on the Hedonistic than on other schemes. For though it is certain that a present pleasure has value, it is not certain how its value compares with the value of other absent pleasures. Further, pleasure, as we saw, is simple like yellow but is also complex like yellow. It has various dimensions, and no clear principles for their correlation. We find no more ground for hope of a 'scientific ethics' in pleasure than in other directions.[1]

---

[1] Again it is Sidgwick who has most illuminatingly discussed the difficulties in the comparison of pleasures. See *The Methods of Ethics*, Bk. II, ch. 3.

CHAPTER IV

OBLIGATION

AT this stage our results are briefly these. Value, though objective, lacks the characteristics necessary to the development of the systematic and precise account found in the fields we call 'sciences'. We must believe that we can know value, but we cannot cherish the hope of constructing a science of it. We might cherish a small hope of this could we believe that value is a single sort of thing, such as pleasure or the satisfaction of desire. But we cannot believe this; and even if we did, this hope would be faint indeed. For the reductionistic theories also retain, under their first principle that value belongs to just one kind of thing, the recognition of various value species or dimensions, for the systematic correlation and ranking of which no clear principles are provided.

The two following chapters may seem to be directed by a contrary bias. For in these I argue for a certain kind of reductionism: I argue that obligation is to be analyzed in terms of value, and that there is just one basic obligation, the obligation to realize what is of most value, or what is best. However, this account preserves the earlier results. For I contend that, though in a given case there will be one act (or several acts) of which it is true that it is the act (or each is equally an act) which does realize what is best, still we have no scheme or rules which enable us to make such judgments with scientific precision. Thus the doctrine here, as in the preceding chapters, may be seen as a compromise. There the compromise was between what might be called 'extreme relativism', or the position that there is no objective property to which value judgments refer, and 'extreme objectivism', or the position that value can be known quite scientifically. I shall not consider with respect to obligation the view of the extreme relativist, for his doctrine on obligation raises no new fundamental

issues ; what I have said against this position with respect
to judgments of value can be applied to judgments of
obligation.   Instead, the view which it will be illuminating
to criticize is that of the 'Deontologist'.   This is the view
that the obligatory or right is a distinct ethical category,
and that certain rules of obligation carry their own authority, quite independently of the tendency of these rules,
when obeyed, to maximize good.   This doctrine may,
somewhat ironically and metaphorically, be viewed as a
peculiar and violent fusion of elements of extreme relativism
and extreme objectivism.   It resembles extreme objectivism
with respect to value in that it holds that rules of obligation
provide a degree of certainty and precision in ethical
knowledge comparable to the certainty and precision provided by our scientific knowledge of natural laws, and
comparable to the certainty and precision that would be
provided by a successful Hedonic calculus.   And the
doctrine resembles extreme relativism in that it marks off
discrete value realms, between which we are left without
any principle of mediation ; much as the extreme relativist
marks off domains of value judgment which share no single
standard of truth.   In contrast, what I recommend is that
there are true judgments of value, and that these judgments
provide the ground for determining true judgments of
obligation.

I shall begin with some general and neutral topics concerning obligation ; these will lead in Section 6 to the
opening of this central dispute with the Deontologist.

1. *Terminology*

The words 'obligation', 'duty', 'responsibility', 'ought'
and 'right' are often used as roughly equivalent. But there
are differences about which it will help to be clear.   Consider first 'ought' and 'obligation'.   The noun 'obligation'
has the adjectival form 'obligatory' and the verb form
'obligate' and 'is obligated'.   What a person has an
'obligation' to do is 'obligatory' and is something he 'is
obligated' to do.   'Ought' is roughly the equivalent of
'is obligated'.   However, there are differences in what the
'is obligated' and the 'ought' suggest.   (1) 'Obligation'

more suggests a class of acts, 'ought' a specific act. When we say that a person has an 'obligation to his children', we have in mind a whole class of acts which he ought to perform. And it is usually a bit less natural to say that a person 'is obligated' to do a given act (say, to keep an appointment) than to say that he 'ought' to do it. (2) 'Obligation' suggests a past act by which the obligation has come about or by which it has been 'assumed'. It is slightly more natural to say that a person 'is obligated to keep the appointment' than that he is 'obligated to help a stranger in distress'. We speak of a 'fulfillment' or 'violation' of obligation, meaning a kind of completion or failure to complete that which began with the past commitment or 'assumption' of obligation. But of course we would also agree that he 'ought' to help the stranger and that he 'ought' to repay the debt. (3) 'Obligation' suggests an act the breach of which is more serious, and for which, therefore, punishment is provided. We might say, loosely, that a person 'ought' to do a given act but is 'not really obligated' to do it. This might be paraphrased by saying, 'It would be better if he did the act, but its omission is not serious, and he should not be punished for it'. On the other hand, we would agree that if he is 'really obligated' to do it, then he 'really ought' to do it. (4) Most important, 'obligation' is used always or chiefly in what is called the 'moral' sense. If a person is looking for his key case we may say to him, 'You ought to look on the bookshelf', meaning not, 'You are obligated to look there', but 'It may be there; so if you want to find it, you might try looking there'. On the other hand, we ordinarily use 'obligated' in a sense in which it would be tautologus to say 'morally obligated'. We do sometimes use this latter phrase, but then we do so to stress the seriousness of the moral obligation. On the other hand, the phrase 'morally ought' adds a new specification to a mere 'ought', it declares that the person is 'obligated' to do the act, even if he does not want the act itself or its results. Because the term 'obligation' does suggest the 'moral ought', I shall usually prefer to use it. But whenever I use the term 'ought' without specifying a non-moral sense, I shall intend it as the equivalent of 'obligated'. It is often convenient to use the shorter expression 'He ought to do X' instead of 'He is obligated to do X'.

Let us now consider the words 'duty' and 'right'. 'Duty' functions like the term 'obligation', except that 'duty' expresses a more serious obligation. We use 'duty' to describe those things to which we are most obligated. Thus we might say, loosely, that we have a 'duty' to care for our children, while we are only 'somewhat obligated' to give part of our earnings to charity. 'Right' is sometimes used as the equivalent of this last phrase, to mean a lesser sort of obligation. We might say that it is 'right' to give to charity, but a person is 'not positively — or at least highly — obligated' to do so.

But the important relations of 'right' are to 'ought'. Often their uses are equivalent. To say that a thing is 'right' is to say that a person 'ought' to do it. Also, 'right' shares with 'ought' the non-moral as well as the moral use. However, there is this important difference: 'right' often has a merely permissive force, whereas 'ought' has a commanding force. In a given situation there may be alternative 'right' things, but there is always only one thing of which we use the word 'ought'. In a given situation we may say that 'X is the right thing', but then we may admit that here 'Y is also the right thing' and again 'Z perhaps is also the right thing'. But we could not say that 'He ought to do X', but again 'He ought to do Y', and so on. This implies that a person may omit the 'right' thing without having brought about the opposite or 'wrong' thing, while a person cannot omit doing the thing he 'ought' to do without having done a thing that was 'wrong' and that he 'ought not' to have done. 'Wrong' is an exact equivalent for 'ought not' as well as for 'not right'. Further, this opposite, 'wrong', always has alternatives. Although there is only one thing which the person 'ought' to do, there are always many things which he 'ought not' to do, or which are 'wrong'. Thus, the 'right' thing and the 'wrong' thing have alternatives as well as an opposite, while the thing which we 'ought' to do has no alternatives but just opposites. Finally, the 'ought' will always coincide with one of the 'right' alternatives. Thus in the same situation there may be three classes of things: (1) those which are *wrong*; (2) those which are *right*; (3) that one which the person *ought* to do.

Another concept that is closely related to that of obligation (and of 'ought', 'duty', 'right') is that of responsibility. But their relations are complex. The concepts of both obligation and responsibility have both noun and adjectival forms, but the primary meaning of obligation is carried in the noun form while that of responsibility is carried in the adjectival form. Consider the relations of 'obligation' to 'obligatory' and of 'responsibility' to 'responsible'. 'Obligation' applies to a kind of act; one speaks of a person's 'obligations', meaning the sorts of acts or areas of conduct in which certain things are expected of him. 'Obligatory' applies to a particular act within this range. A person has certain general obligations, and in accordance with these a particular act is obligatory on him in a given situation. 'Responsibility' and 'responsible' likewise apply primarily the one to a general class of acts and the other to a particular act. Moreover we may in certain cases use these two nouns equivalently and the two adjectives equivalently. However, we discover clear differences in their meanings. The concept of responsible stresses the personal aspect, while the concept of obligation stresses the non-personal aspect, of the things which the person is to do. If we say 'Jones has obligations to many people' we tend to think of the concrete character of the things which Jones is to do, while if we say 'Jones has responsibilities to many people' we think of the personal burden Jones is under. This appears more plainly in the contrast of the adjectives, 'obligatory' and 'responsible'. 'Obligatory' can only qualify an act, while 'responsible' naturally qualifies only a person. We employ 'obligatory' to mark out that act among the possible alternatives which the person is to do. While we employ 'responsible' not to designate this act so much as to indicate that the person is to do it. We say 'the obligatory act here is such and such', while we say 'the person responsible here is so and so'. The adjectives do seem to entail each other: the person is responsible for an act which is obligatory, and the obligatory act is one for which the person is responsible. However we shall see presently that this principle requires qualification.

2. Judgments of Responsibility and Moral Judgments of Praise and Blame

A judgment of responsibility is a precondition of a moral judgment of praise or blame; and it is in order to establish this condition of a judgment of praise or blame that we are concerned to make assessments of responsibility. Responsibility is not the sole condition of such a moral judgment. In addition we must establish that the act for which one was responsible was right or wrong. Usually we investigate responsibility only after we have judged the character of the deed itself. Having judged a deed wrong or bad, we want to know whether the person was responsible for it; hence whether it was a *morally* wrong act, and whether the person is to be blamed. We must establish the same conditions for a right act; but we do not ordinarily speak of 'establishing a person's responsibility' for a right act. (In exceptional cases we do this — as will appear in the later discussion of choice.) Doubtless the explanation is that praising is a less drastic action than blaming. It is more important that we ground our judgments of blame than our judgments of praise, for our condemnations cause pain, and we can only justify causing pain when the act does something besides this. Praise, on the other hand, gives pleasure, and unless the acts of praise have ill side-effects, we can afford to be liberal with them. Praise itself is an immediate benefit, blame an immediate injury. Thus there is less chance of acting wrongly if we praise a person for an act that he has done involuntarily than if we blame him for it. This accounts for our feeling that we must take special care to establish responsibility before passing blame. Still, the entailment holds equally between responsibility and both blame and praise. Neither sort of moral judgment is grounded unless responsibility is established. Finally, the entailment is mutual between both terms and responsibility. As the judgment of moral praise or blame is ungrounded if the judge has not established responsibility, so the judgment

K

of responsibility is pointless unless the judge goes on to ascribe praise or blame.

Since judging responsibility is a preliminary to judging moral merit or demerit, it follows that the purpose of judging responsibility must be primarily to provide for correct moral judgments, and its ultimate purpose must be the same as the purpose of making these judgments. Further, praising (and blaming) is something that we do, and something that we are held responsible for doing. Such utterances are, using Austin's term, 'performatory'. We recognize obligations to perform certain acts of praise and blame. The question why we praise and blame thus takes two forms : (1) What are its actual motives ? and (2) What are its moral justifications ? The second is a very large question, which we can answer only gradually. As for (1), several things are obvious. These motives would seem to be manifold, and to vary with the person and the situation ; but like nearly all sorts of verbal expressions, it would appear that they may (a) express a momentary feeling (of love, hatred, fear, anger, pride, humility, etc.) ; (b) record an attempt to state the truth ; or (c) be a means deliberately chosen to influence someone, either the person judged or some other hearer of the expression. Let us call these, respectively, the emotive, descriptive and rhetorical uses of moral judgments. We can imagine occasions on which each of these uses is justified. But one use, the rhetorical, is primary. We praise and blame persons primarily to influence the way our hearers feel or act.

The occasions on which we make judgments of praise and blame are of several sorts : (1) when we are emotively moved to express ourselves in this way ; (2) when we reflect on or aesthetically contemplate praiseworthy or blameworthy objects ; (3) when we attempt to teach someone to act properly ; (4) when we simply want to give pleasure or pain to someone. We may call (3) the rhetorical-practical use and (4) the rhetorical-emotive use. There is no reason to outlaw uses (1) and (2), and there may be reason, under certain circumstances and with certain limitations, to recommend them. But use (2) would not require a verbal utterance, and use (1) would not require the communication of

the utterance, while uses (3) and (4) would require communication. Moreover, (4) can be accomplished more
effectively by judgments of praise and blame than by any
other device. We could, of course, achieve all these ends
by some means other than praise and blame. We might
(1) express ourselves in dance or song; (2) contemplate
other features of persons than their praiseworthiness or
blameworthiness; (3) teach by stating the value of things
without praising the pupil for his aptness; (4) please and
pain in manifold ways. But praise and blame provide an
especially natural, cheap, effective and — when used dis-
criminatingly — relatively harmless teaching device. We
constantly employ the device, and we do not feel the qualms
about employing it in this way that we feel about employing
it in these other ways. This will become clearer if we
notice the difference between judgments of praise and
blame and judgments of value, or of good and bad. It may
help to call the former 'moral judgments' and the latter
'ethical judgments'. The chief use of moral judgments is
rhetorical, but it does not follow that this is also the chief
use of ethical judgments.

The crucial difference between the two sorts of judgments appears in this, that to praise a thing is to imply or
assert that it has value, but not conversely. First, suppose
for the present (though we shall presently question it) that
any sort of thing — human or non-human, abstract or
concrete — may be praised or blamed. One may praise
an artwork, an animal, a quality like courage, an act, a
person. Now to praise one of these things is to praise it
for its value. It is also true that if we explicitly assert that
the thing is good or bad, valuable or disvaluable, this is
usually equivalent to some utterance of praise. The assertion 'Smith is good' would ordinarily be taken as expressing
some degree of praise. Still such an utterance falls short
of what we most typically understand by praise. For it
would not be nonsensical for a hearer to follow the above
assertion with, 'Do you mean to praise him?' Further, the
reply to this might be, 'Not exactly; still he *is* good'. Let
us first try to state what the difference is, then try to account
for it.

The difference is that saying a thing is good focusses attention on the quality predicated of the thing; while to praise the thing is to turn attention to the thing which has the quality. The thing cannot be praised except by reference to the good quality, nor can the good quality be mentioned without some reference to the thing's possession of the quality. Still there is, at the least, a difference in attentive focus. This comes out in a second difference, which is that we think of value as the predicate of a judgment while we think of the object of praise as also the focus of an act. We merely 'judge' value; while we also 'declare' praise. Further, we can judge value without expressing or communicating this judgment, while we cannot praise without making the praise public. Praise of God is no exception, for in private worship God is conceived as being audience to our praise.

These differences are traceable to a further difference, which is seen in the oddity of our blaming a non-human object. We speak of 'praising' a painting, but never of blaming it. But in their strict use these terms are correlative — where one is applicable the other is, at least logically, applicable. This suggests that the term 'praise' is used in a special and extended sense when it is applied to such a thing as an artwork. That this is so is supported by the oddity of our speaking of praising an inanimate natural object, as a tree or the moon. (When the poet praises such things, he personifies them.) We might say that someone had praised a tree found in the middle of a forest, but we should note this is an unusual thing to say. Our reaction would be : 'The tree is indeed strong, beautiful, etc., but in what way does it "deserve" praise?' The natural object of praise is a person. Praise of the painting is an indirect way of praising the painter. And if we were to praise the tree or the moon we would have to praise God who alone can make one.

Still why do we not 'blame' the painter in the same indirect way in which we praise him? The first thing to observe is that praise and blame are primarily moralistic terms — they apply to persons who perform or fail to perform acts for which they are responsible. But the use of the term 'praise' is then extended so that it applies to all sorts of non-moral personal qualities, as beauty, health, intelligence, etc. To praise a person for these is to give him a special credit which is inappropriate. But no one finds very objectionable the giving of undue praise. On the other hand, it is very objectionable to level undue blame. Thus one negative term of the pair is held to its narrower meaning, while its positive opposite is given considerable range.

Praise and blame are, then, in the strictest sense moralistic, and have special conditions of application which are referred to in the concept of 'deserving'. Assessment of value requires us to look only to the act or object evaluated, while assessment of moral value and declaration of praise in the strictest sense requires looking at the person to ascertain whether the conditions of 'desert' have been met. These are the conditions of responsibility.

A further point. We praise certain qualities which we also praise persons for having. How are we to understand such praise? Here, I suggest, the practical purpose of praise is most evident. Such praise is meant as a recommendation to the hearers that they acquire these qualities. It is as if the speaker, in praising the qualities, is offering a promise of future praise to those of his hearers who acquire these qualities. Praise for a quality, as courage, benevolence, honesty, is to be understood as containing the implications that (a) the quality is good, and (b) that one who has the quality is worthy of praise. The occasions on which these virtues are praised — as by ministers, parents, teachers — show that their chief purpose is rhetorical.

Mere value judgments, on the other hand, may be made on much different sorts of occasions, as when a person is simply reflecting on certain persons or certain qualities. But even if this were denied, and it were held that the use of all ethical judgments is to influence conduct, a crucial distinction remains between the sort of influence exerted by value-assessments and by declarations of praise. The former are used not only to influence others but to guide one's own conduct. Whereas a person does not praise himself in order to guide his conduct. Supposing that we can praise ourselves in the same sense in which we can praise others (which is doubtful), certainly we do not use such self-praise as a way of guiding our action in the future but rather as a way of reassuring ourselves about action in the past.

Thus we may assert value judgments about objects or acts simply to state what is good or of value. We may then praise persons for acting in conformity with these value judgments. The mistake of those who interpret all ethical utterances as persuasive is the mistake of confusing judgments of praise with judgments of value. If we did pass value judgments solely in order to exert influence, a natural question would be why we desire to exert influence. And the natural answer would be, to get people to do what we want. If there are no value judgments prior to and independent of our judgments of praise, this must be the end of the matter. But if there are independent value judgments then the answer may be that we praise them to get them to do what we think it would be good or right for them to do.

Thus, to say that expressions of praise are meant to influence is not at all to link these judgments to propaganda. What distinguishes judgments designed to influence is that they are not made in the interest of knowledge but in the interest of action. Judgments from the sciences may be made in the interest of action, but this is not thought to be what chiefly distinguishes or justifies them. Whereas it is what chiefly distinguishes judgments of praise and blame.

3. *Judgments of Obligation*

Let us now consider the relations between responsibility and obligation. The thing for which a person is responsible is the performance of obligations. Thus the general purpose for holding other people obligated is the same as the purpose for holding them responsible — namely to ground judgments of praise and blame, and thereby to influence them. But a person is not always held responsible for the performance of all his obligations. This gap can be regarded in one of two ways, either as existing between responsibility in particular acts and one's general obligations, or between the noun uses of both terms and their adjectival uses. The latter view is perhaps the more strictly correct.

On this second interpretation, a person can at the same time have several obligations and several responsibilities, but he cannot at the same time be responsible for (or have) more than one obligatory act. The reason for this is that a person is responsible for doing only what is possible, and it is not possible to perform several acts at once. This constitutes a fundamental gap between our notion of these nouns and the corresponding adjectives, and particularly between the noun 'obligation' and the adjective 'obligatory'. We speak of a person's having 'conflicting obligations', as if a person could be obligated to do the impossible — to perform several physically incompatible acts. We certainly do not think this : we do not think that a person who has conflicting obligations is obligated to perform them all.

It is, of course, a paradox to say that a person has an obligation (namely some one or more of the conflicting obligations) which he is not obligated to perform. But we must make a choice of paradoxes : we must say either (not both) that a person can have an obligation which he nevertheless is not obligated to perform and not responsible for performing ; or that he is sometimes obligated to do the impossible, to perform several conflicting obligations. The former violates only our sense of logic and language ; the latter violates our moral sense. To eliminate the paradox we might stipulate that 'obligation' be used only in the general sense, to apply to kinds of acts, while 'responsible' be used only in the particular sense, to apply to the particular one of the general obligations for which the person is responsible. We should then never speak of particular obligations or obligatory acts, and never of general responsibilities or kinds of acts for which one is responsible. But it would be futile to propose this linguistic reform. And once the sources of confusion are clear, reform is unnecessary.

What we must do is remember that obligation and responsibility involve two quite distinct concepts, both meeting in the concept of an act, but one (obligation) taking the act in the aspect of its internal character and consequences, the other (responsibility) taking it in its aspect as the product of a human agent. This alerts us to the existence of two sets of criteria, one defining the general sorts of acts which we will call a person's obligations and for the performance of which we will in most cases hold him responsible, the other set defining the general conditions under which we will call a particular act obligatory on the person and for the performance of which we will hold him responsible. That these are different is apparent in the fact that often the conditions establishing a person's obligations, as to be grateful or keep a promise, are events which happened in the past; while a person's responsibility always depends solely upon his conditions at the moment of action. Our major task is to state these conditions. Let us call them the conditions of obligation and the conditions of responsibility.

4. *Subjective Obligation*

One worrisome puzzle in ethics, that concerning 'subjective obligation', has arisen from confusing the conditions of obligation and of responsibility. By an 'objective obligation' in some given case is meant that act which the person ought to do, provided he has adequate ethical and empirical knowledge. By 'subjective obligation' is meant the act which the person thinks to be his objective obligation. The problem is : given a case in which a person's knowledge is inadequate, and he is mistaken about his objective obligation, what ought he to do, his 'objective' or his 'subjective' obligation. This question cannot exist for the agent in the given case, since here he does not know that the two differ. But it can exist for an observer who sees that there are two possible things which might have occurred : (1) the agent might have done his objective obligation accidentally or by compulsion or by yielding to a desire and acting contrary to what he thought to be his objective obligation ; (2) or the agent might have intentionally done his subjective obligation (which he mistakenly thought his objective obligation). The observer can ask : which in this situation ought he to have done — the act which was in fact right and obligatory, or the act which he thought right? The answer, plainly, is that he *ought* to have done what is right, his objective obligation. But we cannot hold him morally *responsible* for doing it. There is one set of criteria which tells us what is right, and another set which tells us what he is responsible for.

This is, again, somewhat paradoxical. It is paradoxical to say that a person has an obligation to do an act for which we do not hold him morally responsible. But this is because our general notions of obligation are formed on the assumption that a person is aware of his obligations. On the basis of this assumption we go on to assume a necessary connection binding obligation and responsibility. But actually we do not insist upon this bond. We recognize that there are cases where ignorance of the facts may break the connection between a general obligation and a person's responsibility for fulfilling it. Similarly with 'subjective obligation'; we recognize that a person's ignorance of his obligation exempts him from responsibility for performing it.

But there are further questions. (1) Is the performance of subjective obligation itself ever an object of praise? (2) Is the performance of subjective obligation always a condition of praise and reward? (3) Is the failure to perform one's subjective obligation sometimes or always or never an object of punishment or blame? (4) Does the performance of subjective obligation always exempt a person from blame and punishment?

(1) I think we never do praise a person simply for doing what he thinks right, but only for doing (or attempting to do) acts which are specifically good in some way or other. (2) However, we do not praise him unless he did think what he did was right. For example, if we praise a person for an act of generosity, we only do so if he thought the act was right. But what we praise him for is not his doing it because he thought it right, but because it was right in some specific way or other. That this is so is shown by the fact that we do any number of right acts (and do so with the thought that they are right) which no one thinks warrant praise. But the matter is confused by the fact

that we do praise the closely related sort of act and tendency of 'conscientiousness'.

Conscientiousness includes doing what one thinks right, but it also includes doing the act under a particular sort of condition, namely in the face of obstacles, either internal (such as contrary desires) or external (such as contrary public opinion). Conscientiousness is chiefly a virtue of the will. Conscientiousness may, however, entail the exertion of will as much in the pursuit of knowledge of what is right, as in action on judgments as to what is right. So let us describe conscientiousness as the energetic pursuit of what is right. This virtue is manifested, then, only when effort is called for. By contrast, the performance of subjective obligation involves an exertion of will (and 'conscientiousness') only in some instances. And it is only in these instances in which the act of subjective obligation is combined with conscientiousness, or is an act which (while not involving effort) is well-intentioned in some more specific sense, that we are inclined to give praise.

We need an adjectival term with which to describe the act of subjective obligation in distinction from the conscientious act. 'Well-intentioned' will not quite serve, for by this we should ordinarily understand an act which is motivated not just by a tendency to do what is thought right but by more specific sorts of tendencies (such as honesty or generosity) which we suppose generally lead to acts which are right. For example we should not call a Fascist's acts of persecuting Jews 'well-intentioned', however sincerely he believed these acts right; for these acts do not manifest a specific tendency which we think can lead to right acts. Rather, we would describe as 'well-intentioned' a person who was animated by such impulses as tolerance or generosity (as well as by a desire to do what was right); for these impulses do usually lead to right acts. We might, however, say of the Nazi that his intention, when considered on the most abstract level, was a good one. At least it was a better intention than that of the Nazi who did the same acts from a motive of personal expediency. But we would say that the specific intentions of both Nazis were very bad indeed. Perhaps we may, then, describe an act so far as it is a performance of subjective obligation as an 'abstractly well-intentioned' act, and distinguish it from an act which is prompted by specific tendencies generally leading to right acts, which we shall call 'specifically well-intentioned'.

Following this (artificial) terminology, we see that acts may be (a) 'abstractly well-intentioned' but neither 'specifically well-intentioned' nor 'conscientious'; (b) 'abstractly well-intentioned' and 'specifically well-intentioned' but not 'conscientious'; (c) 'abstractly well-intentioned' and 'conscientious' but not 'specifically well-intentioned'; (d) 'abstractly well-intentioned', 'specifically well-intentioned' and 'conscientious'.

My contention is that we never praise acts of class (a), but we do sometimes praise acts of all three other classes, and further that we never praise an act of any class other than these. In short, abstractly good intention is always a necessary condition, but never a sufficient condition, of praise.

This answers the earlier questions (1) and (2). It leaves us with the peculiarly difficult questions (3) and (4). It would seem that we do punish acts which the agent thinks right; but it would also seem wrong to do so. In the case both of the most serious and most trivial offenses, as a traitor or a violator of a minor traffic regulation, we punish the person despite our belief that he was abstractly well-intentioned. But it would seem that if a person does not know what is right, he is not subject to blame or punishment. It does seem to offend our sense of justice to punish an act which the agent did under the impression that it was the right thing to do.

Various ways out of the difficulty may be tried, but none will work. One apparent way out is to say that the penalty is legal and not moral. This will not do: for if we think that the laws assigning these penalties are good laws then we think it is right to punish the person, and if we think they are bad laws then we think it is not right to assign such punishments.

Another apparent solution is to say that whenever it seems right to punish a person for an act of subjective obligation, it is because this act is really the result of an earlier act which violated subjective obligation; and that, although the recent act is the occasion for the punishment, the real object of punishment is not the recent but the earlier act. Some cases of punishment can be so accounted for. We may justify punishing the motorist who had an accident because he fell asleep, because earlier he knew both that he was sleepy and that it was not right to drive in this condition. But not all cases can be disposed of in this way. Suppose that the motorist exceeds the speed limit because he becomes preoccupied with a difficult problem, and suppose that it has never occurred to him that this could happen. We should think it right to punish him according to the rule for such violations. Now one might argue that still there must have been some earlier occasion on which he had a thought that it was right to do something that would not lead to this result. The thought, perhaps, that he ought to train himself as a driver so as to make it impossible for his mind to wander while driving. But this principle, if extended to cover all such cases, becomes the principle that a person sometimes has the thought that it is right to do those specific things which if done will prevent the person's ever having any sort of wrong moral opinion or his lacking the right moral opinion. This would require a degree of detailed knowledge of one's future behavior which it is absurd to suppose human beings could have. Plainly a person cannot foresee or act to prevent all his future moral mistakes.

One other possible suggestion is that the treatment imposed is not a punishment (but perhaps only a penalty). But the confinement of the traitor, and the fining of the motorist, are forms of injury intentionally inflicted for an act considered wrong. So surely they are cases of punishment. One may argue that these injuries are merely immediate and lead to the ultimate benefit of the person punished. That the punishment does have this effect is plausible in the case of the motorist; it tends to make him less liable to act in a way which can lead to his bodily harm. But the principle is less plausible when applied to the traitor. First, the injury of a prolonged confinement is a serious injury even if the prisoner be given every comfort and opportunity except the power of free movement in the society. This case is not like that of the insane person, whose confinement is in the interest of himself as well as others. It might be less serious as an injury than the benefit that would be realized by his coming to change his mistaken moral opinion. But is such a change at all likely? It might be argued that if it is very unlikely that with the most effective means of change (psychoanalysis, perhaps) the traitor cannot be led to alter his wrong moral views, then he is and was insane, in which case his confinement would not be a punishment. But this seems far-fetched; for his deviant conduct is not of the widespread sort which characterizes those persons classified as insane. Nor can one hold that his punishment is beneficial to him because it prevents his committing wrong acts and thereby contributes to the improvement of his character; for the mere preventing of wrong action does not remove his disposition to commit these acts, and it is his dispositions which constitute his character. We must conclude, then, that this is a case in which we punish a person for an act which he thought right.

But though the case does show that the performance of subjective obligation is not always a complete excuse, it does even here constitute some excuse. Knowledge that the traitor was animated solely by a desire to do his duty does not cause us to believe that he should not be *punished*, but it does cause us to believe that he is not to be *blamed*. This comes out in the distinction we make between the traitor and the professional spy, whom we place in the same category as the thief. Still one may say that it is not right to punish a person whom one does not blame — that it is not right to punish or blame him at all. But it is sometimes right to punish persons whom we do not blame. A sergeant may be right to punish an entire platoon in a situation where one member has done something wrong and where the other members refuse to inform on him, even though no one blames the other members for this. And we punish children who do not know that what they did was wrong (but at most know that the act is disapproved of and forbidden), but we do not blame them.

Finally, when we consider the consequence of not punishing the traitor we see that punishment is right. The alternative would be the endangerment of other members of the community. But it is not right to allow the presence of a condition which endangers the community. The issue then is whether it is more of a wrong to punish a person who has done what he thinks right or to neglect public welfare. The latter seems plainly more of a wrong, and seems so because the resulting evil would be worse.

But we are still left with a paradox. Are we to say that the person who does what he thinks right is responsible for his act in those cases in which we punish but do not blame him? If we say that he is not responsible, we imply that a person can be punished when he is not responsible. If we say that he is responsible, we imply that a person can be blameless for a wrong act for which he is responsible. Both are paradoxical. I think we must reject the second paradox and accept the first, as disturbing less other principles which we accept. One such principle is that being responsible entails being able, and it does not seem that a person is able in a full sense to do the morally right act unless he knows what this act is. He may have every other capacity necessary for bringing about the change which the act would bring about. But so long as he does not know what act is right, he cannot do the act as the right act. He is able to do an act which resembles the morally right act in every other feature than that of being morally right. But if he does not know what this act is he can only do this act with the thought that it is not right. In short, he can do the objectively right act or the subjectively right act, but not both. Thus it is strictly impossible for him to do the act which is completely right. And so we cannot hold him responsible for it. We conclude, then, that responsibility, though it is a necessary condition for blame, is not a necessary condition for punishment.

We may remove part of the appearance of paradox by distinguishing two senses of responsibility, one wider, which we can call 'moral responsibility', in which blame but not punishment entails responsibility, and the other a narrower sense, to be called 'practical responsibility', which

includes an ability only to do the objectively right act.
'Moral responsibility' will always include 'practical responsibility', but not conversely. Thus we can rightly
punish, yet rightly withhold blame from, persons who are
'practically' but not 'morally' responsible.

5. Subjective Obligation and Punishment

If this account of subjective obligation is correct, it
provides some means for deciding the general question of
the purpose of punishment.

Broadly there are two theories of punishment — the
Retributive and the Corrective. The Retributive theory
holds that the person is punished because he deserves it;
and he deserves it because he did of his own 'free will' a
wrong act. The Corrective theory is but a more particular
form of what I have called the Rhetorical Theory of praise
and blame. The theory is that the person is punished for
a wrong act as a means of influencing him or others to
correct his or their conduct. Thus the retributive theory
rests upon the theory that we have a special sort of free
will; if this latter theory can be shown false (as I shall later
attempt to do) the retributive theory of punishment has
been undermined. However, the retributive theory can be
attacked more directly, as not accounting for the sort of
acts which we do think punishable.

On the retributive theory what we punish is the act of
free will. We punish the person not for bringing about a
bad state of affairs in the world; we punish him for intending and attempting to do this. Now, if this is our
ground of punishment, we should consider the object of
intention not merely in its non-ethical description by the
intender but in its ethical description. I mean, we should
consider the agent's intention as directed not merely to a
certain event but to this event considered by him as right
or wrong, or good or bad. The theory should ask, for
example, not merely whether a person intended to kill
someone, but whether he considered the killing as something that was right or wrong. Indeed what will count
chiefly in determining whether his intention is good or
bad will be this ethical ingredient. If what makes the

person culpable is his ethical intention, then what makes him culpable should be the most distinctively ethical element in his intention, and this is his intention of doing what is right or wrong. If, then, we punish the person for bad intentions which, being the free acts of his will, are acts which deserve punishment, then we will punish only acts which are not abstractly well-intentioned. But this is not in fact the way in which we do punish adults. We consider intention, but only in its specific ethical description or in its non-ethical description. And this is explained by the corrective rather than by the retributive theory.

I shall try to show this, and generally to refute the retributive theory, by establishing the following points concerning our failure to punish in terms of conscientiousness. (1) Abstractly good intention does not occur in degrees, while punishment does occur in degrees; (2) so far as we do consider intention in assigning punishment we consider specific intentions, and this is explained by the purpose of improving conduct; (3) there are special difficulties in establishing the existence of abstractly ethical intention in particular acts; (4) the one area in which we do reward and punish in terms of abstractly ethical intention, namely in the case of children, is explained by the purpose of improving conduct.

(1) That in punishing we do not punish solely with reference to abstract ethical intention is evident in that punishment is apportioned in degrees, while an abstractly good or bad intention cannot occur in degrees. We can speak of a more or less abstractly well-intentioned person, but not of a more or less abstractly well-intentioned act. The abstractly well-intentioned act is the intentional act of doing that which the person thinks right. There may be several deeds which he thinks equally to qualify as fulfillments of duty, but then the doing of any one of these will be perfectly abstractly well-intentioned and the failure to do any one of them will be perfectly lacking in such an intention. The acts themselves and their consequences can have all degrees of rightness or wrongness, goodness or badness, but the abstractly good intention cannot reflect these degrees. For the person's duty is to do that act

which he regards as most right or obligatory or dutiful; doing an act of any less degree of obligation will be a violation of conscience. Since, then, his abstractly good intention depends upon the person's conception of this act, and since he can have but one relevant conception of this, what he does will be either just abstractly well-intentioned or its opposite. This allows that he may be a more or less abstractly well-intentioned person, meaning that more or less of his acts are so, but not that each act is itself more or less abstractly well-intentioned.

However, it may appear that, because the element of thinking and trying are present in the act of subjective obligation and because these exist in degrees, this act likewise can exist in degrees. But we can see that the degree of these elements do not affect the act's being abstractly well-intentioned.

First, thinking is susceptible of degrees. We can think more or less, and we can believe with more or less conviction. But neither the amount nor certainty of thinking affects subjective obligation. Suppose the person thinks that a given act is probably right. If he thinks he has as much certainty on the matter as he can get, then he is subjectively obligated to do the act. If he thinks that by thinking further he can become more certain, then he is subjectively obligated to think further. But this means that his immediate subjective obligation, what he thinks immediately right, is to think about what will be right in another imminent situation. In either case he thinks but one thing right, and he is obligated to pursue but this one thing; he is not obligated in varying degrees to pursue one of several things. The person either thinks that he has enough certainty that a deed is right to attempt it, or that he has not enough certainty. Hence he is subjectively obligated either to attempt the deed or to attempt to obtain more certainty about whether to attempt it.

Similarly, although trying also exists in different degrees, it does not follow that the person can be subjectively obligated in corresponding degrees. A person will sometimes think it right to do what requires a great amount of effort and sometimes right to do what requires very little. If he

L

is obligated to carry from a burning building a child or a woman or a man, his obligation will not depend on which of these things is harder. But though different acts will require different degrees of effort, there will not be acts which, depending on these degrees of effort, are in different degrees subjectively obligatory. It follows that punishment, which does distinguish degrees of obligation, cannot be directed to the violation of subjective obligation.

(2) The purpose which does explain our general practices of punishment is that of improving conduct. In punishment we consider whether an act was premeditated, and we provide a more severe punishment for the premeditated act than for the act done in ignorance or on impulse. This is explained by the purpose of improvement. The deliberate act expresses a more settled tendency than does the impulsive act, and requires a greater force to alter. The severest penalty is thus assigned to the person who acts with full knowledge, for he will be the hardest to change. What is considered in premeditation are specific rather than abstract intentions. But the principle applies to both : it is harder to change action which is based upon settled judgments of what the person desires or thinks it right to do. And so far as action is alterable by punishment, and alterable partly according to the degree of severity of the punishment, the severer punishment of intentional action is accounted for by the corrective theory. Further, the abstractly well-intentioned person, providing he is intelligent, mature and educated, is harder to reform than the merely specifically ill-intentioned person. For the person who acts from abstractly good intentions (though in ways specifically wrong) acts from the most settled and ultimate sort of conviction, and a sort which it is hardest to change. Moreover, the zealot is protected against a reform in his own views by his own zeal to reform others. In this the person of the most strenuous conscience is like the person with no conscience. And it is another evidence of our general adherence to the corrective theory of punishment that we treat the two — the heretic and the 'hardened criminal' — in the same way.

Another possible defense of the retributive theory is to

OBLIGATION   147

hold that a well-intentioned person can act wrongly only
from a deficiency in his non-ethical knowledge, never from
a deficiency in his ethical knowledge. That is, the abstractly well-intentioned person will always be specifically
well-intentioned. On this account, there would never be
a conflict of subjective and objective obligation so long as
the person possessed all relevant non-ethical knowledge.
Whenever a person acted wrongly, it would be because
either he failed to do what he thought right, or because he
lacked knowledge of the non-ethical features of the moral
situation. Now one does not punish a person for the latter
sort of error; hence the only wrong for which a person
might be held punishable would be an abstractly ill-
intentioned act. But this account makes the fantastic
assumption that all sane adults know what is right, their
failure to do it being just that their wills are weak.
This is incredible. If people did always know what was
right, then they could not seek to discover what was right
and fail to find it. But they often do.

(3) Even if it were desirable to reward and punish a
person for his abstract intentions, it would be a difficult
thing to do. As Kant pointed out, in all those cases where
duty coincides with interest, it is impossible to know
whether a person is acting from interest or from a sense of
duty (a thought of and a desire to do what is right). But
it is also difficult in other cases. Suppose a person acts in
a way contrary to his actual duty. How shall we know
whether his motive was his own contrary belief about his
duty, or his yielding to a strong desire? How can he himself know? We might be able to know this if we had a
sure way of knowing his actual desires. For then, if his
desires run counter to the thing he appeared to do from a
sense of duty, we could conclude that the act was really
done from this purely dutiful motive. But, particularly
since the advent of psychoanalytic inquiry, we have become
aware of the difficulty of being sure what are a person's
desires. Psychoanalysis makes available a total dissolution
of the motive of conscientiousness by reducing it to more
rudimentary desires for love and hate, and to be punished
and to punish. However, we do not need to go this deep

to see the difficulty. For if a person sincerely asks himself whether his apparently most purely dutiful acts were really so — whether, for example, in an act sacrificing some obvious personal interest he were motivated purely by a desire to do what is right, and in no measure by a desire for the approval of others or of himself — he will feel considerable doubt.

(4) There is one area in which we do accept an abstractly good intention as a total excuse. This further shows that we punish to correct, and that our failure to punish or reward adults on the ground of their abstractly good intentions is due to its ineffectiveness as a corrective. This area is that of the behavior of children. We may begin by punishing and rewarding children before they have clear ideas of right and wrong. Here punishment and reward are plainly devices to teach morality, or to give them the ideas of right and wrong in general, as well as to mark out specifically what is right and wrong. Once children have a conception of right and wrong, and are capable of abstractly well-intentioned action, we do not punish them for abstractly well-intentioned acts, however bad their consequences. There is an obvious reason for this different way of treating the child. This is that the child has not been provided with correct specific moral opinions, and hence that he is to be improved, not by punishing him for not using a knowledge which he did not have, but by giving him this knowledge through direct moral instruction.

Still the corrective theory will seem offensive to many persons. (1) Some will find it offensive because they hold that it rests upon the false psychological premiss that punishment does correct the person punished. (2) Others will object to it because they believe that it would sanction punishing an innocent person in order to improve (or prevent the deterioration of) the behavior of others.

(1) Professor Ebersole has argued that punishment is never justified in a 'strong sense' because we cannot *know* that it will reform the person punished.[1] But if we were only right to do actions which we knew for certain would

---

[1] 'Free Choice and the Demands of Morals', *Mind*, 1952, p. 257.

only have a given result, then there would be no (or exceedingly few) right acts. But justifiable or right action depends upon grounded belief and not upon complete certainty. Thus if the purpose of punishment were reform, we could justify punishment by at least a high degree of probability that it will reform. And we have this probability with respect to many acts. In general, the probability is greatest in respect of minor offenses. Punishment and the threat of punishment are most effective where the motive to commit the punishable act is weakest, and generally we are most weakly motivated to do those acts (as violating traffic laws) which are minor offenses. It seems obvious that punishment and the threat of punishment prevent many such acts which would occur in the absence of punishment or the threat of it. But in the case of major offenses, often the offender's motivation towards the act is so intense that no punishment or threat is extreme enough to counterbalance it.

If this is so, it involves the apparent paradox that on the corrective theory we ought to punish least the greatest offenses. But the paradox is merely apparent. For the implication here is not that the punishment for major offenses ought to be least severe. Indeed the greater the offense the greater the force required to counteract the motives to commit it. What is implied is that for the more serious 'crimes' punishment is least often the proper method of treatment. The person whose motivation is sufficiently strong to lead him to commit a major crime is a person whose motivation resembles the obsession of the insane person, and to the degree that he approaches insanity to that degree is he to be dealt with as a patient for treatment and not as an object of punishment. The result, then, is that, on the corrective view, although punishment is less often right than is usually supposed, it nonetheless is right in a great many cases.

There is, of course, a difficulty about the range of the concept of punishment, and apparent difficulties in the corrective account may arise here. Ebersole imagines a case where 'If we possessed a sensitive brain-wave machine which would predict whether a person would commit a crime and what sort of censure and punishment would prevent it, then we would have no need to be concerned about a person's past' in administering punishment. Professor Mabbott calls this a *reductio ad absurdum* of the corrective theory, on the ground that 'It is impossible to justify punishing or blaming people who have done no wrong'.[1] Now in that this is impossible Mabbott is surely right. But the conclusion is only that Ebersole is unduly extending the concept of punishment. Plainly what he has in mind is simply administering some sort of hurt to the prospective ill-doer. But so described, there is nothing morally offensive in such an action. People often voluntarily choose a present hurt to prevent a future evil. And they do this sometimes to forestall a future moral evil. A person who knows he has a 'criminal' tendency may ask that he be confined to prevent his acting on the tendency. Such inflictions of hurt are therapeutic measures and not acts of punishment.

(2) But Mabbott also objects to the corrective theory on the ground that this theory in one form would justify punishing an innocent scapegoat for some crime which he did not commit, so long as this led to discouraging other potential criminals. The first thing to observe is that the case presented is not one that falls within the range of the theory's application, so that strictly the theory is committed to no view of such a case. This is so, because the case is not one of punishment, for a punishment (and hence the corrective method of punishment) applies only where a wrong act has been done. The theory was not constructed to cover questions as to the general use of injury. One might, however, construe the corrective theory as a particular variation of a more general theory which might be called the teleological theory of injury. The latter theory would be just that injury is in itself bad and hence an act of injury is right only when it leads to a greater good. And it would appear that the truth of this theory is necessary to the truth of the corrective theory of punishment. Thus if on the teleological theory of injury, the injury of the

[1] 'Free Will and Punishment', *Contemporary British Philosophy*, Third Series, ed. H. O. Lewis, p. 298.

innocent scapegoat would be justified, while it is not in fact justified, both the teleological and the corrective theories would be shown false. What then of the case of the innocent scapegoat? The reply is (1), that no convincing case of an innocent scapegoat has (to my knowledge) been presented; and (2), if there were a case in which injuring an innocent person (and taking into account the injury to the feelings and characters of others and to social stability springing from the violation of equity) would result in a greater good, then it would be right to inflict the injury.

(1) Consider this example from Professor Carritt's *Ethical and Political Thinking*. '. . . The utilitarian must hold that we are justified in inflicting pain always and only to prevent worse pain or bring about greater happiness. This, then, is all we need to consider in so-called punishment which must be purely preventive. But if some kind of very cruel crime becomes common, and none of the criminals can be caught, it might be highly expedient, as an example, to hang an innocent man, if a charge against him could be so framed that he were universally thought guilty; indeed this would only fail to be an ideal instance of utilitarian "punishment" because the victim himself would not have been so likely as a real felon to commit such a crime in the future; in all other respects it would be perfectly deterrent and therefore felicific' (p. 10).

The example is entirely unconvincing. First Carritt supposes, as is necessary, that none of the actual criminals can be caught, but still supposes that punishment of an innocent person might lead these criminals to desist from their crime. But if they have not been caught, knowing that someone else has been punished (even supposing they did not know this person was not one of their number) would not lead them to desist. It would not even prevent the crime from spreading. For potential criminals are not deterred from crime by the knowledge that the crime in question is punished sometimes, and in this case only once. They will be deterred, if at all, only by the conviction that the crime is punished frequently or usually, and that their own punishment for committing the crime is not merely possible but highly probable. Thus the corrective view would not justify even the mistaken punishment of an innocent person in the sort of case Carritt imagines.

(2) Still, the objector may retort that his criticism does not require that we be able to produce a case where injuring an innocent scapegoat would result in an improvement of conduct. The point is, he charges, that if there were such a case the teleological theory must declare that such an injury is right, whereas we can see plainly that it would not be right. Well, it is true that the corrective theory would be committed to holding that such an injury would be right. But surely it *would* be right. Let us imagine the fanciful case somewhere described by William James. Suppose that the happiness of all mankind could be secured by the unceasing torment of one lonely soul. Would it be right to inflict the torment? Of course it is impossible not to boggle at the example. First, do the rest of mankind know the price being paid for their happiness, or do they not know? If they know, then the example is hardly even conceivable, for we should think that this tormented soul would weigh on their conscience and poison this happiness. Or is this happiness a sheer complacency which is without conscience? In this case the happiness might not seem worth much, or not worth this much. But suppose they don't know. Suppose first that only the person who is tormented knows; suppose he has entered into a pact with a divine being to shoulder the sins of everyone. Well then it is questionable whether his torment would be a thorough one — it would rather be the peace of the saint. And it might well be a right act on his part. In any event it is certain that if such a deal were offered, saints would not be wanting who were ready to take it up. But suppose, on the other hand, that only two persons know — the one tormented and the one who inflicts the torment. Now we have at least two tormented souls, and we must put the question with respect to these two. So put, I think we should say that the tormentor would be right to inflict the torment. It is right to deal 'unjustly' with an individual when so doing works a substantial benefit for all mankind.

But the net result of such fantasies is that they are

merely fantastic, and that they can shed no real light upon the justification of inflicting injury. For they generally require that we separate our estimate of the injury inflicted upon the scapegoat from our estimate of the injury to our feelings of sympathy, brotherhood and equity with other human beings, and of the great social benefits resulting from these. All of these latter values would be sacrificed to some degree whenever we sacrificed a scapegoat to our pleasure or contentment. And when we add the loss of these to the positive evil suffered by the scapegoat, the possibility of a real case being found in which infliction of injury on an innocent person would result in a greater good appears highly unlikely.

6. *Obligation and Good*

Several things about obligation may be taken as generally agreed on. (1) What is obligatory is some act by some person. Nothing other than a person can be obligated, and a person can be obligated in respect of nothing other than his acts. Animals are not held under obligation, nor are very young children. And persons are not held under obligation for their feelings or states of character, except in so far as these are considered as results of acts for which they are obligated. (2) There are certain rules of obligation, as that one ought to keep his promises, tell the truth, care for his children, pay his debts, be kind to people, etc. (3) There are degrees of obligation, and some of these rules are more authoritative than others ; for example, the obligation to keep promises is more authoritative (more of an obligation, a stronger obligation) than the obligation to be courteous to strangers. (4) Such rules of obligation may conflict in a particular situation, such that the agent can only observe one rule by violating another. The degrees of obligation in a particular situation may not correspond to the general degrees of obligatoriness of the rules. It may be, for example, that although one generally has a greater obligation to keep his promises than to be kind to people, still on some particular occasion the latter may be the greater obligation.

These principles would, I believe, be accepted by almost

all theories of obligation. The special problems begin here. The chief point of dispute is whether there is a single additional ordering principle both among the general rules of obligation and among particular alternative possible acts within an actual situation of choice. There are basically two views. The 'Teleologists' hold that there is such an ordering principle, namely the principle of the greatest good. General rules and particular acts of obligation are justified so far as they promote the greatest good. This is the principle by which we should order the rules generally and resolve particular cases of conflict. Ultimately, then, on this view, there is but one obligation, namely to promote the maximum good. The opposed view, that of the 'Deontologists', is that obligation is not thus reducible to good. It maintains that obligation and good are distinct and irreducible ethical ultimates, or that good is reducible to obligatoriness (in which case again there is no single principle for ordering obligations, but only degrees of obligatoriness which must be directly perceived). The chief expositor of the teleological view is G. E. Moore, that of the deontological view is H. A. Prichard. The teleological position is, I shall argue, the correct view and the view of common sense. Even in philosophy it was unquestioned (I believe) until Prichard's famous essay, 'Does Moral Philosophy Rest on a Mistake?' I shall, accordingly, organize my argument for the teleological position in the form of a defense against the attacks brought by Prichard and other deontologists.

7. *Can an Action be Both Right and Good?*

One apparent difference between an obligatory act and a good act is that obligatoriness seems to depend upon certain past events while goodness seems to depend either just upon the intrinsic character of the act or on its future results. This is indeed true of many kinds of obligation. Promise-keeping, caring for relatives, acts of gratitude — these depend upon some past event. Whereas a good act such as generosity or courage depends only upon what it is or upon its consequences. However, certain obligations likewise depend only upon their present character or future relations. For example, truth-telling, helping the afflicted, courtesy. These obligations do not, like promise-keeping and the rest, depend upon some past act by which the obligation has been incurred.

Further, these examples furnish strong evidence that rightness is reducible to goodness. For (1) we are equally ready to call these acts 'right' and 'good' or to say both that the person 'ought' or is 'obliged' to do them and that it is 'good' for the person to do them. (2) The only distinction we should make is this. We would say that there are acts which are good which still no one is responsible for doing, these being either impossible or beyond normal capacity. There does then exist a plain and crucial distinction between the good act and the one for which the person is responsible. But there is also, as we saw, a distinction, though a less obvious one, between what we call obligations and what we hold a person responsible for. Thus in this, too, the good act resembles the obligatory or right act. (3) Further, common opinion would regard it as a truism that the right act is the act which does the greatest good ; that it could not be right for a person to do an act which would realize a lesser good when he could do one that would realize a greater good ; and that in the case of apparently conflicting obligations the agent will be choosing the same act, and the act which is both right and good, if he chooses that act which is most obligatory and which will realize the greatest good.

Prichard and Ross, however, strongly argue that the right and the good cannot be the same. I shall first present the general difficulty which confronts their view, and then consider their positive arguments both in their more general form and in their application to specific obligations such as promise-keeping.

In *Moral Obligation* Prichard maintains quite flatly that an action can never be 'good' but only 'right'. But on the surface this is just paradoxical. Surely we do think that the 'rightness' of an act is a kind of 'goodness'. We would not hesitate to say that a 'morally right' act is a 'morally good' act, and conversely. It is true that we do use 'right' to describe acts and nothing else, while we use 'good' to describe both acts and other things. But what this suggests is that 'rightness' is a species of 'goodness'. However, Prichard contends that what we mean when we say that an action is 'good' is that its *motive* is good; further that the peculiarly 'moral motive' is the motive of doing the act which is felt to be 'right', not 'good'. He argues that if there were not such a distinct thing as 'rightness' this peculiarly 'moral motive' could not exist. 'If the motive in respect of which we think an action good is the sense of obligation, then so far from the sense that we ought to do it being derived from our apprehension of its goodness, our apprehension of its goodness will presuppose the sense that we ought to do it. In other words, in this case the recognition that the act is good will probably presuppose the recognition that the act is right, whereas the view under consideration is that the recognition of the goodness of the act *gives rise* to the recognition of its rightness' (p. 6).[1]

But this is not the dilemma it is represented to be. What is involved may just as well be two kinds of good, the good of one kind being dependent on the good of the other — the particular good in which the *motive* of duty consists being dependent upon the different particular good in which the dutiful *act* consists. Clearly the act of duty (or its good) could not consist of the motive of duty (or its good), for the object of a motive (or of a 'desire' or 'sense') cannot be identical with that motive. But when there are two things of the same order one of these can take the other for its object. In particular, an act of performing one's duty may be one kind of good thing, while a *sense* (or motive) of duty is a good motive to possess or produce this particular sort of good. What Prichard's argument shows is that what makes an act right (or good) cannot be the motive of doing the act because it is right (or good). The argument does not show that an act's rightness may not be one kind of good, and a motive to do the act as right another kind of good which is dependent on this first good.

[1] Prichard made this argument in the early 'Does Moral Philosophy Rest on a Mistake', but he repeated it in a fuller form in 'Moral Obligation', Section VIII, where he says flatly, 'we cannot do a duty from the sense of duty' (p. 158).

Prichard's argument would be an effective refutation of the view that the only good thing is the pursuing of the good. Such a doctrine would be self-contradictory: if the only good were the pursuit of the good, then there could be nothing good to pursue, hence no pursuit of good, hence nothing good at all. But it is not a refutation of the doctrine that right actions are one member of the class of good things, of which another member is good motives.

Prichard stresses that desires and motives differ from actions in that desires are passive, and it sometimes seems that this difference is his sole ground for holding that the 'rightness' of actions must radically differ from the 'goodness' of desires. No doubt the difference between the passive and the active is a great difference; but things which differ in this way might still have something in common. A momentary state of feeling also greatly differs from an enduring disposition for this same feeling, but this does not prevent the two from being alike in important ways or from both being good. Indeed, could we suppose that a desire, such as benevolence, might be good, when the object of this desire is not good? We ordinarily believe that desires and their objects roughly correspond in goodness. Both tyranny and the desire to tyrannize are bad; and both justice and the desire for justice are good. For the present argument it does not matter whether the value of the object or of the desire is primary. Nor does it matter that the correlation does not exist in every case. (These variations are discussed in the chapter on Desire.) What is crucial is the fact that the two are generally correlated — that when we say that a desire for something is good, we imply that the thing is good. This shows the anomaly to be the contrary of what Prichard maintains. It would be in fact an anomaly if a desire to do one's duty should be good when doing one's duty were not good but only 'right'.

8. *Is the Good Something that Ought to Be?*

In another version of the same argument Prichard maintains that we cannot suppose that what is good ever 'ought to be'. He argues as follows: 'An ought could not be derived from anything but another ought. Hence if we ought to act to realize good, this ought of the act must derive from the good's being what "ought-to-be". But neither the good nor an act nor anything else "ought to be"; for "ought" in the sense of obligation is something that belongs only to the person who ought to do the act.' But the argument requires the premiss that the 'ought' of the act must be *derived* from the ought of the good. If the ought of the act can *consist* in good, as common sense holds, then this *good* of the act may derive from the *good* of the act's objective. Prichard first assumes that the ought must be something wholly different from good, then asserts that the ought cannot be derived from good. But if the ought (the right or obligatory act) is itself a form of good, there is no problem of this derivation.

We can better see the connection of the right and the good by considering uses of this expression 'ought-to-be'.

Prichard finds the expression self-contradictory. But since it is commonly employed both by ordinary people and (as Prichard notes) by philosophers, we must suppose that it serves a use. In fact, we shall see that the expression enables us to say something which is not so well said by the more accurate expressions which attribute good or obligation to something.

Besides the objection that the ought-to-be character could not strictly belong to an act or thing but only to a person, Prichard mentions the objection that this character could not belong to anything that does not exist, such as a future act; for a thing which does not exist cannot have any character at all, even the character of 'ought-to-be'. Thus he says that the only possible way of preserving the ought-to-be character would be to attribute it hypothetically. Accordingly, if we were to try to say something like 'X's act of educating Y ought to exist', we should have to modify it to the form: 'If X is, or will be educating Y, his educating Y is, or will be, something which ought to exist' (p. 93). Prichard is right in saying that any meaning an ought-to-be expression could have would have to be hypothetical, but he evidently dismisses this as a real possibility. The fact is that we do use the expression in this way.

Certainly we do not seem ever to intend just the sort of statement he mentions, but he does not modify the statement sufficiently. He retains as the predicate 'ought to be' when the predicate intended is rather 'good'.

When we say '*N* ought to exist' we do not mean, 'If *N* did exist, then *N* *ought* to exist'; but I suggest that we do mean, 'If *N* does exist, then that would be *good*'. The latter form may seem almost equally odd, for it may seem to come to, 'It would be good if what is good (*N*) did exist', which is equivalent to 'It would be good if good (in this case, *N*) would be'. The statement seems odd because tautological; but it is not tautological. The tautology would be, 'It would be good if it would be good', while the actual statement is 'It would be good if good would be'. This is not to say twice that the same thing is good, but is to say that if a thing is good, then the coming to be of that thing is good. This statement may be important in a particular case, and may be true or false. It might seem always true that if a thing is good, then its origination is good; but this is not so; for a thing may be good, yet its origination be equally the origination of something else which is more bad than it is good, and then its origination would not be good.

To say that a thing ought to exist, or that its origination would be good, is sometimes to say rather pointedly that someone ought to originate that thing. But the 'ought-to-be' form has other uses which depend on its allowing an important omission which the direct 'ought' form cannot allow. Motives from which we sometimes might wish to avoid this specification are rudeness, politeness, indignation.

Consider someone saying under different circumstances, 'There ought to be air in this room'. Suppose first the speaker is in bed ill, and says this to his nurse. His meaning is: 'You ought to open the window; indeed you ought already to have done so, and you have shirked your obligation in neglecting it'. If he does not intend to convey this, then he should simply say, 'You ought to open the window'. In a different situation, the expression might be a form of politeness. Suppose a lady says it in the presence of a gentleman and with reference to a heavy window. Here the expression means : 'Opening the window would show you to be a person who fulfills his obligations'. Consider a third use. The speaker utters it to a group of persons each of whom has made unavailing efforts to open the window. Here the sentence means : 'Someone has shirked his obligation in not having made it possible to open the window'. In all of these cases there is a statement of obligation, but a statement which for some reason does not specify that a certain person is obligated. In the first two cases the person who is obligated is made quite aware of it by the verbal form, but the speaker wishes to veil the reference; in the third case the speaker does not wish to veil the reference, but does not know exactly to whom he is referring. All are useful statements of obligation.

The difference between the 'ought-to-be' and the 'would-be-good' forms can be brought out by considering other possible uses of the expression, 'There ought to be air in this room'. Suppose it is said by someone in a burning building with no fire-escape. His actual utterance has meaning only as expressing his desire for air and his fear of being without it. As a statement of obligation, it would have to mean 'There ought to be someone who ought to give this room air', which is false. It is like the statement, 'There ought to be a way to travel to Mars', which, since there is no one who is obligated to provide the trip, is plainly false. But suppose the speaker said instead, 'It would be good if there were air in the room', or 'It would be good if there were a way of going to Mars'. These statements may be true; they are only idle.

Thus the 'ought-to-be' form is indefinite in its referent; it asserts that a thing ought to be, but clearly what it means is that a person not named ought to originate that thing. And it is false if there is no such person who might be named. The 'would-be-good' form is conditional; it does not assert but hypothecates goodness in a thing, and it is idle if there is no condition under which the thing could be realized. The 'would-be-good' form, because it refers primarily to the thing apart from the agent, preserves its sense, even though losing its interest, when we can indicate no obligatory act; while the 'ought-to-be' form, because it refers primarily to the obligatory act, preserves no sense when there is no possible obligatory act. Thus the forms are connected by the fact that the only important or interesting 'would-be-good' statements are those in which the referent could be actualized, and hence which provide grounds for making an 'ought-to-be' statement.

The closeness of the connection of the two forms is seen further in that both are significant only when they refer to particulars. We cannot say that courage or peace either 'ought-to-be' or 'would be good'. We can only say that the courage of this individual or group of individuals, or peace somewhere or other, 'ought to be' or 'would be good'. This suggests that the 'would-be-good' form is most closely connected with this 'ought' form and not with the direct 'good' form. For we can say quite generally that, in some sense, courage or peace is good.

The relation of good and ought is further clarified by another and perhaps more common use of the 'would-be-good' and 'ought-to-be' forms. In this use the speaker does not assert anything, but poses a question. Here again the forms are very similar but also different. A speaker may say that 'air in the room' 'would be good' or 'ought to be', when he is not certain whether the originating of this thing by opening the window is something that would be good or that he ought to do. He is really asking, 'I ought to open the window, oughtn't I?', or 'The air would be good, wouldn't it?' But the two expressions have different emphases, one on the act and the other on the thing to be originated by the act. Suppose that opening the door would be easier but would not provide such good air. Then the declarative form, 'There ought to be air in this room', would mean: 'I really ought to open the window'; and the conditional statement, 'It would be good if there were air in this room', would mean: 'Really the air from the window would be better'.

The general conclusion to be drawn is that the good and the ought are connected by the intermediary forms of the 'would be good' and the 'ought to be'. The 'would-be-good' statement is a stage on the way to the 'ought-to-be' statement, which is in turn a stage to the concluding

M

directive 'ought' statement. In the deliberative process, the person may begin by saying that in general circulating air in a room is good, then that more air in this room *would be good*, then that there *ought to be* more air in this room, and finally that some particular person *ought* to open the window. The direct 'good' form asserts no obligation; the direct 'ought' form does state an obligation; the 'ought-to-be' and the 'would-be-good' forms do not explicitly state an obligation, but the former implies it and the latter suggests it. Thus the good and the ought are connected by natural transitions, which are made explicit by the intermediate forms of the 'would be good' and 'ought to be'.

9. *Are Particular Obligations, Obligations to Realize Good?*

Ross argues in detail that some particular obligations are not analyzable in terms of good. He agrees that there is an obligation to promote good, but he holds that there are 'special obligations' distinct from this, in particular 'duties towards individuals, based on special relations between them and the agent'.[1] He mentions three such duties : (1) to compensate for injury ; (2) to repay benefits ; (3) to fulfill promises. But he pays most attention to the duty to keep promises, devoting to it an entire chapter organized around the criticisms of Mr. Pickard-Cambridge. The latter had argued that the reason promises ought to be kept is that thereby various goods are produced and evils are avoided, namely : (1) the gaining by the promisee of the promised benefit ; (2) the pleasure caused to the promisee by the fulfillment of his expectation ; (3) the heightening of the promisor's reputation for trustworthiness, with the greater power to do good which this will bring ; (4) the benefit to society caused by his increasing the general confidence that promises will be kept. Ross denies that the promotion of good (and the avoidance of the corresponding evils) is sufficient to explain the obligation to keep promises. I think Ross is right, that these

[1] *Foundations of Ethics*, p. 76. Unless otherwise indicated, all quotations are from this book. Ross argued the same general view in his earlier *The Right and The Good*, but the later book does introduce some modifications.

goods are not sufficient. But I shall argue that both writers overlook certain other values which are also realized by promise-keeping and which, combined with the above four values, do fully account for the force of the obligation. These are the values of (5) telling and knowing the truth and (6) consistency of character. These are generally recognized to be goods of character; and fulfilling promises tends to realize them. Mr. Pickard-Cambridge's list includes the good of improving the promisor's reputation, but it does not include the greater good of improving the promisor's character.

These values of truth and consistency are not peculiar to promise-keeping; they are realized also by the keeping of resolves — which may explain why they were overlooked as an element in promises. To resolve to do a thing is to intend to do it, and this includes a belief that one will do it. A promise is a resolve which is communicated to someone as affecting that person's interest. Thus promise-keeping realizes not only the four goods peculiar to promise-keeping, but the two further goods realized by resolve-keeping.

Further, these goods of resolve-keeping, though not peculiar to promise-keeping, are the only goods which are inseparable from promise-keeping. Goods (3), the promisor's reputation and power for good, and (4), preserving an organized society, are certainly important goods and are commonly affected by promise-keeping and promise-breaking. But Ross is right in urging that the teleologists have exaggerated their weight as factors in the obligation to keep promises. For some promises are secret, and these goods could not be affected by the keeping or breaking of secret promises. Good (1), the gaining by the promisee of the promised benefit, is less rarely unaffected by promises, but a change of circumstances might render the thing promised indifferent to the promisee when the time arrives for the promise's fulfillment. Likewise with good (2), the promisee might have become so occupied with other things that it is of no interest to him that the promise is or is not kept. But it is not the same with the goods involved in resolve-keeping. No promise-keeping can fail to realize them. These goods may be rendered insignificant by the presence of greater competing goods, but nothing can reduce them to zero. In Ross' terms, they must always be sources of '*prima facie*' obligation. A person is under some obligation to tell the truth and to be consistent, and so far as he breaks an obligation to keep a promise, he has at the same time broken these other obligations. These obligations, and their corresponding goods, account for that force which remains in the promise-keeping obligation after we have subtracted obligations to realize the other four goods.

In his discussion of promise-keeping Ross gives but incidental notice to these goods of truth and consistency. And apparently he does not consider them to be goods realized by promise-keeping. He rightly says that one can break a promise without telling a lie; 'for it is only when a promise is made with the intention of breaking it that a lie is told' (p. 112). But it remains true that one cannot break a promise without having told a falsehood, for the promise asserted that something would happen which, when the promise was broken, did not happen. Generally, no doubt, lies are worse than mere falsehoods; but falsehoods are usually somewhat bad. Other things being equal, we would rather have believed and told the truth. And to keep a sincere promise is to have believed and said something true.

A promise is not merely a prediction; it is, as we have been well instructed by the late Professor Austin, also an act. To make a promise, or to keep a promise, is to do an act which is right or wrong. But to promise is also to say or imply a proposition which is true or false, namely that the thing promised will be done. This can be made evident as follows: To a person who had promised something obviously impossible, it would be a proper reply to say not merely, 'You can't *keep* that promise', but more forcibly, 'You can't *make* that promise'. A person's believing that he cannot do certain things deprives him of the power to promise these things. He may utter the words 'I promise', but the promise is spurious. He has only gone through the motions of promising. And his wrong consists, not in his later failure to fulfill the promise, but in his

originally pretending to promise. We should not blame a
person for failing to do something that was impossible, but
we should blame him for having said he would do an
impossible thing; for it was possible for him not to have
said this. Further, we should say that he had done wrong
even if in fact he later did what he had 'promised'. The
evidence that a promise has been made is then not whether
the proposition it contains about the event promised is true,
but whether the promisor believes it to be true. A promise
is therefore inseparable from such a proposition which is
believed. Hence a good that will be realized if the promise
is kept is that this belief will have been true. It may be
only a small good to have true beliefs, and this good is
certainly a very small reason for keeping a promise. But it
is some good and some reason. It partly accounts for our
feeling that if there is no other good to be gained or lost by
the keeping of a promise, still one ought to keep it.

Having told the truth in a promise will also be having
preserved 'consistency' between our words and deeds.
And we think this to be good not merely because it pro-
motes social harmony, but also because we think an in-
tegrated character to be something which is good in itself.
Ross gives passing notice to the value of consistency, but it
is not clear what argument he means to construct. He says
that 'The duty of fulfillment of a promise is not a duty of
maintaining consistency between one's words and one's
deeds'. To be sure, the duty of being consistent is distinct
from the duty to fulfill promises, in that there are other
ways of being consistent. But it is not separable from
promise-keeping, for any case of keeping a promise must
be a case of being consistent. Another point Ross makes
is that the duty of promise-keeping is the stronger duty.
But this is not in question. If promise-keeping includes
consistency and if the obligation to keep promises includes
the obligation to be consistent as one obligation among
others, certainly the more inclusive obligation will be
stronger. What Ross in fact seems positively to be arguing
is that the obligation to be consistent is not really very
strong, contrary to the obligation to keep promises; for
when we find a case where we think we may honorably

break a promise, there the obligation to be consistent is not strong enough to deter us. But of course if we have already decided that it is right in the given case to break a promise, then we must at the same time have decided that it is right here to be inconsistent, for we cannot do the former without the latter.

Consider a case in which changed circumstances may seem to change the obligation. Suppose Jones promises Smith to bring him a copy of a book a week later; in the meantime Smith receives another copy and Jones learns this. Now whether this removes Jones' obligation will depend on the terms of his promise. If he promised merely to deliver the book, with no consideration of Smith's use for it or of Smith's use for more than one copy, then Smith's receipt of the other copy does not remove the obligation. But if Jones' promise was to deliver the book in order that Smith could read it, then Smith's receipt of another copy does 'remove' the obligation. But this is because the obligation has been fulfilled. For the promise was in effect to enable Smith to read the book so far as delivering the book would serve this end. If delivering the book to him will not serve that end, then, in not delivering the book *because* he sees this end would not thereby be served, Jones is doing what he promised.

The particular sort of change of circumstance which Ross says would remove a *prima facie* obligation to keep a promise is a change in the promisee's desires. But there are only two ways in which a desire or an expression of desire could affect a promise. One way would be if it brought into existence another obligation, as an obligation to accede to the person's desires. The other way would be if the promise were a promise to do a thing only on condition of its being desired by the promisee. It is true that we customarily think of promises only as promises of something desired by, or at least beneficial to, the promisee. Promises of evil are called not 'promises' but 'threats'. The question, however, is whether only promises to gratify desires, and not threats, can impose obligation. Surely a threat also can impose obligation. Parents and political organizations issue threats, and we think the declaration of the threat does impose some obligation to abide by it. Parents are sometimes said to shirk their obligation when they do not carry out their threats. Of course, it is sometimes better to violate threats, as also it is sometimes better to violate other promises.

We should not leave this topic without mentioning another factor in the dispute between the deontologist and the teleologist. This is a difference in the strength of obligation which they feel to be imposed by a duty such as that of promise-keeping. There is nothing in their theories which would prevent their agreeing in every instance as to whether a given promise should be broken or kept. But I think it unlikely that they would agree. Deontologists seem to feel that there is a special sanctity about such obligations, and it is no doubt a partial expression of this feeling that they insist that these obligations are intrinsic, irreducible to any other ethical element. This comes out strikingly in a particular example offered by Ross. The case is that of a poor man who, after persuading another person to pay over to him a sum of money, then comes into a fortune. Ross cannot bring himself to say what common sense would surely say, that the changed circumstances make it now right for the person to break his promise. Instead Ross introduces various irrelevancies. He writes : 'I think that a man with a very delicate sense of honour would consider that he ought to pay for his own carelessness in making the promise unconditionally. But alternatively it might be urged that the promise was in spirit a promise to pay 100 pounds to a poor man, and ceased to be binding when the man had become rich. In either case, the *prima facie* obligation to keep promises does not seem to be placed in question. And surely, whatever we may think that the promisor ought to do, we should agree that if he does pay, the other ought to return the money' (pp. 97-8).

But first, to tell us what a man of a 'very delicate sense of honour' would do does not tell us what a man ought to do, unless a man ought to do what he would do if he had a very delicate sense of honor. And Ross, though he thinks this sense of honor is morally good, fundamentally distinguishes between moral goodness and obligatoriness, such that a person may do what he ought yet not be morally good, and conversely. So does Ross mean to say that this act of payment would be the right act, or only that, if the person did do the act, honor would be a good motive from which to do it? In any event, the point about honor is irrelevant, since the sense of honor is not a duty. Ross then mentions another obligation, that of not making promises carelessly. But certainly he cannot hold that the obligation to fulfill a particular promise is the same as, or is implied by, the obligation not to make promises carelessly; for on his view the obligation to keep promises is not dependent on any other obligation. The same reason renders irrelevant Ross' point about the obligation of the promisee. For if the obligation to keep a promise is 'intrinsic', then the promisor's obligation to keep it cannot depend on what would be the promisee's obligation if the promise were kept. The oddest thing of all is that Ross mentions a solution perfectly accordant both with common sense and with the deontological view, but makes little of it. This is that the promise was *in spirit* to pay the sum to a poor man. The only explanation of his gliding over this would seem to be that Ross does not want to suggest in any way that the man here ought to break the promise. He wants instead to go on and remind us how strong is a new obligation on the promisee if the promisor does keep his promise. But surely common sense would say that the promisor ought to break the promise — he ought not to give the promisee this opportunity to compete with him in the delicacy of their senses of honor.

10. *Obligations to Oneself and Moral Decisions*

To reach a moral decision is to decide what one ought to do. We make many decisions which we do not consider 'moral', e.g. where to take a vacation, whether to buy a Chevrolet or a Ford, whether to request a raise in salary, etc. In general, we regard a decision as moral only when it involves obligations. Further, generally we think of obligations as concerning others, not oneself, and concerning something rather serious. However, we do speak of a person's obligations to himself. We may say that a person

OBLIGATION

'owes it to himself' not to yield entirely to the interests and pressures of others, or that he 'has an obligation' to develop the potentialities of his nature. A more doubtful question is whether one can have an obligation which is concerned solely with securing his own pleasure. If so, then all practical decisions would turn out 'moral', including those above. The issue here comes back to that between the teleologist and the deontologist. For assuming that pleasure is something good, if we have obligations to maximize good, we should have an obligation to maximize our own pleasure as well as that of others, and decisions about this would be moral.

Certainly we should find it odd or humorous to be told, 'Jones decided that his obligation was to do this act because it would give him more pleasure than the other'. But we can explain this oddity in terms of the general purpose of judgments of praise and blame, and of the connection between these judgments and obligation. We praise and blame for the performance of obligations in order to influence. But praising a person for pursuing his own pleasure, or blaming him for not doing so, cannot generally influence him in any desirable direction. Human beings are so strongly inclined to pursue their own pleasure that the problem of influence is to curtail this tendency rather than encourage it. Thus we do not generally conceive of the pursuit of one's pleasure as an obligation which we must impress on persons and as something for which we will hold them responsible. However, in particular cases we may so conceive it. We may tell a person that he ought to get more pleasure out of life, and we may blame him for not doing so. We should do this to one who seemed to us so preoccupied with his obligations to others that he fails to give sufficient attention to his own welfare. We do think that a person 'ought' to look after his own welfare. Of course he will be better able to fulfill his obligations to others if he is happy himself. And Kant said that we had a duty to be happy, so that our unhappiness would not tempt us to neglect our other duties. But we do not think that a person's obligation to himself is wholly derivative from his obligation to others. Rather we think simply that each person ought to be as complete and happy a person as he can. This is at the root of our condemnation of such qualities as sloth and self-pity, and of acts such as masochism and suicide.

It follows that every decision concerning value will be in a certain sense 'moral', and will involve 'obligation'. In fact, of course, we rarely regard our decisions as moral, and it is best that we do not. We reserve the terms 'moral' and 'obligatory' for the more difficult and critical cases. These terms are strong; they connote serious responsibility and the possibility of serious blame; and ordinarily we will best perform our obligations if the matter of decision is not represented as this much of a crisis. The categories of morality and obligation apply to the whole of life; but life goes best if we refrain from introducing these categories at every turn. We can afford to be much more liberal in the use of the concept of good or value, because it does not directly bring in, as does obligation, the possible blaming of persons. Probably the most immediate thought which the notion of obligation carries to a person who is considering his obligation, is that failure to do it exposes him to blame, from others or himself. And this is indeed what we want the concept to do, and what makes the concept useful. But it is also what makes it appropriate to use it only infrequently.

11. *Rules of Obligation*

This connotation, and this use of the concept of obligation, explains the character and the number of the general rules of obligation, and explains why, because our ideas about obligation are dominated by these rules, we are inclined to overlook the derivation of obligation from good.

On the deontological view the rightness or obligatoriness of an act is decided by reference to a rule of obligation. For example, if Jones is asked how he justifies his paying over to Smith his entire salary for the month of January, a proper reply would be that he promised this to Smith, and that it is a rule that one ought to keep his promises. So far all is very clear sailing. But there is an obvious sort of case where the mere reference to a rule is not enough to provide or justify a decision, namely a case where two rules of obligation apply and prescribe contrary acts. It is a rule that one ought to feed and clothe his children, and let us suppose in the case above that if Jones obeys the promise-keeping rule he cannot also obey the care-of-children rule. If Jones' action were justified simply by 'the following of the rule', then each action would be both right and wrong, for each would conform to one rule and violate another. In such a predicament the only way of saving the principle that right action is rule-following action is to provide a second superior rule or set of rules to apply in case of conflict between members of the first set. An obvious rule to apply here is just the teleological principle of maximizing good. This principle admitted, the teleologist could welcome the use of the general rules of obligation as preliminary guides to, but as never the final arbiter of, right action.

The deontologist will not accept this, but neither does he provide any other rule for deciding between incompatible rules. The only thing left is for him to say that in a case of conflicting obligations the person can compare their force and know directly which is superior in obligatoriness. Prichard does seem to say this. However this would seem to deprive the rules of all real authority, even of a preliminary sort. For if one can know directly what is the superior obligation (by considering the features of the particular case), what need is there to employ these rules at all?

This difficulty appears in an aggravated form if, as Ross holds, *one* of the rules of obligation is the rule to maximize good. The difficulty now is that there is required not merely some method of deciding between the rules of obligation, but some method of commensurating degrees of obligation with degrees of good. Ross holds that right and good are distinct ethical ultimates; but at the same time he supposes that a single unit (of what, is not clear) can measure both. This is plainly contradictory. If we can express both rightness and goodness in terms of a single unit, then either they must be the same or there must be a third ethical ultimate which is common to both. Ross' assumption that they can be commensurated appears in the following. He writes : 'We may then, if we like to put the matter so, think of the responsibility for conferring a promised benefit as being n times as binding as the responsibility (which would be one merely for maximizing good) for conferring an exactly similar unpromised benefit, where n is always greater than 1, and, when the promise is very explicit, is much greater than 1. It will follow that it is always our duty to fulfill a promise, except when the uncovenanted benefit to be conferred is more than n times greater than the covenanted benefit' (p. 117). Let us analyze this. Ross is considering a case where there is (1) a benefit x which can be conferred, and (2) a promise to confer this benefit x. He is supposing that there is an obligation in respect of both (1) and (2) ; obligation (1) is just an obligation to realize good, obligation (2) contains both obligation (1) and the additional obligation to fulfill a promise, the amount added by the latter being symbolized by 'n'. Ross next considers (3) a different second benefit y which has been unpromised, and supposes that this new unpromised benefit y may exceed the (1) unpromised benefit x by the same quantity, 'n', as the (2) benefit x plus the promise of it exceeds the unpromised benefit x. Clearly this is to suppose that an amount of good added to the unpromised benefit x may exactly equal the amount of obligation added to x by a promise to perform it. Note that Ross first speaks of the 'responsibility for conferring the promised benefit as being n times as binding' and then of the unpromised benefit as being more than 'n times greater'; which is to imply that the same unit can serve to designate degrees both of rightness and of goodness. But then there must be a single value-characteristic, and the deliberator will decide what to do by deciding what possible act will realize the greatest quantity of this value-characteristic.

Ross' difficulty here could be avoided only if he were to repudiate either the principle that the maximizing of good is a rule of obligation, or that there is any way of commensurating the amount of good the act would actualize and the amount of obligation which the act carries. Repudiating one or both of these principles would be to deny something which seems obvious and which Ross takes for granted, namely that in making decisions we do sometimes refer to the greater good.

A recent writer, however, asserts flatly that this sort of teleological consideration is not allowed. In an essay entitled 'Two Concepts of Rules',[1] Professor John Rawls writes : '. . . It strikes us as wrong for a person to defend breaking a promise by a general appeal to consequences. For a general utilitarian defense is not open to the promisor : it is not one of the defenses allowed by the practice of making promises' (p. 15). Rawls does not argue this in detail and by examples, and when we consider cases we see that the view is false. We can think of cases where a person is right to break a promise when by doing so he can realize more benefit for the promisee or for other persons. An early section of the *Republic* provides one sort of case. Suppose Jones has borrowed Smith's gun, promising to return it on demand ; then Smith suddenly appears, in a demented state, and demands the weapon's return. We would think it right for Jones to consider the possible consequences and, in view of these, to break the promise. Another case : Smith owns two phonographs, and having no use for both, tries to sell one for $200. Failing at this, he lends the phonograph to Jones, who promises to return it in one month (when he, Jones, will be given a phonograph). On the day before the return, a friend, Brown, hears the phonograph, and Jones tells him that it belongs to Smith, who wants to sell it for $200. Brown says he will buy the phonograph. Brown is leaving the area that night and Smith cannot be reached. Jones takes Brown's money and the next day delivers to Smith the money instead of the phonograph. Jones breaks his promise ; but surely he is right to break it, and he is right because doing so benefits everyone concerned.

Rawls' view on promises is part of a more general view of rules which he calls the 'Practice' view. This view represents rules as defining a 'practice' (such as promising or punishing). The view is that the practice and its rules may be justified teleologically (or, in Rawls' terms, 'by the utilitarian principle'); but a particular act is justified only by the rule. 'A practice necessarily involves the abdication of full liberty to act on utilitarian and prudential grounds' (p. 24). Rawls' doctrine would seem to be that one can justify changing a rule on the utilitarian principle, but so long as the rule remains unchanged, one can in no way justify an act which deviates from the rule. 'The point I have been making is . . . a logical point. . . . It is simply that where a form of action is specified by a practice there is no justification possible of the particular action of a particular person save by reference to the practice. In such cases the action is what it is in virtue of the practice and to explain it is to refer to the practice. There is no inference whatsoever to be drawn with respect to whether or not one should accept the practices of one's society. One can be as radical as one likes but in the case of actions specified by practices the objects of one's radicalism must be the social practices and people's acceptance of them' (p. 32). The principle here would then be: an act can only be right which follows the rule, until one succeeds in getting the rule changed.

This produces the odd situation that, for the reformer who is trying to get his society to change a rule, the reformer must believe that the act which conforms to that rule is right even while he is urging that the rule itself which requires such acts is wrong. In this event, how could he argue his case? The usual way of arguing for reform is to argue that the rule requires wrong actions; but on the Practice theory the reformer cannot argue this. Further, if one cannot think that any of the actions required by the rule are wrong, what occasion would arise to lead him to criticize the rule? Surely our concern to change a rule is occasioned by our coming upon particular cases, or perhaps even a single striking particular case (a 'test' case), in which the rule demands an action we think wrong. We criticize and justify rules by the way they work out in particular cases, and we can do this only if we can judge the rightness of the actions in these cases independently of our judgment of the rule. We conclude that Rawls' Practice view makes an artificial separation between our way of justifying general rules and our way of justifying particular acts.

The central argument of the Practice view is based upon a failure to distinguish between two kinds of rules, which I shall call Constitutive and Directive rules. This error seems to come in part from taking the model of a rule from games, in which constitutive rules are more important than they are in morality. By 'constitutive rules' I shall mean rules which specify what constitutes engaging in a given activity. For example, the constitutive rules of baseball are the set of specifications which define the game, as that it will consist of two teams, each of nine players, occupying such and such positions, etc. 'Directive rules', on the other hand, specify what constitutes a good or bad, right or wrong, sort of engaging in an activity. In baseball these are directions about how to make a put-out, when to bunt, when to attempt to steal a base, etc.

A confusion of these two sorts of rules appears in Rawls' evident belief that there is no difference between *describing* what one does (which one would do by appeal to the constitutive rules) and *justifying* what one does (which would be done by appeal to the directive rules). Rawls writes: 'It follows from what we have said about the practice conception of rules that if a person is engaged in a practice, and if he is asked why *he* does what *he* does, then his explanation, or defense, lies in referring the questioner to the practice. He cannot say of *his* action, if it is an action specified by a practice, that he does it rather than some other because he thinks it best on the whole. When a man engaged in a practice is queried about his action he must assume that the questioner either doesn't know that he is engaged in it ("Why are you in a hurry to pay him?" "I promised to pay him today") or doesn't know what the practice is. One doesn't so much justify one's particular action as explain, or show, that it is in accordance with the practice. The reason for this is that it is only against the stage-setting of the practice that one's particular action is described as it is. Only by reference to the practice can one *say* what one is doing. To explain or to defend one's own action, as a particular action, one fits it into the practice which defines it' (p. 27).

But this is not a full description of the way one accounts for his action, even in games. For within obedience to the rules the player has many alternative choices of actions, and the player could neither explain nor defend his choice of any one of these alternatives by appeal to the rules. The rule would no more explain or justify one particular move than any other of the possible alternative moves. Suppose the baseball player throws to second base rather than to first in the attempt to make a double play. This throw neither conforms to nor breaks any of the constitutive rules which define the 'practice' of baseball. But the player may or may not be able to justify what he did. To justify it he must refer either to the directive rules, or to his general purpose of winning together with the special circumstances of the particular case. The difference between merely explaining what one does by reference to the constitutive rules, and justifying the same act by reference to the directive rules, is that one would explain the act only to one who did not know the game, while he would justify it to a fan or team-mate or coach. For the latter it is obviously not true, as Rawls maintains, that 'to explain or defend one's own action, as a particular action, one fits it into the practice which defines it' (p. 27). If the coach asks the player why he made the move he did, it will not be an acceptable answer for him to point out that he didn't violate any rules of the game. It ordinarily would be justifiable for him to cite the coach's directions. But this also might be unacceptable, if the occasion were one in which the player could achieve victory by going against the directions. To such an attempted justification the coach's probable reply would be 'In telling you what to do I didn't tell you not to use your head. I told you to win the game.'

We can now observe in detail the way in which the constitutive differ from directive rules, and how the directive rules of a game resemble those of morality. (1) If a person breaks the constitutive rules of a game we do not say that he is a bad player of the game but that he doesn't know the game. But when a person breaks the directive or moral rules we say that he is a bad player or is morally bad.

Being a good player of a game has little to do with obeying the constitutive rules ; rather it has to do with the kinds of actions one performs within these rules. By contrast, obeying the directive rules has much to do with being a good player, or, in morality, a good person. (2) If one breaks more than a minimum of the constitutive rules of a game, then we say that he has ceased to play the game ; while if one breaks a number of directive or moral rules, we do not say that he has ceased engaging in the game or in morally relevant behavior. (3) Perhaps most important, the constitutive rules of a game are consistent, such that one never has a choice of which rule he will follow.[1] But directive or moral rules may conflict, so that one must decide which rule to follow. This shows how there can be a special sort of demand for a justification of obedience to a directive or moral rule. There is a general rule that one keep his promises and there is also a general rule that one look after his children ; but we can imagine cases in which a person may have promised to do an act which will prevent his looking after his children. Here the person cannot follow both rules. If the action is justified by the 'following of the rule', then either action he performed would be both justified and not justified ; for it would conform to one rule and violate another. To satisfy the demand, what one must do here is to look for a higher principle. And the obvious principle is the end for which the rules were framed.

Thus if moral rules were analogous to rules in a game, moral rules would be of two sorts, one constitutive and descriptive, the other directive and justificatory. Further, since directive rules would be framed to secure a certain end (victory, in the case of a game), so on particular occasions it would be right (justifiable) to violate these rules when doing so would promote this end. In the case of morality, this end would be the realization of the greatest good.

But in fact the analogy between rules of morality and rules of games is only partial. Their point of difference

---

[1] Professor Ammon Goldworth brought this feature of consistency to my notice.

N

reinforces the fact that moral acts are not justified by the constitutive rules of a practice. In morality there are no constitutive rules ; there are only directive rules. There are no rules defining what it is to play the 'moral game', within which one can play well or badly. There are only the actions of life which one can perform rightly or wrongly. There is no distinct 'practice' of morality ; there is only life. Morality is not, like recreation, something in which one may or may not choose to engage. If one does not obey the constitutive rules of a game, then one has not played the game at all. But there are no rules the breaking of which would lead one to say that the person had ceased playing the moral 'game'. There are only directive rules, the breaking of which would lead us to say that the person had played the game badly.

It is true that there are *conditions* which must be present in order that the person be a moral agent. The person must be responsible ; he must be able to act and act intentionally. But these conditions of responsibility are not in any sense 'rules', for they are not within the range of the agent's choice of following or not following. A person cannot choose to be responsible. He cannot walk off the field of moral action, as a baseball player can walk off the baseball diamond. He may attempt to divest himself of moral responsibility, but this attempt is itself an act which is subject to moral judgment. We call such persons 'irresponsible', and we hold them morally responsible for their irresponsibility. We do not treat them as nonresponsible, in the way that we treat, say, the insane person. Further, as a person cannot deliberately choose to separate himself from the moral sphere, so a person, as one who is insane, cannot choose to enter the moral sphere — just as a person who lacks the personal conditions (for example, arms or legs) for playing baseball could not by choice become a baseball player. The conditions of moral action compare to the conditions under which a game becomes possible, not to the constitutive rules according to which the game is played.

That there are no constitutive rules of morality appears most clearly in the case of rules of 'manners'. Consider, for example, rules about how persons of widely different ages conduct themselves towards each other. To the extent that such rules become rigid, and to the extent to which obedience of them comes to be automatic and mechanical, to that degree does the code of manners become a kind of game with constitutive rules defining the allowable moves in the game and directive rules as to how to perform these moves well. By contrast, to the extent to which these rules become purely directive, to that extent does manners become a branch of morality.

A basic argument by which Rawls seeks to establish his view that the rules of morality are rules of a practice, is the argument that moral rules cannot be arrived at as generalizations or 'summaries' of past experience; because, so he maintains, the action which the rule covers gets its character, gets defined, only by the rule. 'It is absurd to say, for example, that the rule that promises should be kept could have arisen from its being found in past cases to be best on the whole to keep one's promises; for unless there were already the understanding that one keeps one's promises as part of the practice itself there couldn't have been any promising' (p. 30). But this is an artificial and formal approach to the matter. It is true that our present concept of a 'promise' contains the idea that it is a rule that one keep his promises. But surely this concept has been developed gradually, and we had a concept of something like promising before we had a concept of the strict sort of promising which includes a formal rule that we are obligated to keep our promises. Even now the difference between the original and loose concept, and the later and formal one, is not perfectly sharp. Borderline cases arise in which we do not know whether the rule applies — whether the thing is a promise or not. Is it a promise only if a person uses the words 'I promise'? No doubt it would also be counted a promise if he said instead 'I swear that I will'. What then if he merely declares, in a very positive tone, 'I will' do the given act? Would he say, without further inquiry, that the 'I will' did not constitute a promise? The fact is that we reproach a person in much the same way for not doing what he said solemnly he would, whether he said 'I will' or whether he said 'I promise'. Indeed we may, when he only said 'I will', reproach him with the very words 'You promised'. If to this he replies, 'But I didn't *say* I promised', our reproach only deepens, for we think that, not only has he before shirked his responsibility, but he is now trying to evade the charge of responsibility. There is, it is true, a difference of degree in these expressions. 'I promise' is more weighty, more solemn, and with it a failure to perform is more reprehensible. But the difference is one of degree. There can be the same kind of reliance upon a person's word, and the same tendency to perform what one has said he will perform, and the same obligation to perform, before the 'practice' of promising and promise-keeping has become as formally established and as ceremonial as it is now.

Thus we may understand our adopting this ritual of promising as a consequence of our observing the benefit (on the whole) of a person's actually doing what he said he would. Certainly, there was a saying what one would do, and a doing it, before there was the formal procedure of a promising to do it ; and there was the observing of the benefits which came from a person's consistently doing what he said he would do. There is then nothing 'absurd' in saying that the word 'promise', the concept of a promise, and the rule that one will keep promises, arose as a development from the observation that it is desirable for social harmony that a person keep his word. From such observations, the expression 'I promise' was adopted as a device to provide an especially strong assurance that the person will do as he said.[1]

If this is correct, moral rules are, as the teleologist and

---

[1] The same artificially formal approach appears in Rawls' view of punishment. He writes : 'It is impossible to say what punishment is, or to describe a particular instance of it, without referring to offices, actions, and offenses specified by practices. Punishment is a move in an elaborate legal game and presupposes the complex of practices which make up the legal order. The same thing is true of the less formal sorts of punishment : a parent or guardian or someone in proper authority may punish a child, but no one else can' (p. 31). But surely anyone can punish anyone whom he takes to be an offender. A farmer may punish a thief caught stealing his horse. It may be wrong for the farmer to do so, since he does not have proper authority. But no one would hesitate to call the whipping which he administered a 'punishment'.

utilitarian holds, 'summaries' of past experience of acts which have generally led to beneficial results. A rule of moral obligation is based upon an ethical generalization which states that a certain sort of thing (say keeping one's word) is good. This ethical generalization rests on the observation that this sort of thing has proved good, and entails the prediction that this sort of thing will continue to prove good. On its basis a rule of moral obligation is formulated, prescribing that one ought to pursue this sort of thing. The ethical generalization is probable only, and the rule of obligation hypothetical only, though actual formulations conceal this, as do general statements in science or rules in Law. The generalization is justified by instances in which the particular statements it implies have proved true ; and the moral rule is justified by the ethical generalization. But both are subject to general sorts of exceptions (to conditions in particular cases under which the principle does not imply true propositions about these instances) and to possible mistake, such that new cases might either confirm or disconfirm the principle. Some scientific generalizations are so well established that it is almost unthinkable that they will be overturned, and some ethical generalizations and moral rules are of like firmness. But there are other principles of which we are less sure, and all are subject to excepting conditions. Thus when we say that a certain sort of thing has a particular character, or that a certain sort of thing is right or good, we always understand this to hold only generally, 'other things being equal'.

It is clear that the greater the variety of excepting conditions, and the more specificity with which they are defined, the more complete will be our concept of a principle. The more fully we understand the sorts of conditions under which we would hold it right to break the rule of promise-keeping, the better we will understand the concept of a promise and its rule. But it is also clear that we will never possess a full set of such excepting conditions ; further, that in framing the familiar excepting conditions, and in defining new ones, as well as in settling particular cases which allow a generalization about the kind of condition which permits an exception, we refer to the concept of maximum good.

12. *Rights*

Before leaving the topic of obligation and right, there is a special sense of 'right' to examine — the sense which it has in the expression 'natural right'. This concept likewise is analyzable on the teleological principle. We speak of persons as having a 'right to' (or 'natural right to') certain things. We may say that 'a child has a right to an education', 'a reader has the right to the truth', 'a worker has a right to a living wage', etc. The peculiarity is that in the primary sense 'right' modifies an act, while here 'right' is referred to a person as something which he possesses. A 'right to' seems to indicate a relation between the possessor of the right and the thing to which he has the right. But no sense can be made of any such relation. We cannot conceive of a person's having a relation to something such as knowledge or freedom. We conceive of him having these things, but not of his having a relation to them.

The relation that is involved is a relation to another person. For a person, Jones, to have a 'right to' a thing is for him to have a claim upon someone else, say Smith, to provide it. Jones' right entails Smith's obligation, and Smith's obligation entails Jones' right. This sense of 'a right' (noun) is thus derivable from 'right' (adjective). That a person, Jones, has a right to something, say knowledge, means that Jones' act of acquiring or possessing knowledge is right in the weak sense of being not wrong, and more crucially, that the act of someone else, say Smith, in providing him with knowledge, is right in the strong sense that his failing to provide it would be wrong. This teleological way of conceiving a right as a claim corrects the inadequacies of the views which have been most generally advocated. These views are: (1) that rights are a natural endowment of a human being; (2) that rights are conferred on people by a social order which has power to enforce their observance. The strong point of the first view is that it does seem in some sense proper to the human being to have those things which are his 'rights'. But its weakness, and the strong point of the second view, is that a right which there is no ground for obtaining seems empty. However, the conception of a right as a claim includes both features. A person's rights are natural in the sense that the realization of his natural potentialities requires as conditions the existence of these things to which a person is said to have a natural right. The things to which he has a right are things which are good for him to have. And since persons are obligated to realize good, these conditions are things which persons are obligated to provide. Ethical rights are grounded, then, not in a coercive power but in the obligation they impose on persons who are able to provide these things to which persons have a right. We can now observe some consequences of this concept.

(1) *Our only right is that other persons fulfill their obligations.* The only ethical claim one can make on another is that he fulfill his obligation, which is to maximize good. Thus one can claim that another provide for one's own good only when a greater good cannot be realized elsewhere.

A person may indeed assert a right on the mistaken notion that he has a right to whatever will contribute to his own welfare. The doctrine of natural rights may encourage people to assert rights as if they existed in an ethical vacuum, and may encourage them to feel injured when these rights are not fulfilled. Thus a person may assert that he has a right to an advanced education. He may feel that he has the natural potentialities to profit from such an education and that other people with less natural gifts are receiving this education. But it is pointless for him to assert such a right unless he is prepared to show who specifically is obligated to fulfill the right. It is plain that if he does have this right, he does not have it in a vacuum. He could not have the right if no such education were possible — if the society did not possess higher academic institutions. Second, if he does have the right, then the members of his society must be obligated to provide its fulfillment. And he must, in order justifiably to assert the right, be able to describe the specific conditions which establish this obligation on their part.

Doing this will necessarily involve questioning some alleged rights of others, specifically, the right of persons to dispose according to their own choice of the wealth they have acquired. All social outlays, in so far as they depend upon taxes, involve this alleged right. The existence of this right to acquire wealth can be and has been questioned. It can be questioned on the ground that it is not 'natural', as is the 'right' to a development of one's potentialities. But our present concern is not whether one of these rights is more genuine, or whether in the interest of certain rights we ought to reorganize our economic system, with its practices concerning property 'rights'. The point here is just that the assertion of any right, as to an advanced education, has to be explained and justified, and this usually involves calling into question other rights. For one to assert that he has a right, is to imply that someone else is obligated to fulfill the right, and this is often to imply that the other person does not have some of the rights which he thought he had.

Actually, private individuals do not frequently initiate the assertion of rights; and when they do, they usually have in mind the particular person whom they believe to be under obligation to them. Usually a declaration of rights is the work of an organization, as a political party, a labor union, an association of business interests, or a world congress. The function of these declarations may be in part propagandistic; that is, they may be deliberately adopted means to promote ends of self-interest. But they are not just this. They are only effective as propaganda so long as they are accepted as expressing ethical truths. What they express are in fact not truths about rights so much as truths about ideals. An ethical ideal is a condition which would be good if it could be attained; which there is some hope, but no assurance, of attaining; and for the promotion of which people are accordingly only under a sort of indefinite and loose obligation. The obligation is perhaps really an obligation sometimes to consider whether they have an obligation to work for it. To assert rights in the abstract, without specifying their corresponding obligations, is in effect only the declaration of an ideal.

(2) *A right does not entail that its possessor has a corresponding obligation.* There is a danger in this notion of natural rights which even its propagators recognize, and to correct which a further mistake is made. The danger is that people will adopt an unrealistic view of what is their due, and will make demands on society or the world at large which are either impossible or unjustifiable. To offset this the principle is asserted : To have rights is also to have obligations. But the principle is not strictly true. To have a right always entails that someone else has an obligation ; but it does not entail that the possessor of the right has an obligation, either of the same or a different sort. It is generally true that if one person has a claim upon a second person, then this second person has a claim of some sort upon the first. But it is not always true. Suppose Smith comes upon Jones in a land in which neither is a citizen, and that Jones is out of his mind, in great pain, and on the point of death. We would say that Jones has a claim on Smith for the relief of his pain even though Smith can have no counter-claim on Jones who, being out of his mind, cannot recognize the service for what it is, and being on the point of death cannot repay the service. If the circumstances were the same and their positions reversed, Smith would have on Jones the claim that Jones now has on him. Further, if Jones did live, we would say that he ought to show gratitude. But he has the claim even if he will not live, and hence even if he has no obligation to Smith nor Smith any counter-claim on him. What establishes the claim is just that the welfare of other persons is a good which any person is obligated to realize.

It is true that the case is far-fetched, and that usually a claim does involve a counter-claim. This is perfectly explicable on the principle that rights (claims) and obligations are for the realization of good. This mutuality of claim generally exists because : (a) people generally are able to give mutual benefit ; (b) people want benefit in repayment for benefit, not merely for its material value but as a sign of affection and respect, so that ingratitude hurts them in two ways ; (c) people who are pained by ingratitude are discouraged from repeating benefits to others. Thus the general practice of attaching an obligation to a right leads on the whole to a maximization of good. Accordingly this very abstract rule of obligation — Do not assert a right unless you are prepared to recognize an obligation — is justified by the same teleological principle as the more particular rules of obligation, and hence justified only generally, subject to the particular conditions of the actual case.

Another thing which accounts for the idea that a right involves a self-obligation or a counter-claim is the association of moral with legal rights and claims. A moral claim is a claim for an action to realize good. A legal claim is a claim for an action whose performance is reinforced by the coercive power of the state. Legal claims do often involve counter-claims. Jones can only have a claim on Smith if Smith has, or has had, some legal claim on Jones. But a 'legal claim' requires not a power for the realization of good, but a power to use the power of the state to force the realization of some specific thing, whether it be good or not. The existence of this special kind of claim is, I think, itself explicable by its tendency to maximize good, and by the need for achieving the predictability and uniformity which legal claims provide. But I cannot discuss this here.

There are certain further limitations in rights and obligations which are worth noting.

(3) *There can be ethical obligations and claims only by persons and upon other persons.* Consider first inanimate nature. No one would suppose that one part of nature could make a claim upon another part. But someone might hold that nature could make a claim upon men, and men upon nature. One may say that nature claims mankind's worship or respect. But this is either a figure of speech or it means that God claims the worship of nature as his creation, or the state (which may be either a superior person, like God, or a group of persons) may demand respect for the state's natural resources. Nature itself can make an appeal, or exert an attraction, but not embody a claim. Nor can a person make a claim on nature; when a settler stakes his claim on a piece of land, his claim is actually upon the state. And to say that men claim their livelihood from nature can only mean that they try to

extract this livelihood from nature, not that nature is obligated to fulfill the claim.

What about claims and obligations between men and animals? If animals cannot have obligations, then men can have no claims on them. One might say that one who has taken an animal out of the gutter and given it domestic advantages, has a claim on the creature's loyalty. But probably we would agree that the only claim involved is a claim on the rest of us to convince such a person that he has no such claim.

It is not quite so plain that the animal has no claim on a person for kind treatment. Our actual conduct towards animals is ambivalent. We exterminate insects ruthlessly, but we make some effort to treat the higher animals 'humanely'. The word 'humane' itself seems ambiguous. Does it mean a quality persons should exhibit in their treatment of animals, or a quality animals have which determines how we should treat them? Should we treat animals with humanity or as part of humanity? And besides the contrast in our treatment of different sorts of living creatures, there is the contrast in our treatment of creatures of the higher sort. We are ruthless towards animals in a wild state, while we often treat kindly the same animals in a tame state, and animals of an identical kind may be produced for slaughter or fondled as pets. Finally, we not only feed on the slaughtered beasts, but feed them to the animal objects of our charity.

These several apparent inconsistencies can be reconciled by the principle that strictly claims can be made only by human beings. What follows is that animals could support claims only in the degree to which they approach humanity or personality. Two principles, both derivable from this, will explain our varying treatment of animals. First, we regard the higher animals as making more of a claim than the lower animals; second, we regard domestic animals as making more of a claim than wild animals. We feel more of a claim by the tiger for our kind treatment than by a mosquito. We recognize more of a claim in the tame tiger than in the wild one. The higher beast is more like a person, and domestication of an animal makes it more human. We can see the principle working in our attitudes towards plants and minerals. We may feel a sort of claim by a plant upon our care, and more by a plant which we have domesticated; whereas we feel no claim at all exerted by a mineral.

Our claims and obligations are, then, limited to persons or to things which resemble persons. There are two other quite general limitations which may be overlooked. (4) *A right does not entail a right either* (*a*) *to relinquish this right or* (*b*) *to declare this right.* A right to a thing does not entail a right to refuse the thing or to refuse the fulfillment of the right. We are inclined to think of rights as the same as freedoms; and we often use interchangeably the term 'right' and 'free' in the expressions 'right to *X*' and 'freedom to *X*'. Some rights are merely freedoms to avail ourselves of a certain opportunity. But the right does not involve a right or a freedom to accept or refuse the fulfillment of the right. If, for example, one has a right to move freely, then he has no right to deprive himself of this right. He has a right to move about or not to move about; but he has no right to have someone determine that he will move about or not. It is sometimes said that there are certain rights which a person cannot relinquish. But the fact is that there are no rights which a person can relinquish.

We can see this in two ways. (1) A right entails an obligation on someone. If we had the right to renounce a right then we should have the right to require that this person who is under obligation violate his obligation. But it cannot generally be right to require others to violate their obligations. (2) If a person has a right to a thing (such as knowledge or health) then this thing must be good for him. But generally he cannot act rightly in refusing to accept something that is good for him. Just as a promise is not cancelled by a person's not wanting the promise kept, so a right is not contingent upon a person's wanting the right fulfilled.

It also may be assumed that a right to a thing entails a right expressly to declare that right. But this is not so. A patient may have a right to the treatment of a doctor whom he has not paid for previous treatment, even when the

patient has no right to declare this right. And in general
one has all sorts of rights which it would be wrong to insist
upon. Insisting on a right may be a poor means of getting
the right's fulfillment, but if the right is a right, then it
would be best if it were fulfilled. Thus it cannot be right
to declare a right when this would prevent its fulfillment.

To sum up. In this last section I have tried to show
how we appeal to the teleological principle for an understanding of the concept of rights; just as we appeal to this
principle in other general areas of obligation, as that of
punishment (Section 5). I have also tried to show our
dependence on this principle in our understanding of the
concepts of: an obligatory act (Sections 7 and 8); specific
kinds of obligatory acts, such as the keeping of promises
(Section 9) and attending to one's own welfare (Section 10);
a general rule of obligation (Section 11). The principle
obtains further support when we consider the reasons
which we invoke in reaching and justifying practical decisions. To this topic we now turn.

CHAPTER V

DECISION

1. *The Elements of Practical Reasoning*

PRACTICAL decisions are decisions as to what to do. Because action occurs in a particular situation, the practical problem of deciding what to do is always a particular decision. Even when the decision concerns a series of events, and is a decision of policy, still the object of the decision is something particular. It is a conclusion as to what to do in this moment or in this series of moments.

The deliberator uses general principles, but he uses these to illuminate the features of the particular case, and not to make a deductive (or inductive) inference. There is such a thing as moral reasoning, but, as Aristotle said, the judgment must ultimately rest with 'perception'. We can generally describe the elements of good moral reasoning, and we can mention ways in which this reasoning can go wrong. But we cannot state general rules of correct moral reasoning which, if followed, guarantee a correct decision. In practical decisions, as in historical judgments, the primary logical factor is truth rather than validity. Nevertheless the general elements of a valid practical argument can be described.

The practical argument will contain a conclusion to the effect that a given act is the correct or 'right' thing to do. It will also contain at least two premisses, a particular premiss stating that the act has a particular feature, and a general premiss stating that things which have such a feature are right. For example : (conclusion) Jones' paying Smith $1000 on January 1, 1960, is right because (particular premiss) this act is the keeping of a promise and (general premiss) keeping promises is right. In actual discourse we use enthymemes ; we say 'The act is right because it has been promised', omitting mention of the general rule. Further, when we speak of 'reasons' for a decision or act we ordinarily have in mind the particular premiss, though it would seem that anyone would agree that it only serves as a reason in so far as the general premiss is presupposed. It will be convenient to have for these two premisses labels which include the word 'reason'. Practical reasoning involves the giving of reasons. Let us call the particular premiss the 'descriptive reason' and the general premiss the 'practical reason'.

It follows that there are three steps in practical reasoning: (1) noticing a particular feature or set of features of the moral situation and of the acts possible in it; (2) remembering a general practical principle about things with this feature; (3) applying the principle to the particular thing in question. We might call these phases respectively: (1) perception, (2) conception, (3) inference. Correct moral reasoning involves correct performance of these three steps, and moral reasoning can go wrong through (1) misperceiving a feature of the case; for example, thinking it involves a promise when it does not; (2) introducing a false rule or principle; for example, supposing that it is right to keep the promises made by other persons; (3) making an invalid inference, for example, inferring that it is right to punish Jones because breaking promises is wrong, and Jones broke a promise. A correct argument here would require the additional general premiss, 'Wrongs deserve punishment', or replacing the one general premiss with the different one, 'Breaking of promises deserves punishment'.

On this account, what is distinctive of practical reasoning are steps (1) and (2). Practical perception is not quite like other sorts of perception, though it resembles in certain ways the aesthetic perception of the artist and in certain ways the scientific perception of the psychologist. People differ in their powers of practical perception, as they do in their powers of aesthetic and psychological perception. This is most apparent when we consider that a great many of our practical decisions are about what act will produce pleasure or pain for another person; and that some persons are especially dull at perceiving how their acts affect others in this way, while other persons are especially acute in foreseeing these effects. These differences seem partly a product of training, partly a natural gift. In any event, this element of moral reasoning does not raise any important theoretical problem. Step (2), however, which involves the use of a general practical principle, raises again the question of what the nature of this principle is. Put in the terminology of 'reasons', what is a 'practical reason'?

The main views are: (1) the Imperativist view that there are in the strict sense no moral reasons (C. L. Stevenson); (2) the 'Pro-attitude' view, that the best or most conclusive reason is that the thing decided on is the object of a desire or 'pro-attitude' (P. H. Nowell-Smith); (3) the Deontological view, that this reason is a reference to a rule of obligation; (4) the Teleological view, that this reason is that the act will realize maximum good. I shall argue generally for the truth of (4), though with important qualifications. The Deontological position has already been sufficiently considered in the previous chapter, and the grounds for the Imperativist position have been discussed in the chapter on Value. It remains here to consider what can be said for the Pro-attitude and the Teleological accounts.

2. *The Best Reason*

It often happens that in the actual process of deliberating or arguing we do not employ in the particular premisses a term which even implies an evaluation or rule of evaluation. But the more general context will always imply some evaluation.

The terms used as central in reasons for decision may range from (1) explicitly evaluative terms, such as 'good', 'right', 'desirable', 'virtuous', 'generous'; through (2) implicitly evaluative terms, such as 'easy', 'inexpensive', 'effective'; to (3) terms such as 'blind', 'bereft', etc., in which an evaluative element is present, if at all, only by suggestion; to (4) purely descriptive terms, such as 'heavy', 'blond', 'cool', etc. Evaluation is the primary and almost sole use of the first set of terms; it is a frequent use of the second set; an occasional use of the third set; and a rare use of the fourth set. However. the reason explicitly stated

for an act may employ a word from any of these sets. As
an example from set (3), one may, as his reason for helping
someone, mention that the person is blind, or poor, or has
recently had a death in his family. And as his reason for
choosing a position, one may use a term from the descriptive category, as that the place of work is cool, or the
vacation long.

Still another sort of term can be used which outwardly
is more evaluatively neutral than any of these. One can
mention as his reason for a choice just the proper name of
the thing chosen. Such reasons perhaps show most clearly,
however, that a non-evaluative reason cannot be complete.
If as my reason for going to a lecture I give the name of
the speaker, or as my reason for choosing a friend, the
person's name, or as my reason for purchasing an artwork
the name of the artist — plainly something more is implied.
It is implied as a general premiss either that I think these
are good or obligatory, or that I happen to like them.

Each of these — that the thing is desired, or is obligatory, or is good — is sometimes a good reason. But the
reference to good is the best reason. For it is by reference
to good that we understand why desire and duty provide
good reasons; and in the case of conflict between the
reason 'it is best' and the reason either 'it is a duty' or
'it is desired', the right choice will be that which is based
upon the first of these reasons. We have considered the
reason of good versus the reason of duty in the preceding
chapter. We can consider now the reason of good versus
the reason of desire.

One fairly common reason given for an act or choice is
that the person wants the thing chosen. In his recent
Ethics, P. H. Nowell-Smith argues that this kind of reason
is the only 'logically good' reason. He adopts the term
'pro-attitude' in place of 'wanting', 'desiring', or the like,
as being more inclusive than these. And he stresses that
by 'logically good' reason he means something more general
than 'morally good' reason. The latter is a 'reason which
justifies an action and exempts the agent from moral censure'
while 'logically good' reasons are not 'propositions that
entail a decision to act but propositions which are such

o

that, once they are granted, it would be logically odd either to ask for further reasons for doing something or for a further explanation of why someone did it' (p. 104). His conclusion is : 'The proposition that any statement which gives a logically complete reason for choice must include a reference to a pro- or a con-attitude is . . . a frank tautology' (p. 114).

Now it certainly seems odd to suppose that uttering a tautology about a choice could 'explain' it, or that once a person had uttered a tautology, it would be 'logically odd' to ask for further reasons. If the only good reason for a person's choice is necessarily (tautologically) entailed in its being a choice, then the oddest thing of all is our ever asking him for this reason. For we must know this reason already. Asking a person why he chose a thing becomes a perfectly senseless business.

Nowell-Smith goes on to say that all propositions other than those affirming pro-attitudes, which pass for reasons, are incomplete. This includes the reason that the act is a 'duty' or is 'best'. The reference to 'duty' provides a reason in the sense that it contextually implies 'a pro-attitude'. The case of 'good' is a bit different. If I say a thing is 'good', I do not, according to Nowell-Smith, just imply that I have a pro-attitude toward it; I 'express' this attitude. This would seem to make 'good' a 'logically good' reason for choice; but Nowell-Smith asserts the opposite. 'The answer "because it is best" . . . does not just imply a pro-attitude; it expresses it. But it does not only do this. If this were all I wanted to do I should have to say "because I happen to like it more than the others". It contextually implies that I have reasons for my choice; but it does not say what they are and therefore does not explain my choice' (pp. 160-1). He continues : 'We are tempted to say that it gives the best possible reason . . . the trouble is that the reason is *too* good. It is like saying that I was frightened because it was a terrifying experience ; and, as an explanation, it operates in much the same way. Just as "because it was terrifying" shows that my fear was not an unusual one and contextually implies that the object had certain unspecified "good-making" properties, and that my choice was not a peculiar one. Any of these contextual implications could be expressly withdrawn, especially, as we shall see, the last; but in default of such withdrawal my audience would be entitled to assume them' (p. 161). But why should the fact that 'good' implies all these other things disqualify the term as a reason, so long as it does also express that the person likes the thing? It would appear that Nowell-Smith's objection to 'good' is just that it is tautological in reference to choice (as 'terrifying' is tautological with reference to 'fear'). It would seem as if he wants the reasons to mention the 'unspecified good-making properties' — after he has argued that no such reasons can, apart from a statement of a pro-attitude, be 'logically good' reasons.

But let us leave these special difficulties and consider Nowell-Smith's positive thesis that a pro-attitude is the only sort of logically good reason for choice. It is true that 'because I desire it' does often function as an account of choice. But surely it is not the only sort of good reason. It is thought to be a good reason for some choices; for others 'because it is best' is considered a better reason.

With respect to these reasons — (1) 'because I desired it' and (2) 'because it was best' — we can distinguish three sorts of cases: (a) cases where (1) seems the better reason, (b) cases where (2) seems better, (c) cases where either would seem satisfactory. Here are some examples. (a) If someone asks 'Why did you choose the sharp cheese instead of the mild' it would seem a better reason to say 'because I like it' than 'because it is best'. (b) But if the question is 'Why did you reprimand your helper for slowness', to say 'I wanted to reprimand him' would not be thought a proper reason while it would be proper to say, 'Because it was the best thing to do in the situation'. (c) Finally, if one asks 'Why did you buy the Beethoven recording instead of the Brahms?' it might be an equally good reason to say, 'The Beethoven recording is better' or 'I just prefer Beethoven'. Moreover the same sorts of replies might seem equally good in a more serious case. Suppose the question is: 'Why did Smith resign after the unfair treatment of Jones?' We might find equally acceptable the reasons: (1) 'Because he didn't want to work at such a place', or (2) 'Because it will accomplish most good'.

Both reasons are acceptable, but is one better? There are two ways in which a hearer might continue. He might ask for reasons showing the truth of each of these reasons. And the person might reply, in the case of (1), by mentioning specific unpleasant features of such a place, or in the case of (2), by mentioning specific beneficial consequences of his resignation. Or the hearer might question whether the reason offered were in fact a good reason. He might say (a) 'But why is the fact of your wanting to leave' a good reason? or (b) 'But why is the fact of the act's being beneficial' a good reason? It is plain that (a) here is natural while (b) is 'logically odd'. We would expect Smith to reply to (a), 'Well, perhaps it isn't a good reason', while to (b) he would rightly demand, 'What could be a better reason?' The fact is that if a person referred to his desire as accounting for his action, he would not intend this as a 'good reason' in the sense of being a justification of his decision; while he would intend a reference to the act's benefits to serve as a justification. The desire may account for the resignation in the sense of explaining its cause. But the beneficial consequences explains why the act is right. And it is the right act which one tries to arrive at in the process of practical decision. The deliberator is not concerned — not primarily concerned, anyway — with determining what will motivate him to choose whatever he does choose; rather he wishes to decide what he ought to choose. His falling back upon the reference to desire often is meant just to convey his opinion that no question of what he 'ought to do' is involved — that this is one of the cases in which he can forgo engaging in practical decision and instead follow his impulses.

The reference to desire does not always indicate this, for there are cases of practical decision, involving a considerable process of deliberation, in which the problem is just to know what object is most desired. But if in this case the reason offered for the eventual choice is 'because it is most desired', this is a good reason only if the case is one in which it is reasonable to think that the greatest good consists in the gratification of the person's desires.

This becomes evident as we consider the case of conflict between the person's desire and the greatest good. Suppose Smith admits 'Though I thought it best not to choose the thing, still I desired it so very much that I went ahead and chose it'. Smith has here explained what caused him to make the choice, but he would not say this with the intention of showing that his choice was rational or based on a good reason. It is true that he might thus refer to his strong desire as a way of pleading that he ought not to be held responsible. But he would do this only when he thought the choice was bad, and not based on a good reason. He would never say, 'My choice was really a rational or good one, because I did desire the thing so much'. Thus if the reference to his strong desire is meant to 'justify' anything, it must be meant to justify *him* for making the choice (even though bad) and not the *choice* which he made. On the other hand, if Smith said, 'I had no desire for the thing but I did think it best', plainly he would intend this as a good reason. The reference to desire while good is absent is not thought to provide a good reason, while the reference to good while desire is absent is thought to provide a good reason.

It will now be clear how we are to explain the case where 'because it is desired' is a better answer than 'because it is best'. The explanation is that there is a large class of cases where what is best is that the person act on his desire. In such cases action on the reason 'because I desire it' is in fact equivalent to securing what is best. The gratification of desire, and the experiencing of pleasure, is itself something that is good. And there are many cases of choice in which the only significant difference in value between one choice and another is the difference in the pleasure they provide the agent. In these cases, for the person to deliberate in terms of the general principle of maximizing good might well lead him to mistake the sort of good involved, and in any event would introduce complication and delay. It would be a sign the person were needlessly confusing the issue if he accounted for his choice in such cases by offering the reason 'because it is best'.

As a final move the advocate of the pro-attitude account

might try to turn the tables as follows. I have here proposed that the reference to desire is sometimes an acceptable reason because the case is one in which the maximum
good consists in the person's satisfying his desires. The
objector might assert that it is just the reverse : a reference
to good is acceptable because what is understood by 'good'
is the maximum satisfaction of desires. But this involves
the general theory of value which I have attempted to show
mistaken in the chapter on Desire. It does not, however,
affect the present argument, and there is nothing in this
present account to bring it into opposition with the Interest
Theory of value. For the Interest Theory itself recognizes
a distinction between the reasons 'because I desire it' and
'because it is best'. The former refers only to the agent's
desire, hence to a small part of the possible good ; so that
on the Interest Theory likewise 'because I desire it' must
be generally inferior as a reason for decision to 'because it
is best'.

There is yet another possible, but wholly implausible,
position. This is that good is something distinct from what
is desired, but that the only good reason for choosing a
thing is not that it is good or that it is desired, but that it is
desired as being good. But this is a very far-fetched view,
and I doubt that anyone has ever held it. One may agree
that the good is desired, but the reason for choosing what
is good is just that it is good, and not that it is desired as
being good.

We turn now to the difficulties in the specific application
of this reason referring to what is good.

3. *Practical Decisions and Technical Decisions*

It may seem that practical decisions are at least of two
sorts, decisions as to one's obligations and decisions as to
what is best. And we might regard the former as chiefly
decisions on what to do, the latter as chiefly decisions on
what to choose. There are decisions in which one's choice
is from the start felt as constrained by the pressure of
obligations ; in other cases the decision is felt to be free of
these limiting and negative pressures, and to involve not
the possibility of a violation of duty if one chooses wrongly

but only that of loss if one chooses something less than what is best.

But of course this distinction cannot be basic, since our obligations are obligations to do what is best. That the difference is one of stress is apparent in the fact that we may feel guilt for having chosen something less than the best, no less than for having fulfilled something short of our greatest obligation. Though no one else may blame us, we blame ourselves. Nonetheless, the distinction is useful for expository purposes, and we may mark it by calling a decision in which a sense of obligation is most prominent a moral decision and a decision in which a sense of potential value or good is most prominent an ethical decision.

There is another sort of decision about what to choose, which I shall call 'technical', namely decisions about what is the best instance of a 'good of a kind', as a good hammer or a good typewriter. These decisions cause comparatively little difficulty, and it might occur to us that practical decisions as to what is good to choose could be reduced to some kind of technical decision. But this is not possible.

Technical decisions resemble practical decisions in that they are based on reasons about what is good. These reasons are the criteria of some good of a kind. By contrast, a decision about what to choose may involve a number of kinds of thing which are not subsumable under some more general kind, with its specific criteria. Criteria for kinds of things themselves differ in definiteness. For example, the criteria of the following have a decreasing order of definiteness : baseballs, apples, automobiles, administrators. But there are criteria for a good instance of each of these kinds, and the criteria are non-ethical. For other kinds of things — namely acts and persons — the criteria are not of this sort, and these are the objects which choice most fundamentally concerns. What the person has to choose is a good act and to become a good person. But we cannot choose a good act on the basis of certain features of these acts which make them good. For the good act (hence the good act to choose) is just the act which is good to choose. And the good person is the person who chooses good acts. Here again we encounter the ultimacy of the concept of good.

A decision about a good instance of a kind is called 'technical' rather than practical because such decisions need not be a decision about what to do. A practical decision may require a technical decision. For example, a practical decision whether to risk one's life in an attempt to save a drowning person may involve deciding whether the technical means available, as a rope and a small boat, are good enough to give a chance of success. But the technical evaluation of the means is one thing, and the practical choice another. This is more evident if we alter the example to suppose that there are several ropes and boats available, and that the attempt would be a risky business even with the best equipment; so that after having decided whether to make the attempt one has still to decide which are the best means. In some cases the practical decision will be partly dependent on the technical decision. If one judged that the technical equipment were totally inadequate to the act considered, he would decide not to attempt the act. In other cases the two decisions are independent; as when there is no question of the availability of adequate means, the practical question being whether to use the means in the way considered. But in both cases the decisions are distinct; the decision made on one will not necessarily employ the decision made on the other. The clearest indication of this difference is that we think there are experts in the various sorts of technical decisions, while there are no such experts in practical decisions. This is partly because technical decisions express just one's knowledge of the subject-matter under judgment and of how things belonging to this subject-matter are good and bad for the accomplishment of certain goods; while practical decisions express not just one's knowledge of good or bad but one's good or bad motives. But also, while in some cases the right practical decision may be to choose a thing which is the best instance of a kind, in others the right choice may be of an inferior member of the kind, or of a thing which is a member of no conceptual kind and for which we have as yet no technical criteria.

4. *The General Objects of Choice cannot be Hierarchically Graded*

But though the technical judgment is distinct from the practical one, it may seem that we might achieve on a perfectly comprehensive scale the same sort of thing which the technical judgment attempts within the range of a limited class. As the members of a kind differ in their value, so it may seem that kinds of things themselves can be graded in value, such that the right thing to choose would be, not just the best member of any kind, but the best member of the best kind. The problem for practical decision then would be not selecting among goods of a kind, but among kinds of goods. We have already mentioned Nicolai Hartmann's attempt to rank goods in a hierarchical scale. But the difficulties of deciding on this sort of principle are overwhelming. There are so many kinds of goods, and so many factors among each kind, that it is folly to think we could ever obtain a complete set of principles. We can observe this in detail.

First of all, on a much more general level than that of goods of a kind, we can distinguish four major categories of good things which are possible objects of practical choice. Suppose a person does a generous act. We can distinguish (a) the *act* itself (i.e. the particular change in the world which the person causes) ; from (b) the *motive*, or quality of character from which the act arose or which the act tended to produce ; and from (c) the *feeling*, with its element of pleasure or pain which accompanies the act ; and from (d) the *event* composed of the act and the feeling as an incident in the person's life history.

There is a general tendency for these sorts of things to correspond in degree of value. An act which is very good is apt to manifest a good quality of character, to be accompanied by a good feeling, and to contribute to a good life. However, these concomitancies hold only generally. Let us take a case. Suppose a person gives a large sum of money to charity. The act is good, for it changes the world in a good way. But it may manifest a bad quality of character — possibly a neurotic need to be approved of, or a desire to keep the money from another recipient. We say here that the act was good but the person was not. Likewise the same act may be accompanied by a bad feeling. If the person gives the money only to prevent the government from taking it in taxes, he may feel considerable pain at his benefaction. Finally, the gift may not contribute any positive value to the person's life. Supposing he has inherited the money and is concerned only to keep of it as much as he can, the disbursement would not contribute to the sort of life we consider good.

In this example it may seem that the discrepancy between the value of the act, on the one hand, and of the feeling and the life on the other, arises solely from a discrepancy between the value of the act and the motive. That is, it might appear that, if the person's motive were good, the act would have to evoke a good feeling and make a positive contribution to a good life. But this is not so. The same discrepancy can exist between motive on the one hand and between act, feeling and life on the other. Suppose that the motive is the good one of courage. A person swims out to save a drowning person, but the result is that the icy water prevents the rescue and causes the death of the would-be rescuer. The act does not make a good change in the world; the feeling of the rescuer during the experience is one of pain, frustration and regret; and the result on the person's life is to destroy it.

Likewise, there is no difficulty in thinking of cases in which the feeling is good, namely extreme pleasure, when the act is bad, the motive bad and the result on the person's life bad.

It is harder to know whether an event may contribute value to the pattern of a person's life, when the event is bad in all other respects. I can think of no case in which it would. But it remains true that its value may be discrepant with the value realized in other categories, since, as in acts of self-sacrifice, its value may be negative when the values of all the other sorts are positive.

Among these four categories of value there is another sort of distinction which is crucial, namely that between what we call egoistic and non-egoistic values. The good of the act is actualized entirely outside the agent, while the goods of the motive, the feeling and the life are solely within the agent. However, this does not simplify the problem of deliberation. Moralists sometimes speak as if in deciding on the right act the person ought to consider solely non-egoistic values, but on any form of teleological view this is wholly implausible. For if the right act is that which maximizes good, then the agent must be concerned with realizing good wherever possible. Some moralists also speak as if these egoistic values can be realized only if the person does not attempt to realize them. That is, they suggest that one can be virtuous (manifest or cultivate good qualities of character), only if he considers solely how to produce the best results for others; that one can get pleasure only by forgetting it; that one can save his life only by not trying to save it. There is some wisdom in these homilies, but as universal principles they are false. Occasions may arise in which a person has to decide whether he will act to produce immediate and clear benefits for others or to cultivate a good quality in himself. Likewise he may sometimes get more pleasure if he considers which activity will give him more pleasure. And he may contribute to a better life by consciously considering how to do so.

This distinction between the egoistic and non-egoistic values brings out another radical source of complication. The non-egoistic values include effects on one or many persons, and in respect of each of the categories of good. Our acts can increase or reduce the values of other people in respect of their acts, motives, feelings, lives and social relations. We can regard these as factors of the value of the person's act, and hence as dimensions of value which he must consider in comparing alternatives to reach the most rational decision.

The members of the other categories also have sets of various attributes which constitute distinct dimensions of value, though the number of and nature of these is far from clear. I shall briefly consider these in the case of a feeling and a life.

Most attention has been given to these dimensions in

pleasures. Their number and nature is a matter of dispute, but all seem to agree that degrees of intensity and duration are two features of pleasures. Further, it is agreed that both features contribute to the pleasure's value, and that they are often discrepant; such that if the question is to get pleasure, the deliberator may have to decide whether to choose the intense short pleasure or the weak enduring one. Common opinion also recognizes various factors as contributing to the value of a life. Lives, like pleasures, are generally thought better the longer they are. However, we also think that some lives, like some careers of professional boxers, would have been better had they ended sooner. For we think a life ought to have a development. Like a play, it ought not to drag on and on after its climax. Let us call this feature *progressiveness*. Also, a life should be *happy*, not tragic; it should have a balance of pleasures over pains. And a life is thought better if it is *full* — 'well-rounded'; if, that is, it includes a variety of different sorts of things. Finally, a life is better when it is *complete*, allowing the person to realize all or most of his potentialities. These are then some dimensions of value in a life. It is clear that their degrees of value will not always run parallel, and that a person may have to choose to lose the highest degree of value in one dimension in order to obtain a high degree of value in some other.

There are, then, manifold sources of practical perplexity. Deciding on the right act may involve comparing alternatives which are members of a single category, and these, moreover, in terms of different dimensions, or alternatives of different categories. Thus a complete set of principles would have to tell us how to relate every member of every dimension of every category to every other member of every dimension of every other category. Not only would their number have to be fantastically large, but it is quite incomprehensible how we should go about commensurating the elements. How, for example, should we commensurate a pleasure of a certain intensity with an incident contributing in a given degree to a progressive life? It is obvious that we will never have anything remotely resembling such a table of ethical values.

5. *Rules of Prudence*

In place of this hierarchical scale, about all that common sense provides is the prudential principle that the more enduring goods are generally the better. This is applied wholesale both within dimensions, within categories and between categories. Enduring mild pleasures of any kind are counted better than intense short ones, and the longer kind of pleasures (such as art) better than the short intense ones (as of sense). Again, the goods of a character and a life are counted better than those of a single act or experience. But this is of very limited application, and is subject to all sorts of exceptions — as are all of the more special ethical principles which make up the wisdom of common sense.

At this point we might attempt to formulate a more complex and adequate set of principles, and a set which would enable us to make more particular comparisons. For example, we might propose that generally the value of love is better than that of developing one's intellectual or artistic potentialities, and this might function to help us reach true decisions in particular cases. But it is doubtful whether it would help us in more cases than the exactly contrary principle. And even if the principle were correctly applicable in a large percentage of cases, still it would not always give correct decisions, nor would the principle itself inform us in what cases it is subject to exception. In very difficult moral problems, then, we are simply thrown back upon an original estimation of what is good.

Most, if not all, of the ethical principles of common sense may be understood as either recommending the general superiority of some value or practice, or the general evil of some practice. '*Honesty* is the best policy.' '*Love* thy neighbor.' 'Do unto others as you would have them do unto you' (justice). These are completely deficient in telling us how to decide actual cases. They only tell us to be just, loving and honest in general. They do not tell us when to be honest in preference to being something else. If we could always follow these and all other such problems consistently, they would provide adequate guides. But if we could, we also should have little need for such guides. The fact that we cannot follow them consistently is just what makes moral decision, and life, difficult.

When we consider the overwhelming complexity of values, and the extreme generality of ethical principles, we can understand the use and authority of the rules of obligation. Confronted with this complexity and with only the vaguest direction as to how to compare and sum up values, a person must conclude that it is folly to think that on any occasion he could with utter certainty choose that single one of all possible acts which will maximize the good. Alongside this, one thing that is clear is that, in order to produce any value, one must on most occasions act to produce something that is definitely known to be good, even though it is not known to be the greatest possible good. The rules of obligation enable him to do this. They spare him the necessity of frequent and prolonged deliberation. Instead of providing explicit statements of comparative value, or principles for arriving at such statements, they provide something more direct and practical. They speed the person into immediate action by simply telling him to do such and such. But this does not mean, as the deontologists have held, that they are their own justification, with their own sort of inner holiness. They are but imperfect guides, justified by the light they shed. Every deontologist (except the Kantian) must recognize this, in so far as he recognizes that no one of the rules of obligation is inviolable.

CHAPTER VI

RESPONSIBILITY

1. *The Voluntary*

WE saw in the chapter on Obligation that the concept of responsibility is integrally related to the concept of obligation. Generally a person is responsible for the performance of his obligation; and generally a person is obligated to do a particular act only if he is responsible for it. It is the same act which is obligatory and responsible. But the conditions of the two are not the same. An act is obligatory in so far as (besides being responsible) it realizes good ; while this act is responsible in so far as (besides being obligatory) it is 'voluntary'.

This relation between the obligatory and the responsible has another important aspect. We hold persons responsible in different degrees for particular acts, and this degree depends not merely upon the degree of voluntariness of the act but upon its degree of obligatoriness. We are most responsible for acts of the highest degree of obligatoriness and voluntariness, and least responsible for acts of the lowest degrees of obligatoriness and voluntariness. The degree to which a person is responsible for an act may be increased or diminished by an increase or reduction in either factor. For example, threats are regarded as coercing and depriving of voluntariness in certain degrees, and the more terrible the threat the less voluntarily can one act under it. A threat of death is in general more terrible than a threat of poverty, and a threat of death to oneself and one's family is more terrible than a threat of death to oneself. Likewise, obligations have varying degrees. An obligation to protect the welfare of one's nation is greater than an obligation to protect the welfare of one's club. Thus a person would be less responsible in yielding to a threat to his property at the cost of releasing information which would endanger or destroy his club, than at the cost of giving out information which would endanger or destroy his nation. In both cases he would be less responsible if the threat were not to his property but to his life, and still less responsible if the threat were to the lives of himself and his family. Thus, whether and how far a person is responsible depends upon the degree of his obligation as well as upon the degree of his voluntariness. Our concern here is with the conditions of voluntariness.

The term 'voluntary' appears to be a shorthand way of referring to more specific conditions. But the term, despite its vagueness, is useful as a correlative to the term 'responsible'. Though one speaks of a 'responsible act', it is strictly the person who is responsible for an act. The sort of act for which he is responsible is one which, besides being an obligation, is 'voluntary'. However, I shall continue to use the phrase 'responsible act' to designate that act which is both obligatory and voluntary. What then constitutes voluntariness?

The first and in many ways the most satisfactory account of the concept is that of Aristotle, who divides voluntary acts into two classes : (1) those which are not compelled and (2) those which are not done in ignorance. I shall propose the similar but more positive account, that voluntary acts are those which (1) we are *able* to do and (2) are *intentional*. In order to be responsible for an act X, (1) the person must have done the act (in which case, unless the act occurred by chance, he was able to do it) or, if he has not done it, he must have been able to do it, and (2) the act or the failure to do the act must have been intentional.

Three sorts of objection are made to such a view : (1) that there are no universal conditions of responsibility; (2) that there is no such thing as responsibility; (3) that one universal condition of responsibility is a special faculty called 'free will'. I shall call the first the 'Ascriptive' theory; the second the 'Extreme Deterministic' theory and the third the 'Libertarian' theory. I shall take up the first and second in this chapter, and the third in the next chapter.

2. Are All Conditions of Responsibility 'Negative'?

The first of these views has been presented by Professor H. L. A. Hart in his essay, 'The Ascription of Responsibility and Rights'.[1] Hart maintains that there is no limited set of universal positive conditions of responsibility, but rather an inexhaustible list of specific and varying defenses which nullify responsibility. Thus the question whether 'Smith hit her' and was responsible is chiefly the question whether 'any of a vast array of defenses can be pleaded by Smith or his friends which, though they do not destroy the charge altogether, soften it, or as lawyers say, "reduce" it' (p. 162). Examples of such defenses are that his act was 'accidental', 'inadvertent', a 'mistake', 'in self-defense', 'under provocation'. Nor can we construe these defenses as signs of the absence of a common element which is a positive condition of responsibility, such as intention or voluntariness. For such concepts are either themselves 'only understandable when interpreted in the light of the defenses' (p. 163), or they are a very special sort of event (Hart mentions Prichard's concept of 'setting oneself') which is not common to all cases of responsible action. On this view, then, it would appear that terms such as 'voluntary', 'able', 'intentional', which we have been accustomed to employ as names for very general and positive conditions of responsibility, must either be abandoned or interpreted as names for quite specific sorts of defenses, similar to such concepts as 'accidental', 'inadvertent', etc.

This view is, I believe, mistaken; but it can only be refuted by the detailed analyses in subsequent sections of the general concepts of 'able to do' and 'intention', showing that these are always required as positive conditions of responsible action. There is a preliminary point, however, which will serve both as a partial concession to Hart and as a partial explanation of his error. It is true that responsibility is a 'defeasible' and a negative concept in the sense that we ordinarily inquire whether the person was

---

[1] Reprinted from the *Proceedings of the Aristotelian Society* in A. G. N. Flew's *Logic and Language* (First Series), Blackwell, 1955. All quotations are from the latter.

P

responsible only when there is some ground for thinking that he was not responsible. First, almost all ascriptions of responsibility are for blameworthy acts, and these are acts for which the person may be concerned to show that he was not responsible. Second and more important, the cases when a person is not responsible are exceptional. The fact is that we are responsible for most of our actions. Because this is so, ordinarily no one thinks it necessary to question whether a person was responsible — we can safely assume that he was. The question arises only when there is some indication that the case was unusual and that he was not responsible. What this shows is not that responsibility is a 'negative concept', but only that our main concern with it is negative. It shows, not that responsibility is conceived in terms of conditions for its absence, but that the positive conditions of its presence are so general that, in the absence of evidence to the contrary, their existence can be assumed.

But further, the negative conditions will not provide all we need. For we do not want merely to excuse persons from responsibility and from the blame that goes with a wrong act for which they are responsible. We want also to praise them for certain acts but only for those acts for which they are responsible. And we may sometimes be in doubt about this. So that we want to know not merely whether a defense can be brought to exculpate from blame, but whether positive conditions are present which justify praise.

I shall next describe this condition of being able to act, and then consider the argument of the Extreme Determinist that there is no such condition. We shall not be ready to consider intention until the very end.

3. The Two Positive Conditions of Responsibility

Several concepts seem to be involved in the concept of responsibility, that of (a) 'able to act', (b) 'free' or 'uncompelled' and (c) 'act of oneself'. Further, these concepts seem to entail each other. An act which (c) the 'person' does, or which 'he' or 'he himself' does, seems to be one which he is (a) 'able' to do, and one which he is (b) 'free'

or 'not compelled' to do. But in actual use we do not
hold to these implications. Each of these terms has its
own criteria or rules of use, and these rules are different.
We can think of cases where we would apply each of the
first three terms but not the others: (1) (a) but not (b) —
'He is really quite *able* to get up, but his doctors are *compelling* him to stay in bed'; (2) (b) but not (a) — 'No one
is *compelling* him to remain in bed, but he just is not *able*
to get up'; (3) (a) but not (c) — 'He was quite *able* to act
as Smith did, but still the *act* was done by Smith and not
by himself'; (4) (c) but not (a) — 'He himself did the *act*,
it is true; but it had to be by chance, for he was not *able*
to do it'; (5) (c) but not (b) — 'He was *compelled* to sign it,
it is true; but still *he* did *do* it'; (6) (b) but not (c) — 'The
fact is *he* didn't *do* it; he was *free* to do it'. We can also
imagine the details of a case in which we might use any of
these expressions such that we would not hold the person
responsible for the act (or failure to act) referred to.

This might suggest that the negative of each of these
terms provides an excepting or nullifying condition, according to Hart's principle, while none is a positive condition of
responsibility. There is, however, another solution. This
is that none of these terms stands for a sufficient condition
of responsibility, but one of them together with some other
term may provide such a condition. It may first occur to
us to try some combination of these three, but this will not
work. For suppose we combine them all, conceiving an
act which the person is able to do, and which he does, and
which he is not compelled to do. We can still suppose that
such an act is done unintentionally, by chance or accident;
and we would not hold the person responsible for such an
act. This gives us the clue: the other term required to
complete the condition of responsibility is 'intentional'.
Given 'intention', we can dispense with all other terms
except 'able'.

But we cannot dispense with 'able'. Combining 'acting' with 'intention' will not be sufficient. For a person
can be responsible both for acting and for not acting, providing he is able to act. If the person is able to act, and
if he intentionally does not act, then (assuming the act is

obligatory) he is responsible. A person who does act intentionally is responsible, but in this case he is able to act. Acting intentionally entails being able to act intentionally, but
intentionally not acting does not entail intentionally acting; and one can be responsible for both intentionally
acting or not acting. Thus what is required for responsibility is the conjoining of intention not to acting but to the
ability to act. Acting 'freely' or 'without compulsion' is
inadequate for the same reason that 'acting' is inadequate;
namely that one is responsible if he intentionally and freely
refrains from acting, when he is able to act. Finally, we
obviously do not get a sufficient condition of responsibility
by combining 'freely' and 'intentionally', except in conjunction with 'act' or 'able to act', for both 'freely' and
'intentionally' are significant only in conjunction with acting or refusing to act. Shall we conclude, then, that a
person is responsible for an act if he is able to do it and if
his doing it or not doing it is intentional? Or do we need
to add that he must have done it or been able to do it
'freely' (or 'without compulsion'), as well as 'intentionally'? I think not. For, as I shall argue in the next
chapter, the notion of 'free to act' is equivalent to 'able to
act' in one of its senses. And in cases (as in (1) and (2)
above) where the terms 'free' and 'able' are contrasted,
this same contrast might also be expressed by the use of
'able' in two of its senses, which I shall call the 'personal'
and 'situational' senses. Let us now consider these.

4. The Ability to Act

Whether a person 'can' act or is 'able' to act depends
upon conditions both of himself and of his external situation. We use these terms to refer to both such conditions.
If we say, 'Tom can run' or 'Tom is able to run', we may
mean either that Tom has a personal ability (power, capacity) to run; or we may mean that the situation permits
his running. I shall call the former the 'personal' sense of
'can' and 'able', and the latter the 'situational' sense. We
establish the personal ability by examining not merely the
person's present state but his past behavior, while we establish the situational ability by examining his particular

external situation. To determine whether a person has a personal ability to do a thing we investigate whether he has done it in the past, or has done things of the same sort, and whether at the moment under consideration he was in a state like that in which he had done such things in the past. We would also want to know whether the outside circumstances were like those in which this sort of thing is usually done.[1]

It might occur to us to assign the 'personal' sense to the word 'able' and the 'situational' sense to 'can'; and I think there is a slight tendency to use the terms so. For example, we might be more apt to understand the sentence 'He can speak' as meaning that the situation permits it, and the sentence 'He is able to speak' as meaning that he possesses this ability. This difference in use is exceedingly slight, the way in which we take either term depending chiefly on the context. However, the difference does come out when we change from the verb 'able' to the noun 'ability'. If we say 'He can speak' we might be thinking either of conditions of the situation or of the person, but if we say 'He has an ability to speak' we are plainly thinking of the person, not of his momentary situation. For this reason it would be a bit odd to say, 'He has an ability to write this afternoon', but not odd to say either 'He is able to write this afternoon' or 'He can write this afternoon'. Still, we shall sometimes want a noun for this dual sense of 'can' and 'able', and 'ability' seems the only term available. Thus I shall unfortunately have to strain the term to speak of a 'personal ability' and a 'situational ability'. (A 'situational ability' is more fully described as a situational opportunity for a person to exercise some 'personal ability'.) And because it occupies a middle position, I shall prefer the verb 'able' to 'can'.

We may use these terms 'can' and 'able' in either of these ways; but most often, perhaps, we use them in both

---

[1] F. Raab in an essay entitled 'Free Will and the Ambiguity of "Could" ' (*The Philosophical Review*, 1955, pp. 60 ff.) draws a similar distinction to that here between the 'personal ability' and the 'situational ability'. Mr. Raab distinguishes between 'the possession-of-an-ability "could" ' and 'the absence-of-duress "could" '. He has also made an excellent detailed analysis of the way we verify such 'could' statements.

ways at once. To say that 'Tom was able to deliver the message' is to suggest both that he had certain general abilities and that the particular circumstances did not hinder the delivery. A particular context may give stress to just one of these senses. For example, if we say 'Tom is moving to Australia, so he will be able to play more tennis', we understand 'able' in the situational sense, as referring to the circumstances. While if we say, 'Tom is getting stronger, so he will be able to play more tennis', we understand 'able' in the personal sense. But even in these special contexts, which isolate one of these senses, the other sense is usually presupposed. For example, some questionnaires request opinions on an applicant's general abilities, without mentioning the circumstances of a particular situation; but the questions would not be asked nor answered if it were certain that the applicant would find no opportunity for exercising these abilities. There would be even less point in mentioning that a person has a particular opportunity if he has no abilities by which to take advantage of it.

At any rate, we always intend both senses when speaking of responsibility. To say, 'Jones was responsible for the act because he is able to do it', was to say both that Jones had certain personal abilities and that the situation allowed for their exercise. We should not say that Jones was responsible for delivering the message if he could run but the road were blocked, or if the road were open but he could not run. Our primary concern in assigning responsibility is with the particular act — it is the act for which he is responsible, and not the general ability (though he may be responsible for particular acts which lead to his having a general ability). But we establish responsibility for the particular act only by considering the person's general abilities as well as his particular circumstances.

We offer it, then, as a universal principle that being responsible requires a being 'able to act' in both senses. By this we mean that the person has (1) both (2) a situational ability to do a specific act and (3) the specific personal abilities, such as an ability to walk or speak, which are required for the specific act. Sometimes the phrase is used to mean (4) a distinct kind of personal ability, as an ability to 'get things done' or 'to handle practical situations' or something of the sort. In use (3) the phrase is a name for a class of unspecified personal abilities, namely whatever abilities are required for the particular act in question; while (4) is a name for one specific sort of ability (on the level of an ability to walk or to speak) such as would be included in the summary classification of (3). Since in actual use the phrase 'able to act' is applied in all of these senses, and not merely in sense (1), I shall label these uses as follows: (1) the 'unrestricted' use; (2) the 'situational' use; (3) the 'personal' use; (4) the 'special' use. If the context does not make clear the sense in which I am using the phrase, and if I use none of these qualifying adjectives, I shall intend the phrase in the personal sense.

There is a further aspect of the unrestricted ability to act. It must be defined to include whatever negative momentary personal conditions would disable the person from acting. The situation might be of the sort to permit a person's acting in a given way, and his general capacities might be such as to permit him to act in this way, while yet some change occurs in him, such as insanity, emotional shock, or bodily paralysis, which prevents him from acting. So we shall understand this unrestricted ability to act, which is present in voluntary and responsible conduct, to include the absence of any momentary disabilities which affect any particular personal ability. It is to be noted, however, that this general sort of disability obstructs only this ability to act; it does not obstruct (though it may modify) the other factor in voluntariness, namely intention. The corresponding factor in the case of intention is unconsciousness. To be unrestrictedly able to act one must be free of these momentary disabilities, just as to act intentionally, one must not be asleep or unconscious.

5. *The Determinist Thesis*

One sort of theorist, the Extreme Determinist, denies that, in any sense relevant to responsibility, a person is ever able to act. What he asserts is that no one is ever 'able to act differently'; but this just comes to saying that no one is ever 'able to act'. For we should have no use for the second expression if we were never permitted to use the first. We want to say that a person was able to act in a given way when in fact he did not act in that way but differently. If we cannot say this, then there is no difference between saying that the person was able to act in a given way and that he did act in that way. If the only evidence that the person is able to act is that he does the act, then we have no way of distinguishing the two, and we ought to give up the former, more complex expression. But in fact we do have ways of distinguishing a particular case of acting from 'being (unrestrictedly) able to act'. That a person acts on a given occasion (and acts not by chance or accident) shows that he was able to act; but his failure to act does not show that he was not able to act. We have already seen how we do determine that a person has an ability to act. I shall first try to show that the Extreme Determinist's thesis, which denies this ability, is false, and then explain the source of its error.

6. *Can We Do Away with the Concept of Responsibility?*

On the ground that a person is never able to act differently, the Extreme Determinist (whom I shall now call, for short, simply Determinist) declares that a person is never responsible for his acts. The Determinist must then advocate that we discard this concept of responsibility along with the concept of the ability to act. But he can never get us to do this. And the very attempt to do so would be in contradiction with his recommendation. For he will want to hold us responsible for not holding people responsible.

The Determinist wants to change our ways of behaving and talking about responsibility. He wants us not to punish people so much, and not to blame them so much. So he argues: to be responsible is to be fully able to act; but people are not fully able to act; hence they are not responsible; so we shouldn't treat them as responsible. And he supports the argument by pointing out that we are steadily understanding more about how people act; and the more we understand the less we hold them responsible.

He also predicts that in some future time we will not hold them responsible at all. I think that he is right about the way we should change, and are changing, our practices concerning responsibility. But we have to use the concept of responsibility in order to get people to change it. How should we educate children not to hold people responsible, except by holding children responsible for doing this? One might reply that we will accomplish this by praising them for doing the act, instead of blaming them for failing to do it. But surely we shall not praise them indiscriminately; we shall praise them for the voluntary and responsible act, and adjust our degrees of praise according to their ability. As we blame most the act which the person is most able to do, so we praise most the act which the person does even though least able to do. Further, we would in fact find it impossible only to praise, and never to blame. Perhaps we might refrain from punishing or from uttering judgments of blame; but then the mere withholding of judgments of praise would come to be felt as a kind of blame. This is so even now. In situations where one expects a judgment either of praise or of blame, mere silence is felt as dispraise. Thus, if the Deterministic prediction were to come true, it would have to be through eliminating both praise and blame. But that is neither conceivable nor desirable.

Let us now consider how the Determinist supports his view, and where he has gone wrong.

7. *The Determinist's Error*

The Determinist derives his view that persons cannot act differently from his view that all acts are causally necessitated. He reasons as follows: (1) all responsible acts are acts; (2) acts are natural events; (3) all events are caused; (4) what is caused is necessitated; (5) what is necessitated must happen; (6) what must happen cannot happen differently; (7) hence no acts can happen differently. The questionable assertions here begin with (3). But I shall question this and the subsequent assertions only in so far as they are taken to entail that (A) any choice or act which a person makes is the only one possible to him, and (B) so far as an act is caused no other choice or act is possible to a person.

(A) The Determinist may put his argument in this way : Every choice and every act is determined in the sense that for the person only one act is possible, namely the choice and act which the person made or did. But if no other choice or act were possible, then the person was not able to act in any other way ; hence he was not responsible for acting as he did.

There are several points to be made here. First, it is true that to say that a particular act is 'not possible' is to imply that the act is one which the person is 'not able' to perform. But it is not obvious what is meant by saying that the act is 'not possible'. If when predicated of an act 'not possible' means exactly the same as 'not able', and if the conditions for truly predicating 'not possible' are identical with the conditions of predicating 'not able' — then the former expression raises no new problems. And we can accept the principle that to the degree that it is not possible for a person to choose or act in a particular way, to that degree he is not free and not responsible. We do in fact commonly employ this principle without difficulty. We think that there are all sorts of things which it is not possible for a person to choose or attempt. For example, in the case of most persons it is not possible for the person to choose or attempt to kill himself or a close relative. The fact that we are not able to choose to do these things does not distress us. For we do not want to choose to do these things, or to hold other persons responsible for doing them. We think we are better off being unable to choose them. These impossibilities of choice do limit our ability and freedom to act. But there are some abilities and freedoms which we prefer to be without.

However, the Determinist wants to have it that there are no degrees of possibility ; that every action which is done is the only action which is possible, hence that any other action, for which we might (mistakenly) be inclined to hold the person responsible, is not possible. But this is a groundless assertion. There are no grounds for claiming to know, in the case of *all* choices or actions, that no other action was possible. There is not even any ground for claiming to know, in the case of *any* particular choice or action, that no other choice or action was possible. We just cannot know this much. We can feel very, very certain that a person will not choose, say, to kill himself, and we can have very good grounds for believing he will not do so. But, as Hume showed, it would not be an impossibility for the person to do the act, for no contradiction would be involved in his doing it.

The point of statements about what is possible in the sphere of events (as distinct from the sphere of logic) would seem to be predictive. To say that an event 'is not possible' is to say that it 'will not occur'; and to say that a past event 'was not possible' is to say that it did not occur and that in the light of what one now knows one could have predicted beforehand that it would not occur. The grounds for a statement about the non-possibility of an event are then just the grounds for predicting the non-occurrence of that event. But the only grounds we have for prediction are grounds which establish degrees of probability, never absolute certainty. It is true that the more firm are our predictions of what a person will do, the less 'possible' is it that he will choose or act otherwise, and the less 'able' is he to choose or act otherwise.[1] But this is no cause for worry. For these choices are either choices which we do not want to be able to make (as the choice to kill someone) or are choices for which we do not want to hold the person responsible (as the choice, which an insane person could not make, not to kill someone).

(B) The principle from which the Determinist attempts to derive his conclusion that the person is not able to choose or do anything other than what he did is that his act was caused. This principle, though its meaning is vague, is widely accepted; and let us accept it. Let us agree that whenever a person chooses or acts, there is some cause (or

[1] It is, of course, not *our* ability to predict that a person will act in a given way which reduces *his* ability to act differently. Rather, it is the conditions which ground our prediction of (and hence which partially enable us to predict) his action which reduces his ability to act differently. Nor does ability to predict provide an ability to control. Prediction is a necessary condition of control, but it does not itself bring control.

causes) accounting for (or helping to explain) that choice or act. But from this it does not follow that no other choice or act was 'possible' or that the person was not 'able' to choose or act otherwise. Another choice or act was possible if the person chose or acted intentionally and was able to choose or act differently.

There is nothing in an act's being caused or not being caused which is incompatible with its being a choice or an act which the person is able to make or do. If the act occurred (and was, according to the accepted principle, caused) then clearly the person was able to do it. And if it did not occur (hence was not caused) we may still have evidence that the person was able to do it. In order that a person's failure to do an act be accounted for by his not having been able to do the act, these causes must be of a particular sort. If they be of this sort, then we say that what he did (or failed to do) was 'caused' or 'necessitated' in the special sense of being 'compelled'. It is not just causes which disable him, but a particular sort of causes which we call cases of 'compulsion' or 'compelling causes'.[1] These we may classify as : (a) external, when some natural force or person controls one's bodily movements, (b) bodily, as in paralysis, or (c) mental, as in emotional disturbance. If it is not such causes as these which account for the act, then we say that the causes were not of a sort which absolve him of responsibility. Rather, we say that the cause of his choice and act was his own intention and abilities (to act and not to act), and he is responsible because the act was an effect of these.

The Determinist thesis, though relevant to responsibility only as concerns action, is sometimes put in a more general form, the application to human action being presented as a deduction from this more general truth : all events are causally determined (necessitated). Sometimes it is put in the imaginative form : If one could know both the complete state of the universe at any given moment

---

[1] Professor A. J. Ayer has perhaps most clearly shown that in investigating an act's responsibility we do not merely try to establish whether the act was caused. ('Freedom and Necessity', *Philosophical Essays*, Macmillan, 1954.)

and all the causal laws, then he could predict every future event, including, of course, all human actions. The ordinary man makes a remark of this sort when he says 'What happens must happen'. But the ordinary man intends the expression figuratively. It expresses his present mood, not a metaphysical doctrine. This is apparent in that at other moments he asserts the exactly contrary doctrine of a thorough Indeterminism — 'Anything might happen'. As the Deterministic utterance expresses his feeling of resignation, so this Indeterministic utterance expresses his feeling of hope. He does not mean to make a metaphysical commitment on either.

In ordinary life we commonly use statements similar to these, which have Deterministic and anti-Deterministic suggestions, to say something about human conduct which is expressible in terms of the personal and situational ability to act. We may say, Deterministically, 'He must have done what he did' — meaning that his abilities to act were very limited in the given sort of situation. And we may say, anti-Deterministically, of a person who is particularly gifted or particularly lucky, 'Well, with him anything might happen'. What we mean is not that there are no causes operating on this person, but that his abilities or opportunities are extremely great. Thus remarks which have a Deterministic or anti-Deterministic flavor are either metaphorical expressions (as in the preceding paragraph) or are literally descriptive, as here, and in the latter case are to be understood in terms of the concept of the ability to act.

The fact is that we cannot know anything positive about the entire universe, or about all events in the universe. So far as the Determinist principle has point, it has point as a generalization about the fields which we have known. There is a point in reasoning that, because in general fields of knowledge share a number of traits, it is probable that they share the particular feature of being formulable according to causal laws. If causal laws rule in physics, it is reasonable to think they rule in psychology. But their ruling in physics and other sciences, though it would be some evidence for their ruling in psychology, would be very partial and provisional evidence; it would be worth very little if we did not progressively find psychological events subsumable under causal law. In fact we do find this. And we are glad to find it, just as we are glad to find causes in other sorts of phenomena ; for this gives us more control of events. We are quite as in need of control of ourselves as of the things outside us.

But here the metaphysical extension of Determinism comes in to frighten us. If things have causes, then perhaps they can be controlled. If we have causes, then perhaps we can be controlled. We then make the erroneous inference that, since we are subject to causes, we are in fact controlled. If someone knew everything about us and all the causal laws, then he could predict just what we would do ; and, providing he could control what he could predict, he could handle us like puppets ! But there are several points. (1) There is not the slightest evidence that anyone will ever attain this degree of knowledge ; and (2) there is reason to think that the advancing knowledge of human behavior will be the joint possession of a great many persons, so that the danger would not be that of control by a single person or small group of persons. Moreover (3) prediction itself does not bring control ; control requires power as well as knowledge. And generally we do not mind a person's being able to predict what we will do so long as he cannot use this knowledge to control us. Further (4), it is not the causes of our acts themselves which can control our acts ; it is only some human being who can control our acts by means of causes. And (5) this power to control acts (which knowledge combined with physical power does give) can be used to control a person's act no less by the individual himself than by someone else. Knowledge of human nature tends to increase its possessor's self-control as well as his control of others. Finally (6) power to control is no more of a danger than it is an opportunity. For we can control persons (ourselves and others) for good or for bad. What we have to fear, is not the causes themselves controlling us — for causes cannot by themselves do this — but rather our controlling causes and effects for the wrong ends. And surely this is not so fearful as our being impelled to choose and act from causes of which we are ignorant.

8. *The Source of the Determinist's Error*

We can see this suggestion of our being dominated by causes in the word 'determine' itself. Consider the following ordinary statements using this word. (1) 'Jones was determined to return to California'. Here 'determined' has the meaning of 'resolved' or 'decided'. (2) 'It was determined that Jones would return to California'. Here the meaning is that one who knew the conditions (as Jones' feeling about California, or the sort of offer he would receive) would see the necessary connection between these conditions and Jones' return. But the Determinist does not make either of these statements, but rather, (3) 'Jones' return to California was determined'. What is one to make of the meaning of this 'determined'? In the lack of anything definite one is apt confusedly to join both the meanings of (1) and (2) above, namely 'has conditions or causes' and 'has been resolved upon'. The Determinist's utterance has not the meaning of (2), for it speaks of the event itself, 'Jones' return', rather than our knowledge of its conditions. Nor has it the meaning of (1), for it says that the return 'was determined', not that 'he determined it'. It is as if Jones' return is being determined by the condition of someone's resolution, only not his own.

For this reason it is better not to speak of acts as being 'determined' but simply as being 'caused'. No civilized person would think that, because an event had a cause, its cause was necessarily the act of some personal being. But our civilization is incomplete, and we revert to animism on slight stimulus. To call an act 'determined' is to call up this thought of some conscious force constraining us, and since we cannot believe that there are forces 'determining' us in the way we often 'determine' ourselves, we feel inclined to reject the doctrine. The doctrine that acts are caused has no need to raise for itself this obstacle. If it were to have a name, a better name than 'Determinism' would be 'Causationism'.

We can also see more generally why it should be thought that causes deprive a person of voluntariness and responsibility. We have noticed that the question of responsibility comes up in a negative form. Ordinarily we assume that a person is responsible. The question whether he is responsible comes up when there is some indication that he is not responsible. It is then that we ask about causes. We ask whether there are causes which disabled him from acting, and which consequently rendered his behavior involuntary. Thus we associate causes with acts which are involuntary and non-responsible.

The notion that the responsible act cannot be caused is also encouraged by the difficulty of speaking of a person as causing his own acts. There thus arises an opposition between those acts of a person which are caused and those which he does (or which are his). The causes of his acts tend to be thought of as something distinct from himself. We do sometimes say 'He was the cause of it, and so he is responsible'. But the 'it' here is thought of as the external event rather than his act. Thus his acts are thought of as either done by him, and so responsible, or as done by causes, and then not responsible. Consider this example. Suppose a plank falls and hurts Smith, and the question arises whether Jones pushed the plank and is responsible. We might ask whether Jones, or Jones' act, caused the plank's falling. We would not ask whether Jones was the cause of his pushing the plank. Yet we might conclude that something else was the cause of this — if, for instance someone jostled Jones' arm. We say either that Jones did it, or that something else caused it. In the former case we call the act responsible, in the latter not. Thus we connect the act which was caused only with the act which is non-responsible.

But that there is in fact no conflict between responsibility and cause is plain. For we say that a person is responsible for acts which are within his 'control', and by 'within his control' here we mean 'within his power to cause'. A Libertarian may say that the person is not the cause of any acts which are caused just by his 'character', which has itself been caused by past events. The 'self' which causes responsible acts must, according to this doctrine, be a timeless self, otherwise this self will evaporate into an endless sequence of past causes. But this is a mistake. So far as the person's character, or one side of his character, causes his act, it is his present character as now formed. The cause of his character is his past experience. But the cause of his present act is his present character, and not the causes of his present character. The cause of an event is not the causes of the cause of that event, any more than the parent of a child is the parent of the parent of that child. The past causes can only operate through the present ones. Thus regarding the causes of a person's acts as his ('empirical') character is not to regard these causes as in any sense outside the person. Nor is the cause merely 'inside' something else which is the person. The cause is the person, or the person in one of his aspects. The person is the sum of his general tendencies and particular intentions. And so far as his action expresses (or is caused by) these, so far it is voluntary and responsible.

CHAPTER VII

WILL

THE view that acts cannot be responsible if they are caused has also been maintained by the advocate of 'free will', sometimes called the 'Libertarian'. The Libertarian, like the Extreme Determinist, argues that if a person's act is caused by his desire or by his character, and if these are caused by past events, then the true origin of his act is not in himself but in an infinitely remote past. But contrary to the Determinist, the Libertarian asserts that we are responsible for some of the things we do. Hence, he argues that we must have whatever conditions are required for responsibility; and the fundamental condition is that we have an ability to act differently. But he holds that this ability, since it escapes the chain of natural causes, is of a highly special sort. It is not what I have defined as an unrestricted ability to act, but is an ability 'to will' or 'to choose' or to do these things 'freely'. In this chapter I shall consider the concept of willing, and in the next that of choosing, as each relates to responsibility.

1. *The Special Feature of 'Free Will'*

The Libertarian believes that willing is a very special sort of activity. It differs from other capacities in that these vary in degree, while the capacity to will cannot vary, if it is to serve as a universal condition of responsibility. The capacity which is required for responsible action must be present equally in all responsible persons in the moments of their responsibility. Thus this power of moral effort cannot depend upon anything peculiar to the person. The view has to be that whenever a person confronts a problem of moral choice he has whatever power is required to try to do what he believes right. Personal differences will account for the particular moral choices he confronts, and for the particular way in which he conceives them. But he has to have a power to act which is unaffected by any peculiar past or present influences. Otherwise, we could only say that a person was responsible after investigating these particular personal factors. But the Libertarian wants to say that the mature and sane adult (whatever this may be) is, by virtue of this perfectly general condition, responsible for his moral choices. He may not be responsible for what he feels and thinks at a given moment, but he is responsible for what he attempts to do — or for what he 'wills' to do. Hence this power of 'free will' by which he makes these attempts must be a universal human endowment.

I think we do not find any capacity of this sort. We find various capacities and activities which are called by the name 'will', but all of these vary among persons. I shall mention these several ways which we do in fact use the expression 'to will' and I shall suggest adopting as the most favored sense the meaning it has when it is equivalent to 'to try'. But another view which has often been proposed is that 'will' is a name for a form or degree of desire. After considering these several views I shall return to the question whether 'will' could be a universal condition of responsibility.

2. *'Free', 'Able', and 'Free to Will' and 'Able to Will'*

In common use, when we say that a person is responsible for an act because he did it 'of his free will', we just mean that the person acted intentionally and was unrestrictedly able to act differently. Also, outside contexts of responsibility, we use the expression 'free will' to convey the meaning of 'able to act' in the situational or personal or unrestricted senses. Take the sentence, 'You are now free to speak'. We might use this situationally, to indicate that no one will interrupt you or that everyone will listen. Or it might be used to indicate a personal ability, as if a surgeon or psychiatrist were to say it to a patient after treatment. Plainly there is nothing which is unique about this ability, or which renders it independent of natural causes, as is the 'free will' which the Libertarian conceives.

The Libertarian's case is served even less by another

common use of 'free will'. In this use the term 'free' merely adds stress to meanings conveyed by other words in the expression. We often say 'He did it of his own free will' just as a way of saying emphatically that he did it of his will. 'Free' here is strictly redundant, as is 'own'. A person cannot do something 'of his will' and not do it of his own will; introducing 'own' just stresses that the person did it and is responsible. Likewise with 'free', adding 'free' to 'will' (or to 'own will') increases the stress. Both redundant terms may serve to express the speaker's feeling about the matter, or his belief about the degree of opportunity or ability which the person had.

Now consider the expression 'able to will'. The fact is that we do not ordinarily use this in speaking either of responsibility or of anything else. And the reason is clear. We usually use 'able' and 'will' in a sense in which it is paradoxical to combine the two in the phrase 'able to will'. That is, we use 'able' in a way in which it is equivalent to 'dependent on his will'. Thus to say 'Jones was able to do the act' could be conveyed by saying that 'Whether Jones did the act was dependent on his will'. But now if we construe along the same lines 'Jones was able to will the act', we get, 'Whether Jones did the act was dependent on his will to will the act'. And we cannot make sense of a willing to will an act.

There is a further point. We often distinguish the meanings of 'free' and 'able' such that it is not redundant to join the two in the phrase 'free and able'. But in the Libertarian's use in 'free to will' and 'able to will' the two terms are used equivalently. At the most these two terms would indicate different aspects of one thing. The Libertarian might use the expression 'free will' to stress the relation of this will to other things or outside causes — to make the point that the will is 'free' of these in the way that a person is 'free' of outside forces, that is, capable of acting independently of them. While the expression 'able to will' would turn attention to the internal capacity in the exercise of which this independence becomes manifest. This somewhat parallels our ordinary use of these terms, but there is a crucial difference. We use 'free' to stress a

situational ability, 'able' to stress a personal ability. These
two sorts of ability are separate, while 'free' and 'able' in
the Libertarian's use are inseparable aspects of one thing.
We would say that 'John is free to run but not able to run',
meaning that, though there are no outside hindrances to
his running, he lacks the personal ability to move his legs
in the required way. One might even make this distinction
in the case of a highly internal ability, such as thinking.
One might say, after the company had gone and the noise
subsided, 'At last I am free to think' and then add, 'but I
seem no longer able to do so'. But in the case of the 'will'
about which the Libertarian speaks, one would never say
'He was free to will but was not able to will', or 'He was
able to will but not free to will'.

We conclude that in his concept of 'free will' or 'able
to will' the Libertarian cannot be employing the ordinary
meanings of 'free will', 'able', or 'free and able'. Let us
now consider specifically the notion of 'will' and 'willing'.

3. *Willing and Trying*

We use the word 'will' as a noun or as a term in a
noun-phrase in the senses of five other words. It is used
in the sense of (1) 'tried' — for example, in 'I *exerted my
will* to the utmost'; in the sense of (2) 'intention' — in
'It was his *will* that they should quarrel; he brought them
together so that it would happen'; in the sense of (3)
'choice' — in 'What is your *will* in the matter?'; in the
sense of (4) 'desire' — in 'What is your *will*, Master?';
in the sense of (5) 'overt action' — in 'It is of my own free
will that I am here'. Of these meanings the Libertarian
would not regard either (4) desire or (5) overt action as
the sense of 'will' which is intended in the doctrine that
the responsible act is the one which is willed. He might
mean by this act the one which is (2) intended or (3)
chosen; and I shall take up these concepts in the following
chapters. However his meaning would seem to come
closer to (1) tried, and it is this which we have to consider
here.

I believe it is in this sense that we most ordinarily use
the word 'will'. This is what we mean when we say of two

athletes or two workers that one has a 'stronger will' or 'more will-power'. We mean that one is capable of trying harder, or of exerting greater effort.

However the fact is that though we chiefly use 'try' as a verb, to name an activity, we rarely use 'will' as a verb. We use 'will' as a noun, in 'It depended on his will'; as an adverb, in 'He did it willingly'; as an adjective, in 'He is of a very willing disposition'; in a verb-phrase, in 'He exerted his will to the utmost'; or as part of a noun-phrase, in 'It was by a sheer act of will that he did it'. When we do use the term as a verb we use it either in an extraordinary sense, in which it is not quite clear what sort of activity we are referring to, or we use it in a more ordinary way, in which it has the meaning of 'try'.

The extraordinary use is seen in such sentences as 'He willed it so', or 'He willed their marriage' (as in answer to the question, 'What did he have to do with it?'). But the meaning of such expressions is a bit mysterious, and it is appropriate to ask what the person means — to ask: 'What in fact *did* he do', as if his 'willing' the thing were not really a doing of it, but only our metaphorical way of saying that he did it. In such uses, as in 'willing a marriage', the person's 'willing' is recognized to be altogether incapable of fully effecting the event. We never would say that the person 'willed' the sort of thing which those who believe in the efficacy of the will do think the will could effect, namely a movement of his body.[1] We say that a person moved his arm, or tried to move his arm, not that he willed to move (or willed the movement of) his arm. Likewise we would say that he was able (or free) to move his arm, not that he was able (or free) to will to move his arm.

The nearest we come to ordinary or non-metaphorical

---

[1] Or the 'kinaesthetic and other sensations upon which we have learned from experience, the movement of our (body, e.g., our) leg, normally supervenes'. This very curious notion of what we will has been proposed recently by Professor C. A. Campbell ('Self-Activity and Its Modes', *Contemporary British Philosophy*, Third Series, 1956, edited by H. D. Lewis, p. 93). Professor Campbell argues that we are introspectively aware of this as the thing which we immediately will. But the view, besides being quite fantastic in itself, is refuted by asking what could be the 'kinaesthetic and other sensations' which we immediately 'will' when we will thoughts, as the recollection of some memory.

uses of the verb 'to will' are cases such as the following. If a good runner fails to finish a gruelling race, we might say 'He wasn't able to will to run on'. But though we might say this, it would be more natural to say: 'He didn't have the will to run on', or 'He couldn't make the additional effort', or 'He was unable to try any longer'. Used in this way, 'will' has, unlike the above metaphorical use, the sense of 'try'.

There is a difference in the senses of 'try' and 'exerted an effort of will', but this is a difference in two aspects of a single thing. 'Will' is the noun naming the capacity, of which 'try' is the word naming the activity in which the capacity is exercised. Thus, instead of saying 'I simply willed to continue working', it is more natural to say 'I exerted my will to continue working', 'will' here replacing the preceding verb as a noun in the verb-phrase. The reason this is more natural, and the reason why 'tried' or 'exerted effort' would not convey quite the same sense in the above as 'exerted my will', is that 'will' calls attention to the person who has the capacity rather than to the activity which exercises it. 'He had a strong will' comes a bit more naturally than 'He exerted his will', and this latter a bit more naturally than 'He willed'. The concept of 'will' is chiefly of a property belonging to a substance, rather than of an event or activity. But this difference is not of importance to the problem. For whenever there is a capacity of will there are some acts of trying, and conversely; the question being whether this is the sort of capacity and act which is required for responsibility.

But we can find no other relevant meaning of 'will' than 'trying'.[1] If we exclude trying (and for the present, intending and choosing), and if we exclude the mental or

---

[1] 'Try' also seems the preferred sense of 'will' by most Libertarians (for example, see C. A. Campbell, *op. cit.*, esp. p. 91). However, this preference is not uniform. For example, W. G. Maclagan (in 'Freedom of the Will', *Aristotelian Society* Supplementary Volume xxv, 1951, esp. pp. 191-2) seems to conclude that the required meaning of 'will' is not 'trying' but 'deciding'. And H. A. Prichard, after first thinking that the correct rendering for the special kind of activity he had in mind was 'setting oneself to cause', eventually concluded that the right word for 'this special kind of activity' was just 'willing', which term stands for a character '*sui generis* and so incapable of being defined' (*Moral Obligation*, Oxford University Press, p. 189).

physical events which we try (or intend or choose) to perform, we find nothing which we could call the 'willing' to
perform them. I may move my hand or recall a place
where I once was; or I may try (or intend or choose) to
do these things. But I cannot, in some distinct sense, 'will'
to do them. I do not experience any third thing, which
intervenes between the intention to move and the movement, or between the intention to try and the trying.[1]
William James held that what distinguished willing was the
attending to an idea, action naturally following on attention.
We do experience a strain, an effort of trying; and we
experience the idea, or its absence; but we do not experience anything more. One can certainly try to keep hold
of an idea, as when he wants to solve a problem, or to stay
awake, or not to yield to a temptation to which the idea is
opposed. But such willing is just trying.

4. *Willing and Desiring*

The notion that there is a peculiar moral capacity and
activity of free will has been frequently discussed with
relation to desire. Some who have denied that there is
such an activity have said that what is called willing is just
one kind or degree of desire. Although this is a mistake,
'will' is intimately related to desire, and to understand this
concept it is important to understand this relation.

'Willing' a thing, say to thread a needle (Prichard's
example), evidently does require a desire to accomplish the
thing which is 'willed'. How widely we shall construe
'desire', and whether we shall apply it to unconscious
actions, is certainly a question. But in cases of conscious
actions it would be agreed that to will or strive for any
objective is to have some desire to attain it. This fact has
inclined certain thinkers to say that willing is just desiring
or desiring in a certain degree. This cannot be right; for
we can desire a thing, and desire it more strongly than
anything else at the moment, without acting on the desire.
This will happen, for instance, if we know that to obtain

[1] For a curious but impressive argument of this point see B. O'Shaugh-
nessy's 'The Limits of the Will' in *The Philosophical Review*, October 1956,
esp. Sections 2 and 5.

the thing we desire is impossible. Knowing this impossibility may reduce the desire, but the point is that, prior to
this, one may have the desire, and know it to be his strongest
desire, yet not try to satisfy it. The formula then will not
do, that we always 'will' what we most strongly desire.
But the narrower doctrine does seem correct, that one can
only strive for an objective which he desires in some degree,
whether for its own sake or as a means to something
else.

The question this raises is whether besides the desire
for the objective which is 'willed', there must also be a
desire for the 'willing' of it. Prichard maintained the
latter — that, in order to 'will' an object, one must desire
not merely the object but the 'willing' of it. This evidently
was part of Prichard's belief that 'willing' is a very special
sort of activity — a belief which he regarded as incompatible with the belief in the uniformity of nature as a
physical system, and which implied 'the idea that we are
butting into, or interfering with, the physical system, just
as we think of an approaching comet as effecting a breach
in the order of the solar system' (*op. cit.* p. 193). It would
seem that Prichard supposed that if the desire involved in
'willing' were merely a desire for the objective 'willed',
this desire might be accounted for without any breach in
natural uniformity; while if the desire involved were
simply a desire to 'will', this would be unaccountable on
natural principles. At any rate, this desire to 'will' is just
as elusive a thing as is 'willing' itself in the orthodox
Libertarian account. And to make clear that there is no
such thing as this special sort of 'willing', as distinct from
trying, it will be of use to show that there is no desire to
'will', which does not derive from a desire for the thing
'willed'.

We have distinguished several senses in which the word
'will' is used. In two of these senses — to 'choose' and to
'desire' — we can speak of a desire to 'will'. We can
sensibly speak of a desire to choose and of a desire to
desire. But in the case of the other meanings we cannot
make sense of a desire to 'will' as distinct from a desire for
the thing 'willed'. We cannot make any sense at all of a

desire to 'intend'. And we can make no sense of a desire to try to do a thing as distinct from a desire to do that thing. But the sense of 'willing' which Prichard has in mind, as we shall see by his examples, is closest to 'try'.

A person can have a desire to 'will' or try, which is different from a desire for the objective, but such a desire is (a) derivative from the desire for the objective, and (b) only an occasional, not a necessary element in trying. A person may want to do something (say, be pleasant to a superior) which he knows he can do only if he tries hard to do it, and he may not know whether he can try in the required degree. In this case he will desire to try. This desire is distinct from his desire for the objective, but plainly it is derivative from it. The person desires to try as a means to satisfying another prior desire. Further, this desire to try does not always accompany trying. Imagine a situation which is the same except that the person knows that he can try in the required degree. Here there will be no occasion for his desiring to try. He sees what degree of effort is required for the objective he desires, and he simply summons this effort. He does not first desire it and then summon the effort — just as one who wants to write and has a pen lying at hand simply takes the pen and writes.

One might argue that trying always involves a desire to try, on the principle that the use of any means to satisfying a desire always involves a desire for these means. But we have seen that this principle is mistaken. One may want to accomplish a thing without wanting to do so with a given set of means. Here he only uses these means because they are means to what he wants. Likewise with trying. One may want to do the thing without wanting to have to try to do it, while one does nonetheless want to do it enough to exert his will to accomplish it. In this case one would only desire to try, as distinct from simply trying, if it occurred to him that he might not try and consequently might not accomplish the end which he desired.

We may, then, desire to try as a means (though we do not always do so). But I think it is plain that we never

desire trying for its own sake. Exertions of effort are painful. It is not the sort of thing one does for its own sake,
but for its consequences. However, there are two sorts
of consequences which are so closely connected with the
activity that the desire for these may be taken to be a
desire to 'will'. We may try to do something just to see
whether we can do it. But this involves a desire not to
try but to know what we can accomplish by trying. Or we
may try to do it in order to demonstrate, to others or ourselves, how strong a will we have. What we here desire is
to have the will, or have the reputation for having it, rather
than to use it. Thus people may engage in difficult
activities to develop this power of will or a reputation for
it. But none of these is a desire for the activity of 'willing'
or trying itself.

Further, if there were a primary desire to try, it would
be expected that there would be a desire to try in different
degrees. But surely there are no such desires. One sometimes desires to do a thing which requires a great effort,
but the desire is always linked to a specific objective. He
feels like thinking hard or like running hard; he does not
feel indifferently like doing either. Nor does anyone ever
desire to try in no degree, or not to try at all. We sometimes desire to remain inert, which desire is incompatible
with exertion. But here the desire is for something which
excludes trying, the desire is not itself for the absence of
trying.

Let us now consider Prichard's arguments that the
desire involved in 'willing' is not always a desire for a
specific objective, X. In *Moral Obligation* Prichard offers
three objections. First, he writes: 'On consideration,
however, we have to reject the idea that the desire required
is the desire of X, on three grounds. First, if it were true,
we should always will any change which we desired to
happen, such as the sliding of the table, whether or not we
thought that if we were to will it to happen we should
thereby cause it to happen; and obviously we do not'
(p. 195). But this argument is based on the unnecessary
assumption, that a thought that 'willing' could not accomplish X would reduce or remove the desire to '*will*' X,

while not reducing or removing the desire for X. But a thought of the impossibility of accomplishing an objective may reduce or remove the desire for it.

A second objection is offered to the view that the desire required in 'willing' is the desire of the change X. 'Second, we occasionally will a change to happen without a desire for it to happen. This must occur, e.g. if a man ever does an act moved solely by the desire for revenge, willing say, the movement of a switch which he is confident will result in the death of another, not from any desire for his death but solely from the desire to cause it by willing the movement. And even if there are no acts animated solely by the desire for revenge, there are certainly actions approximating to this. At all events, in the case of playing a game the desire at work must be not the desire of some change but the desire to cause it. A putter at golf, e.g., has no desire for the ball to fall into the hole; he only desires to cause it to fall in' (p. 195). Surely Prichard does not state the matter rightly. That the revenger or the golfer desires to *cause* the change does not show that he does not desire the *change*. He may desire both. What he does desire is the change only as it is caused by him. He desires the change as a part of something else which is the whole object of desire, namely the causing-the-change. But Prichard continues: 'This contention is, I think, not met by imagining as Cook Wilson in fact does, that the player desires the falling into the hole as caused by his action, and so desires the falling as part of, or an element in, his action. Its falling is neither a part of, nor an element in, his action; at best it is only an effect of it. And the player could only be said to desire the falling if, as he does not, he desired it to happen irrespectively of what would cause it to happen' (p. 194). It is true that the falling is not a part of the act, but an effect of it; but the falling is a part of a more comprehensive event, namely the *causing*-the-falling, and the falling could be desired as such a part. Surely Prichard is wrong in saying that the falling could be desired only if it were desired irrespectively of what caused it.

Prichard's view here seems explicable only by his overlooking a third thing which is a great part of what is desired in such cases, namely the physical movements which mediate between the effort and the eventual change. The golfer's desire is to *hit* the ball in the hole, not just to '*will*' it in, nor to 'will' the hitting of it in. What the golfer takes pleasure in is his skillful movement or the thought of his skill. The golfer enjoys his power, but the power is not of willing. If what he desired were mere will-power, as Prichard conceives, then he would desire that the ball fall in the hole merely by an act of 'will', without the golf stroke. If this were what he desired he would take up something besides golf.

The revenge case is similar but more complex. We can agree that the revenger does not desire the enemy's death except as caused by him. One might think that the revenger would *most* desire to cause *most* completely the enemy's *most* complete misfortune, but that he would desire any misfortune caused in any way in preference to no misfortune caused by an agency other than himself. But perhaps the latter desire is merely hate and not that special form of hate which is revenge — hate being a desire for mere destruction, revenge a desire to injure another person in return for an injury caused by him to oneself or a person close to oneself. Still Prichard overlooks an important element. The revenger wants not merely to cause the injury but to have the enemy *know* that he had caused it. Thus the revenger wants to do the deed with his own hands, purely in order, by his direct presence, to enforce on the victim vivid knowledge of who is responsible for his suffering. As a means of revenge physical processes have, besides this, two other advantages over mere 'willing'. As temporal, these processes prolong the satisfaction; and as relatively uncertain, they increase its poignance. These would be absent in a merely willed injury. And from the enemy's side, there would not be the peculiar pang of having been paid back. The revenger would have merely the pleasure of hating and the enemy merely the pain of being hated. Thus what is desired by the revenger, as by the golfer, is not merely the 'willing' of the change, but the actual movements (or results of them) which cause the change.

Prichard presents a third objection, and another sort of example. 'Then third, there is a consideration which comes to light if we consider more closely what it is that we will in certain cases, and more especially in those in which we describe an action as one of trying to do so and so. Suppose, e.g., I have done what we describe as having tried to jump a ditch, and so imply that beforehand I was doubtful of success. Obviously I did not will a movement of my body which I was sure would land me, say, two clear yards on the other side, since if I had thought of willing this I should have realized that willing this would not result in my getting across. I willed that movement the willing of which, if I were to will it, I thought most likely of all the willings of movement in my power to result in my landing on the farther bank' (pp. 195-6). Just what does Prichard intend this to show? It does show, in an instance in which the thing 'willed' is somewhat indefinite, that the jumper would not desire to 'will' jumping exactly two yards on the other side, since 'willing' this would not accomplish his desire of reaching the other side (and, though Prichard does not say, presumably he would not desire to land exactly on the other side, for then he might fall short). But many objects of desire and will are vague or approximate. Plainly the instance does not show that what the jumper desires is just 'willing' or trying to jump, and not 'willing' to jump some roughly given distance, say between six inches and two yards on the other side. Not even jumpers in athletic contests desire merely to jump and not to jump any given distance. Even if the object of desire were merely to jump, this would not show that what is desired is 'willing' to jump. What the jumper (in the example) desires is to jump some distance, to accomplish which he sees that he must exert his will in a great degree. Presumably Prichard would wish to describe this as a desire of great 'willing'. But if the great 'willing' is only a means to clearing the ditch, the jumper will not desire the great 'willing' unless he greatly desires to clear the ditch. The correct description of the case would be as follows. The jumper desires to clear the ditch; he sees that to clear the ditch he *must* exert his will greatly or try hard; so he *does* try hard. Will and effort are means to the satisfying of a desire.

There is then nothing to show that 'willing' is a special sort of activity requiring a desire for itself as distinct from a desire for the objective we pursue in action. To apply this directly to our attempt, in holding people responsible, to influence them by judgments of praise and blame — what we intend to influence in this way is just their desire to perform the right acts, and not their desire to *try* to perform these actions. We suppose that if we can sufficiently influence their desire for the acts, this will lead the person to *try* to do these acts.

5. *The Capacity to Try as a Universal Condition of Responsibility*

The crucial question with which we are left is whether 'willing' in the sense of 'trying' can serve, as the Libertarian claims 'will' serves, as a universal condition of responsibility. Plainly it cannot. For the capacity to will, as the universal condition of responsibility, must exist in all persons equally in their moments of moral choice. The Libertarian says that will does exist in this way. But in all senses of 'will' except one, 'willing' does exist in degrees. This one sense is that of 'intention'. Intention is a universal condition of responsibility, but it does not seem that the Libertarian means by 'will' merely 'intend'.

Now it would be odd that, when other capacities vary so greatly among persons, they should not vary in this one capacity. But the Libertarian makes two sorts of claims. One is that we are introspectively certain that we do have a capacity of free will. The other is that we hold people responsible, and praise and blame them, on the assumption that they have this capacity. Both of these statements distort what we actually find.

Let us consider whether we are introspectively aware of an unlimited capacity of will in any of the five senses of 'will' mentioned earlier. It is clear that we do not think we are capable of (5) overtly doing anything whatsoever — we are obviously limited by physical circumstances. Nor do we think we are capable of (4) desiring anything whatsoever. Indeed most things are ones for which we are capable only of aversion or indifference. (2) Intention is something of which we may always become aware in moral choice, but it would not seem to be simply this that the Libertarian means by 'free will', and if it is there is no dispute. (The subject of intention and responsibility is taken up in a later chapter.) As regards (3) choosing, it may seem that we are able to choose to do anything at all which we believe possible. It may seem that if I now consider acts which it is possible for me to perform, I am able to choose to perform any of them. But this is a mistake. It is physically possible for me to take my desk scissors and cut off my little finger. But I am incapable of choosing to do this. Anyone else can think of choices which he is incapable of making. But we shall consider the ability to choose in detail in the next chapter.

This leaves us with the notion of (1) trying. The Libertarian might say that although any person is incapable of choosing certain things, once he has chosen anything he is indefinitely capable of trying to accomplish it. Professor Stuart Hampshire asserts that it is a 'truism to say "He can always try . . ."' But of course one could not try if he were unconscious or if he did not believe that he might succeed in doing what he tried to do. But even assuming these conditions, it is not true that one can always try. A person may in a particular activity reach a point where he says sincerely, 'I just cannot try any longer'. If someone replies, 'You simply don't want to try', the answer is: 'But I do want to try some more, for I want to accomplish what I might accomplish by trying'. And if the objector persists: 'But you don't want the thing you might accomplish by trying as much as you want to avoid trying. Trying is troublesome, if not actually painful. You just want to avoid the pain of trying . . .' — a conclusive rejoinder is, 'Supposing it true that I don't want to try any more, it is still the case that I cannot try any more. For I know that I cannot do whatever is required for continuing to try.'

Thus trying cannot be a universal condition of responsibility. In some particular case, whether a right act is done may depend on whether a person tries hard enough. But if trying is a universal condition of responsibility, then we are all equally able to try in cases of moral choice, and we will all be equally responsible for an act that depends on trying. But we do not think that people are all equally able to try, or capable of trying in an indefinite degree. We think there are degrees of effort which no one is able to exert — for example, no one could be asked to exert the effort required to keep awake for several weeks. Moreover, we think it is possible for persons' wills to become paralyzed with respect to certain activities. We say they have 'phobias' or 'obsessions', thereby exempting them from responsibility, and recognizing that the way to influence their conduct is not by moral judgments. To respond to moral judgments, they must be capable of trying in a certain degree; but they are not capable. These cases are exceptional; most people can try to do anything which they think they can do. Hence it is reasonable to praise and blame them in order to stir them to exert effort toward doing the acts which are right. But we think people's wills are not of the same degree of strength, and we assess their responsibility in terms of this degree.

We can see what it is about trying which has made it seem plausible that we can always try, and which at the same time has made the concept morally central. This is that trying is (or at least appears) more labile than almost any other capacity, and in particular more responsive to praise and blame. Trying is something that we can be more readily led to do as a result of urging by others. Thus trying is a natural target for praise and blame. Exhortation cannot, on the spur of the moment, give us new physical or mental capacities, but it can give us a new impetus to effort. As cheering sections at athletic contests urge their teams to try harder, so we often praise and blame people for their moral behavior as a way of getting them to try to act properly. Thus such praise and blame of responsible acts presupposes some capacity to try in those judged.

Still the concept of will and trying is not entirely necessary to the concept of responsibility. For we also hold people responsible for acts, and praise and blame them for

R

acts, which may not require effort. The universal characteristic of acts to which we ascribe moral praise or blame is not that they are effortful, but only that they are intentional.[1]

[1] Some writers may have vaguely thought of 'willing' as a certain combination of intending and trying. This combination is suggested in Ross' favored phrase of 'setting oneself'. In ordinary life we use this phrase to mean something like an 'intending to try', as when one 'sets himself' to run, or to repel an attack. I think it is just possible that writers, in looking for a special act of will distinct from such things as intending and trying, have been looking for something that would combine certain features of both. Trying is a definite sort of activity, while intending is not. Being responsible would seem to have required always some condition, and this condition would seem to have been the performing of a certain kind of internal act. So writers have looked for an 'act of Will' which would be, like intending, present wherever responsibility was present, while still being an identifiable act, like trying. This attempt to combine intending and trying is considered in some detail in the chapter on Intention.

CHAPTER VIII

CHOICE

ANOTHER capacity which has often been said to be a necessary condition of responsibility is the capacity to choose. It may indeed seem obvious that we can only be responsible for acts which we choose or are able to choose. But I shall try to show that this is a mistake. Choosing, like willing, is only on some occasions a condition of responsibility. What responsibility always requires is an ability to act.

Choosing, though a less unusual sort of activity and ability than willing, is yet in need of analysis. Some writers have wanted to interpret the ability to will as the same as the ability to choose. Writers at the other extreme, who have wanted to deny anything at all like 'free will', have interpreted choosing as the same or as necessarily entailing the sort of action which I shall call an action on choice. In actual use 'choice' sometimes is an equivalent of these words, 'willing' and 'acting', as it is also sometimes an equivalent of 'desire' and 'intend'. However, its meaning is distinct from all of them. Its use in the sense of 'desire' and 'intend' does not raise special problems with regard to responsibility, while the other uses do. Our problem is to show that choosing is a distinct sort of activity and ability; but that it is a describable and natural one, not something quite special, like the Libertarian notion of 'free will'. This will correct the error of those who treat choosing as the same as acting, and who thus regard any question whether a person in some distinct sense chose or was able to choose as quite irrelevant to the question of responsibility. It will also correct the opposite error of those Libertarians who think this always a relevant question as concerns responsibility. I shall argue that choosing and the ability to choose are not, like acting and the unrestricted ability to act, a universal condition of responsibility; but that they are, like the ability to reason or to walk, conditions which are sometimes conditions of the unrestricted ability to act, and are in these cases relevant to responsibility.

1. *Acting and Choosing*

Writers who treat choosing and acting as the same as regards responsibility,[1] do not always make it clear whether they think there is just one ability going by two names (an 'ability to choose' and an 'ability to act') or whether they think there is a difference, but the difference is not relevant to responsibility. But plainly there is a difference, however narrowly we understand 'acting'. It is true that choosing is closely related to acting. To choose a given alternative entails *beliefs* that one *can* act in the given way and that one *will* act in this way. But to choose these acts does not entail performing them. For both these beliefs about one's action may prove mistaken; and one can choose without later acting on the choice. Likewise one can act without having chosen, as when one acts on impulse, not considering the thing done as one among several alternatives.

Further, one can act on an earlier choice, without choosing to act at the moment of action. Suppose one chooses to go to a concert in the evening. In the meantime he may reconsider and choose again. But unless something unforeseen arises, the earlier choice is enough. He will review his choice, or recall it, only if circumstances change, or if he has a change of feeling. He has chosen, and when the time comes he acts. If acting always did involve choosing — if going to the concert required a new choice in the evening to act on the afternoon's choice — then when would the choosing stop ? When the concert had begun ? No, for until the concert is over it is always possible to recall the choice. But an urge constantly to review choices is a symptom of mental disturbance, not a part of normal behavior. (Just as it is abnormal never to choose anew but to go ahead with what one has previously chosen, however radical the change that may have inter-

---

[1] See, for example, Francis Raab, 'Free Will and the Ambiguity of "Could" ' (*The Philosophical Review*, 1955, pp. 60 ff., esp. pp. 60 and 71) ; and P. H. Nowell-Smith, *Ethics*, p. 101.

vened.) Thus we often do act on choice, without choosing to act at the moment of action.

That acting and choosing differ is further evident in the fact that the same kind of act may be done either from choice or not from choice, and that, in order to know whether this act was done from choice, one must do something more than observe *what* is done — he must, at the very least, observe *how*, or in what manner, it is done. It is not necessary here to raise the question whether there is a class of acts not open to public observation. Let us suppose, for the present argument, that there are not — that choice always shows behavioral symptoms. Still these symptoms of a choice are distinguishable from the act chosen. For these symptoms require careful observation, and may be missed, when the act itself is obvious. Further, the symptoms will be similar in cases of choice in which the specific acts chosen differ. To act from choice, then, is not just the same as to act.

Also, being 'able to choose' and 'able to act' are not the same. But the matter is complicated. We have seen that we use 'able' generally in two senses, the personal and the situational. Further, there are conditions for each of these modes of any kind of ability, and both sets of conditions vary from one kind of ability to another — the personal and situational conditions of the ability to run differ, for example, from these conditions for the ability to drink. However it may seem odd to regard 'choosing' as an ability. I think it may be this apparent oddity that has caused writers to identify choosing with acting on choice. It is plain, however, that choosing is an ability. For some persons are better at choosing than others, and some are afflicted with a peculiar inability to choose — they can never make up their minds. What causes confusion is that there is only a personal, not a situational mode of the ability to choose. For there are no situational conditions for the exercise of the ability. In this respect choosing is like thinking, imagining and wishing. Situational events outside the person may, in some sense, encourage or discourage the exercise of these abilities; but no external circumstances can absolutely obstruct their exercise, as they can obstruct the exercise of the ability to run. Thus what we mean when we say 'we give you a choice' is not that we give you a situational opportunity to exercise an ability which you were utterly unable to exercise before, but rather that we give you an opportunity to exercise the ability with respect to a specific set of alternatives which were not available before. We are not saying: 'Here we are giving you the opportunity to exercise your ability to choose', as when, taking the chains from your legs, we say 'Here we are giving you the opportunity to exercise the ability to run'. For you were able to choose (though not the particular alternatives we present) before we set these alternatives before you, while you were not able to run at all before we unbound you.

We do none the less use 'able to choose' in a situational sense, and this use causes trouble. We often say 'You are able to choose' in the above sense of 'We give you a choice'. We mean, not that you have this personal ability nor that the situation allows you to exercise it, but that 'You are able to *act* in any of several ways', or 'You are able to act on your choice'. Suppose a person, being offered a choice of alternatives, says, 'Give me anything'; but then objects to what he is given; whereupon we retort: 'Well you could have chosen'. What we mean is that he could have done a different thing — if he had chosen to do it.[1] Our reason for saying he is 'able to choose' is that we think of his act as following on his choice. We think of it so, for we have drawn his attention to several alternatives, and ordinarily a person does not simply take one at random but considers these and then chooses. The full statement of our thought here is: 'You are able to act in whichever of these several ways you choose'.

Thus we do frequently use the phrase 'able to choose' as the equivalent of 'able to act', or 'able to act on choice',

---

[1] We might here say that the person 'chose not to choose' but this would be misleading. For we may not know whether or not the person chose. He may have said by impulse, 'Give me anything'; he may not have considered and chosen whether or not to make a specific request. And making a specific request is not choosing: it is, at the most, uttering a choice. Similarly, taking one of the pastries from a platter is not choosing to take one; it may be just taking one.

and this encourages us to confuse the two. But we can see that they differ. First, being 'able to choose' does not entail being 'able to act on the choice'. It only entails one's believing that he is 'able to act on the choice'. Second, being 'able to act' does not entail being 'able to choose'. There are two possibilities. One may be able to do an act, and be able to choose the act, but be unable to do the act when he chooses it. For example, one may be able to write on a typewriter rapidly and accurately, and be able to choose to do this, but be able to do it only when he does not choose to do it. Or one may be able to do the act but be unable to choose it (or then to do it from choice). This is the condition of persons neurotically compulsive or anxious. Either they cannot deliberate; or if they deliberate, they cannot decide. The character of Hamlet is a clear example. Hamlet could not decide to kill Claudius, though (as A. C. Bradley shows) he was quite able to kill people, including Claudius, when an emergency aroused his disposition to overt action rather than his disposition to meditate on action.

The ability to choose involves an ability to think and deliberate, and an ability to come to a decision. It is not a simple conjunction of two separate abilities of deliberating and deciding, but rather an ability to deliberate in such a way as to come to a decision. We may deliberate without choosing, but not conversely. 'Decide' is sometimes used as synonymous for 'choose', but it more readily suggests the concluding phase of choice, which follows deliberation; while 'choose' suggests the whole process. Deliberation is a preliminary to deciding; it is a part of choosing.[1] Hamlet deliberated, but could not decide, hence could not choose.

A choice thus involves a (A) deliberating and a (B) deciding. And it is usually followed by (C) an act of carrying out the decision. Now in particular cases we may use 'choice' to mean (A); (B); (C); (A) and (B); (B) and (C); or (A), (B) and (C). Contexts sometimes make

---

[1] The term 'decisive' may cause confusion, for we may speak of a person or an act as 'decisive', when what is meant is not that the person makes a decision or that the act comes from a decision, but only that the act is firm and definite. So a person may be 'decisive' when he has not 'decided'.

clear a stress on one of these. If we say, 'He went off by himself in order to choose a course of action', we stress the aspect of deliberation. 'He chose rightly', stresses the decision. 'He chose a professional career', stresses the resultant act. 'He arrived at the choice of a professional career', distributes stress almost equally among all three. But other occurrences of 'choice' and 'able to choose' may not clearly indicate such stresses, and this may cause confusion. The confusion of (A) and (B) is not serious. For unless both are present, we seldom use the word 'choose' or 'choice' without qualification. If a person deliberated but reached no decision, we would probably say, 'He began to make a choice, but did not arrive at a conclusion'. And there is no great danger of confusing (B) decision and (A) deliberation, since unless the decision was reached by deliberation we would qualify it in a special way, as in the phrase 'snap decision'. But the confusion of 'choice' as including both (A) deliberating and (B) deciding, with 'choice' as meaning the (C) resultant act, is serious. It occurs easily and leads to mistakes about the conditions of responsibility, as we shall see.

2. *Responsibility and the Ability to Choose*

We have now to consider how the personal ability to choose concerns responsibility. First, the responsible act need not be the result of choice. A person cannot be responsible for an act done unintentionally or in ignorance; but to do an act intentionally or knowingly is not the same as to choose to do it. For a person may know what he is doing, and know that he cannot do anything else, and know further that he cannot choose (deliberate and decide) to do it or anything else. Further, a person may know what he is doing, and be able to do something else, yet not choose to do what he does. For example, one person may strike another, but not choose to strike him. He simply never has a thought of not striking him. He observes an offense, and strikes the offender. He may strike coolly and 'deliberately', like a Western cowboy; but still he does not consider or think or deliberate about striking. He just knows what to do and he does it.

Second, a responsible act need not be one that the person is 'able to choose'. In some cases being able to do an act requires being able to choose it, while in other cases it does not. In the case above the person strikes another and is responsible even though he does not choose to strike and even though, were he like Hamlet, he would have been unable to choose to strike. On the other hand, the act may have required his being able to choose it, and he may be excused from responsibility because he was unable to choose it. Maybe he ought to have struck, but began to consider whether he ought, and being unable to choose to do the act, he was unable to do the act; and in that case perhaps he is not to blame. In short, the universal condition of responsibility is being able to do the responsible act, and only in some cases does this involve an ability to choose.

The general independence as regards responsibility of the ability to choose and the ability to act can be brought out by considering the expression and the argument which are ordinarily used by those who say that responsibility requires an 'ability to choose'. What they say is that 'to be responsible the person must have been able to choose differently'. The 'differently' here is odd. A substitute phrase would be 'able to choose in a different way'. Now 'in a different way' might mean either (a) 'in a different manner or style or method' or (b) 'a different alternative'. By (a), we might have in mind something such as slow or rapid ways of choosing, systematic or haphazard ways, or something of the sort. But in ascribing responsibility what one has in mind is obviously not this but (b), that the person could have chosen a different alternative. But then the expression is odd. For if one wants to say just that the person 'was able to choose a different alternative', all he need say is that the person 'was able to choose'. The rest is redundant; to be 'able to choose' is to be 'able to choose among different alternatives', and conversely. In reference to a present choice, we would simply say to a person 'You are able to choose'; we would only bring in the mention of different alternatives if we went on to specify what they were. But with reference to past choices the statement is commonly made, 'You could have chosen differently'. What could it mean ? It must mean more than 'You could have chosen'; for this suggests that the person did not choose, while 'You could have chosen differently' suggests that he did choose. But again if we only want to say that the person *did* choose, why speak of what he might have done ? Evidently what we intend by 'He could have chosen differently' would not be conveyed by either 'He was able to choose' or 'He did choose'. Nor can we mean just a combination including both of these, for then we would just say that 'He did choose'; this would imply that he was able to choose. The only meaning that remains is (1) 'He could have *acted* differently, if he had chosen to do so'; and it is evidently a case of condensation which leads us to substitute (2) 'He could have chosen differently'. That this is the case is seen in that we sometimes make the condensation by substituting in the other direction, saying (3) 'He could have acted differently'. The three sentences are regularly used as equivalent. But while the first and third do not mislead, the second has led to the philosophic confusion of supposing that there is a special 'ability to choose' different both from the ability to act according to choice and the ability to deliberate and decide.

Let us put the point more summarily. To ask, 'Could he have chosen differently ?' is evidently to imply that the person did choose. But if the person did choose, then plainly he was able to choose; and if able to choose, then able to choose differently. The question then is not genuine; its very statement contains its answer. What the asking of the question exhibits is the questioner's confusion of choice and action. On the one hand, he knows that a 'choice' occurred, meaning here by 'choice' an act of the sort that sometimes results from choice. But he wants to know whether in this case the act did or could have resulted from choice. It would be absurd to put his question strictly: 'Could the choice have come from choice ?' Instead he asks the less obviously absurd : 'Could he have chosen differently ?' To replace this confused question we distinguish five clear ones. (1) 'Could he have acted in a different way ?' (2) 'Could he have chosen (deliberated

and decided)?' (3) 'Could he have chosen (deliberated
and decided) *specifically* something different?' (4) 'Could
he have acted differently, and chosen to act, and chosen
specifically something different?' (5) 'Could he have acted
differently, and chosen to act, and chosen specifically something different, and acted differently as a result of choosing
differently?' The failure to distinguish these causes
trouble, and particularly the failure to distinguish (1)
and (3).

We get a clear picture of this trouble in the case of
G. E. Moore. In the *Ethics* (1912) Moore proposed that
the rightness or wrongness of an act turned just on whether
the act was 'voluntary' or a matter of 'choice' in the sense
of there being several 'different actions, any one of which
we could do, *if* we chose'. But in 1942 he was convinced
that the moral wrongness of an act depended upon the
further condition of the person's being 'able to choose
some other action instead'.[1] He credited his changed
conviction to the arguments of Professor A. C. Garnett,
who asks us to imagine the following case. Suppose that
a neighbor while watering his lawn accidently turns the
hose on the parched rose bush of the person next door,
then allows the water to continue to flow on the plant.
'Now suppose that this neighbor were afflicted with a compulsion neurosis that made it psychologically impossible for
him to exercise the choice to interfere with accidental
situations of this kind. It would still be possible for him
to turn the hose back on his own lawn *if* he so chose;
so, on Mr. Moore's definition, the action would still be
voluntary and right.'[2] It seemed plain to Garnett and
Moore that such an act would not have the kind of voluntariness necessary for moral rightness.

But the whole thing is very confused. Notice first the
confusion in Garnett's language. He speaks of it being
impossible for the person to 'exercise the choice' to interfere with such situations. This suggests that the person
has a choice, but cannot exercise it. But if the person made

[1] *The Philosophy of G. E. Moore*, ed. by P. A. Schilpp, Northwestern
University Press, p. 624.
[2] *Op. cit.* p. 184.

a choice, or did choose, it would be pointless of Garnett to suspect him of having not been able to choose. What Garnett's statement must mean is that the situation provides the opportunity for changing the hose, but that the person has not the personal ability to make use of this opportunity. Garnett is evidently misled by the ambiguity of 'choice', which he here uses in the sense not of the act of deliberating and deciding, but of a possible resultant act, while by '*exercise* the choice' he might mean either 'do the act' or 'choose the act' or both. His account of the gardener's case does not make clear what his inability is — whether of action or choice or both. But all that is evident is that the gardener cannot *interfere* with accidental situations, not that he cannot *choose* to interfere with them.

In any event we can see that the ability to choose (deliberate and decide) is not a necessary or sufficient condition for judging the gardener's act morally right or wrong. Rather the necessary and sufficient condition is that the person be able to act, and that he know what he is doing. For first, we would withdraw our judgment of the act's rightness just on the basis of knowing he is unable to act. In the example it is the *act* which the gardener evidently cannot perform. He cannot act to change the hose, even though the situation allows it. It may also be that he cannot choose such acts, but there is nothing in the example to show this. It is quite conceivable that he could deliberate and decide to interfere in such cases, but could not bring himself to do it. But we would then still withdraw the judgment on the basis of knowing just the person's inability to act. Second, we would affirm the judgment on the basis of knowing just the person's ability to act. Suppose the gardener were able to move the hose, and did so knowingly but not after deliberation. He saw what was happening, knew it was a good thing and let it happen. He did not consider alternatives and choose. This lack of choice would not lead us to withdraw our judgment of the act's rightness. But third, if the ability to choose were necessary to the act, and if the person were unable to choose, then we should not judge the act morally right or wrong. Suppose the gardener cannot choose —

either because he cannot bear to think about moving hoses, or because he cannot decide what to do about them. And suppose that this is why he does not move the hose. Then he is unable to act because he is not able to choose, and we exempt him from moral judgment, not because he could not choose, but because he could not act.

We always exempt from judgment a person who does not know what he is doing or who cannot do anything else. Garnett's gardener seems to know what he is doing. But we are told he could not act otherwise. Whether he could have chosen to act otherwise, the account does not show. Whether he could have chosen would depend upon how aware he was of his inability. If a person knows he cannot do a thing, then he cannot deliberate about doing it — one can deliberate about doing only what he thinks possible. (Of course he might fantasize about it, but that is not deliberation.) But Garnett does not tell us whether the gardener knew about his compulsion. Nor do we need to know this or whether he did choose or could choose. For to exempt him from moral judgment we only need to know that he could not act.

It is true that some particular responsible act may depend upon an ability to choose, just as a particular responsible act may depend upon other mental abilities, such as remembering. We may say that someone was obligated to remember that he had an appointment; this obligatory act would require an ability to remember, as well as whatever other abilities are conditions of remembering. Similarly an act may require as one of its conditions an ability to choose — to deliberate and decide. In a given case the crucial ability may be either. It may be difficult or impossible to deliberate, or only difficult or impossible to decide; and in either case it will be difficult or impossible to choose. Specifically, the act in question may be of a sort that will be done only if the person thinks of doing it, and of a sort that is hard to discover, such that if the person is unable to deliberate, he will be unable to discover this act. For example, suppose the act is one of rescuing a person in distress, and that this person is difficult to reach and can be reached only by combining various means.

This particular combination could be discovered only if the agent were able to deliberate about these means and to decide on one of them. He may be unable to do the act either because he cannot deliberate or because, having deliberated and thought of several alternative possible ways of rescue, he cannot decide to attempt one of them. The doing of this act thus requires an ability to pass through both phases of choice. And if the person were unable to do so we would excuse him.[1] Similarly, in the case of Garnett's gardener the act may have required an ability to choose. The act would have required this ability only if the gardener had considered whether to water the plant as one of several alternatives. Had he begun to choose, then he could have done the act (unless by chance) only by deciding to do it. In the latter case the responsible and morally praiseworthy act would have required an ability to choose. Thus the ability to choose is a condition of responsibility in those cases where the deliberative phase of choosing is necessary to discover the act to be done, or where, whether necessary or not, the person, having already begun to choose, can only arrive at the performance of the act (unless by chance) by deciding on its performance.

We conclude then that the ability to choose is sometimes, but not always, required for responsibility. In this respect the ability to choose is on a par with any other ability, as the abilities to speak, to run, to remember, to imagine, to reason. Any such ability will be necessary when it is necessary to the ability to act. Which abilities are necessary depends upon the particular act to be done. If the act can be done without the agent's deliberating and deciding, then an ability to choose is not necessary to it; just as if the act to be done is to speak, an ability to run is not necessary to it. Some abilities always require other abilities. Speaking involves an ability to move the tongue in certain ways; choosing involves an ability to think. But being able to act in the unrestricted sense does not in

---

[1] Conceivably the act might be done by accident or chance — the person might, without deliberation or choice, hit on the right means of rescue. But no one would regard such an act as obligatory — no one would say that a person was obligated to perform a rescue when the only way he could do so was by chance or accident.

general entail any other specific abilities, but always entails only whatever specific abilities are required for the specific act in question.

This shows a way toward settling the differences between the Libertarians and their opponents. Their opponents are right in saying that responsibility always requires just an ability to do the responsible act. But they err in treating the ability to act as just the same, with respect to responsibility, as an ability to choose. They thereby give aid to the Libertarians, by enabling them to make a strong appeal in pointing to the fact that we do have a distinct ability to choose. The Libertarians then go on to make the capacity something both more special and more universal than it is, treating it as a kind of momentary power which descends on us like an inspiration, not out of the past but out of the demands of the moment, and on all the needy alike. A thing so wonderful and so unlike every other human ability cannot be adjusted to what we know of nature and ourselves. An ability to deliberate and decide, on the other hand, is perfectly familiar, and provides a necessary requirement for responsibility in some cases, but by no means in all.

CHAPTER IX

INTENTION

INTENTION is, like the ability to act, a universal condition of responsibility. A person is not morally responsible for an act if he did not intend it. And if he did intend it, and was able to act otherwise, then he is responsible. It makes sense to hold persons responsible only for what they do intentionally; for we hold persons responsible in order to influence them, and our judgments of responsibility are designed to influence only their intentional action.

So much, I think, would be accepted by common sense. But there are also apparent exceptions which would be commonly accepted. For instance, if one is so immersed in his thoughts that he unintentionally drives through a traffic signal, we might be inclined to say that he was responsible, even though acting without intention. To get clear on these matters we shall have first to get clear on what we mean by intention, and this will be a rather long inquiry. This done, it will be fairly simple to see how intention relates to responsibility.

A minor preliminary is to distinguish the 'intentional' from the 'voluntary'. The intentional is one of the conditions of the voluntary: an act can be intentional without being voluntary, as when one is coerced; but it cannot be voluntary without being intentional. However, this latter may seem wrong. Aristotle refers to 'voluntary passions'; and one frequently speaks of things which simply happen to him as 'voluntary'. In her book *Intention* Miss Anscombe uses the example of a person who finds himself drifting out on the lake, and who 'voluntarily' continues to drift. It would be a bit odd to say that he 'intentionally' continued to drift.

But suppose that, by allowing himself to drift, the person will miss an appointment. It would be quite in order to ask: 'Is it your intention to continue drifting?'

The reason that the first use seems odd is that 'intention' is thought to belong to an act, while allowing oneself to drift does not seem to be an act. But in an important sense it is an act, just as pretending not to hear what someone says is an act. The difference between the notion of 'intentionally' and the particular sense here of 'voluntarily' is that 'intentionally' refers to something that a person does, while 'voluntarily' here refers to one's attitude of acceptance toward the event, whether it be something that he does or merely something that happens to him. The difference between 'He did it voluntarily' and 'He did it involuntarily' is that the former implies acceptance of the event, while the latter implies resistance. Whereas the difference between 'He did it intentionally' and 'He did it unintentionally' is that the former implies a correspondence between what he did and his thought of what he did, and the latter implies a discordance between these.

We can now consider what sort of thing it is that one intends.

1. *We are Responsible only for Present Intentions*

We use 'intend' in two quite different senses, which I shall call the 'strict' and 'loose' senses. In the strict sense one 'intends' only a present act of his own, while in the loose sense he 'intends' also external events, including acts by others. The loose sense is also expressed by the verb 'aims' (and by the nouns 'purpose', 'end', 'objective'). The loose sense is usually meant when we use the noun 'intention', the strict sense when we use the adverb 'intentionally' or the adjective 'intentional'. Suppose we see a person sprinkling the lawn. If we ask: (1) 'What are you intending to do?' with the sense of: 'What is your intention?' we mean to ask about his aim or purpose. We do not want him to answer that he is sprinkling water or that he is holding the hose in a certain position. We can see that he is doing this. We want to know what event he foresees as a result of his sprinkling — what is his aim or purpose. Suppose now, noticing an absent expression on his face, we ask the same question: (2) 'What are you intending to do?' with the sense of 'Are you watering the

s

lawn intentionally?' Here we want to know about his thought of the act itself. Both questions (1) and (2) might be regarded as questions about the person's thoughts. In one case the question is about his thought of what will come from (and what he desires to come from) what he is doing. In the other, it is about his thought of what he is now doing. It is evident that these two — 'intentions' and 'purposes' — are different. We cannot have a purpose in an act unless the act is intentional (though this is not to say that we do not have unconscious 'motives'); but we can intend to do an act for which we have no extrinsic purpose. In answer to question (1), the person may say: 'I don't exactly have an "intention"; I just enjoy sprinkling'.

Thus one intends an external event only in the sense that this event is one's purpose in acting. I intend to sprinkle water on the grass; my purpose is, ultimately, that the grass grow. It is the same when we have intentions with respect to other persons. If I order someone to open the window, it is in one sense (the strict sense) that I intend to give him the order and in another sense (the loose sense) that I 'intend him' to obey it. His obeying it is usually my purpose in giving the order. (My purpose might also be to get him to disobey the order, so that I would have grounds for punishing him.)

The oddest feature of the strict concept of intend is that it rules out 'intentions' for the future. If I cannot strictly 'intend' an event external to my present intentional act, then I cannot intend a future act of my own. We do commonly speak of intentions for the future, and I do not want to change that way of speaking; but I do want to stress the differences between these and a present intentional act.

First, we can see that there is an important difference between our 'intending' ('purposing') external events (like the grass growing and the acts of others in obeying our order), and our 'intending' ('purposing') our own future acts. The difference is that when I intend others to act in the future I need not intend that they act intentionally, while when I intend a future act of my own I must intend that this future act be intentional. My purpose in getting someone else to act need not be to get him to act intentionally, but only to get him to act. But it would not make sense to say I intend to do something which I do not intend to do intentionally. If, for example, I say 'I intend to stay awake until 4 A.M', what I must mean is that 'I intend to do (intentionally) whatever is necessary to stay awake until 4 A.M. (as to drink coffee at regular intervals)'.

We do use 'intend' in ways which seem to belie this, but these uses are vague or confused. A person may say that he 'intends' to waken at 7 A.M.; but it is hard to know what 'intends' means here. This waking would not seem to be in the person's power, and a person cannot intend to do something which he does not feel will be in his power to do. He can intend to try to do a thing; but it is even harder to see what one could mean by saying he intends to try to waken at 7 A.M. What the person would seem to mean here is that he 'hopes' or 'expects' to waken at 7 A.M. But intending in any standard use is not the same as either hoping or predicting. Neither of these entails that the person will do anything to bring the event about, while 'intending' does entail this.

There is an oddity in saying that one intends to do an act intentionally, and even more in saying that one intends to intend to do an act. But there is no great difficulty about it (any more than about one's choosing to choose, or desiring to desire, in the future). The oddity is in that the expression 'to intend to intend' suggests that the person is now only half-intending — that he is already preparing an excuse in case in the future he should need one. The fact is that it is rare to mention the intentional character of any acts. There is no reason to mention it. It can be assumed, for ordinarily what we do is intentional. We mention intention when there is some reason to doubt its presence. But in intending a future act there would be no reason to doubt that it will be done intentionally; accordingly it would be odd to mention it.

We can now observe the difference between an intention for the present (or a present intentional act) and an intention for the future. It is that an intention or purpose for the future does not require a thought of the act intended at the moment when one has the intention. One can now intend to go to the bank tomorrow without having any present thought of going to the bank tomorrow. Suppose one earlier considered whether to go and decided to go. Then it would be correct to say that now he does intend to go, even though going is the farthest thing from his present thoughts. But one could not intend to do some present act which was the farthest thing from his thoughts.

The distinction between present intentions and intentions for the future has a bearing on responsibility. I have said that we hold a person responsible only for his intentional acts; and I have now argued that in the strict sense an intention is an intention of a present act, not of a future one. But it may appear that we hold persons responsible not merely for their present intentions but for their intentions for the future — their purposes. For we do say that a person is to blame for entertaining a bad purpose, as well as for acting to realize such a purpose. I suggest, however, that in such cases what we blame a person for is just his present intentional act of forming and entertaining and acting to realize the purpose. We blame him for intentionally dwelling upon a bad desire and for developing the desire into a purpose. A purpose is a present thought of (or disposition towards) a future action. We cannot blame a person for a future action, for the future action does not exist. Nor can we blame him for his present desire, or for his thought of the thing desired or his thought that he desires it, in so far as these are beyond his control. But we do blame him for forming the purpose of gratifying the desire. And the forming of this purpose is a present intentional act.

2. *Acting Intentionally is Acting Knowingly*

To act intentionally is to know what one is doing. Intending is not merely knowing what events one is engaged in — what is happening to one. Nor is it merely engaging in a certain event — merely 'doing' something. It is doing something knowingly. It is the knowledge one has of his action at the moment of action. However, it is misleading to say that it is knowing in a particular way, and also misleading to say that it is behaving in a particular way. For knowing of every other sort does not necessarily entail acting, nor does acting of any other sort entail knowing. This particular sort of knowing is inseparable from acting, and this particular sort of acting is inseparable from knowing.

My intending to do something is the same as my thinking that I am doing it. My intention is the thought I have of my action. (This is not a reduction of 'intention', for the concepts of 'self', 'action' and 'effecting a change' are no clearer or more elementary than the concept of intention ; but it is an explication of the concepts that are involved in the concept of intention.) It is not my action, for my action is an effecting of a change. My intending to do something, say to think clearly, is not my doing it ; for I may, while intending to think clearly, fail to do so. But my thinking I am *doing* it is my intending to do it. 'My doing' here must be taken strictly, as distinct from my having something 'happening' to me. If my hand kept shaking, despite my efforts to control it, my thinking my hand was shaking would not be my intending to shake it. But my hand's shaking is here not something I do, as would be my shaking of my hand. If I do *think* I am shaking my hand, then I am intending to shake it. It would be nonsense to say 'I think I am shaking my hand, but I am not intending to shake it'. My intention is my thought of the change which I am effecting.

We might, then, analyze (a) : 'I am intending to do X' as (b) : 'I am now doing X, unless X is not happening'. To be 'intending to do X' is in some sense to be 'doing X' but it is not necessarily for 'X to be happening'. Certainly it is paradoxical to say 'I did X but X did not happen' or 'I was doing X but X was not happening', but this is because 'do' is used in two very different senses, in the senses of 'intending the event X' and of 'accomplishing the event X'. We might be tempted to try to evade this appearance of paradox by substituting 'attempting' for 'doing' in (b). But this will not work. For we intend many things which involve no attempt. One can attempt only something in which there is a possibility of failure, while he can intend things which he is perfectly certain of accomplishing. There is no word other than 'doing' which comes close to the meaning of intend. (Except 'trying', which we will consider later.)

Consider the following dialogue. A: 'What are you now doing?' B: 'I am thinking clearly.' A: 'But you are not thinking clearly.' B: 'Well, anyway that is my intention.' A: 'It may be your intention, but you aren't doing it.' B: 'But if I am doing anything, and I am doing something, I am doing that.' A: 'You're not. You may be having thoughts and uttering words, but they aren't at all clear.' B: 'I am certainly intending to do more than that, though that may be all that is happening.' A: 'But can you *do* anything more than is happening?' B: 'Well certainly I can intend to do more, and if intending is a doing or a part of a doing, then, yes, I can do more than what is happening. And if intending is not a doing or a part of doing, and as you certainly argue, not a happening, what is it?'

We cannot answer here that it is just a thought of what one is doing, unless we insist on understanding 'doing' in the sense distinct from 'what is happening'; for intending is not a thought of what is happening to oneself. What we arrive at is that intending involves in a unique sort of relation the concepts of the person who acts, the thought he has of his action, and the action itself. Intending is *his* acting, and his *acting*, and his *knowing* (or thinking) he is acting. The concept of intending requires taking each of these concepts in the special sense in which it involves the others. If we take one concept — action, person, or thought — in the inappropriate sense (taking 'action' to mean the event accomplished, or 'thought' to mean the mere cognitive view, or 'person' to mean body), then the formula will be false. Intending is a conscious-personal-action.

The presence of these other concepts in intention is evident in that we may substitute for the word 'intentionally' words for these other concepts. Suppose a person, hit by a falling object, himself falls and hurts another. We may say, (1) 'He didn't do it *intentionally*', or (2) 'He didn't do it *consciously* (or deliberately)', or (3) '*He* "really" didn't do it; something pushed him', or (4) 'He didn't "really" *do* it; it just happened'. (1) is by far the clearest, most explicit, and literal of these descriptions. The others extend and specialize the meanings of 'conscious', 'he' and 'do'. This process of extending meaning is apparent in the need for the term 'really' to qualify these terms. Here we see the metaphysical process in operation. We stipulate a use of one term which prohibits its use without a second term. We stipulate, in effect, that one is not permitted to use the term 'he' or 'act' where he cannot also use the term 'intend' or 'intentional'. But although we can stipulate, we cannot enforce the stipulations, and they are generally ignored. A better method is to adopt the most standard term for the thing in question, then show how it involves the other terms which are sometimes used as its equivalents.

The most striking peculiarity of this element of knowledge in intention is that it is not based on observation. As Anscombe has said, one does not 'look and see' what his intention is, nor does he infer this.[1] This differentiates intention from bodily events, such as internal changes which are not directly observable, and also from past or future actions which are based on inference. From evidence a person may infer what he has done and will do. But it is not from evidence that he states what he intends to do. Suppose one says: 'I will get drunk tomorrow night'. This cannot be both a prediction based on inference from past behavior and also a statement of intention.

Another feature of intention is that the person who has the intention is in a privileged position for saying what his intention is. A person can know what he is doing in a way that no one else can. He can be mistaken about what he is doing, but not about what he intends — what he thinks he is doing. His intention is this thought; while what he knows (in knowing his intention) is that he has this thought of what he is doing. But also, where this

---

[1] I am much indebted to Miss Anscombe's painstaking discussion of the concept in her short volume *Intention*, Cornell University Press, 1957.

belief that one has about what he is doing is true, it will be correct and convenient to speak of his 'knowing' what he is doing.

3. *Objections to the Preceding Account*

Several sorts of objections will be made to this account of intention as acting knowingly.

There is a preliminary question about the use of the word knowledge to describe the sort of awareness one has of his act in intention. Anscombe would disallow our speaking of a person's 'knowing his intentions', on the ground that a thing that can be known is the sort of thing about which one conceivably might be mistaken or doubtful, while it makes no sense to speak of being mistaken about one's intention. One can be mistaken about other people's intentions, and one can lie about his own intentions. But that is all. And one cannot be in doubt about his intention. He may be in doubt about what he will do, but then he has as yet no intention. Thus Anscombe holds that, in asserting that only the person himself 'knows his intention', the word 'knows' here means only 'can say'. 'Knowing' one's intention is like 'knowing' the location of one's pain (about which likewise one cannot, she supposes, be mistaken), and not like 'knowing' the position of one's leg (about which one can be mistaken). She provides, however, no argument to show that we should use knowledge in this restricted way, so as to disallow instances where there could be no doubt or mistake. Nor is it illuminating (as Professor Chisholm points out)[1] to substitute for 'know' here 'can say'. For what is involved is not just an ability to utter the words. Rather we mean that the person is in a position to tell us something which no one else is in such a good position to tell. If the choice is between intention's being something which the possessor alone can 'know' he has or can 'say' he has, 'know' seems the better choice. This is a dispute chiefly about the concept of knowledge, not about intention.

The critical objections to the formula that acting in-

[1] See his review of Anscombe's *Intention*, in *The Philosophical Review*, January 1959, p. 110 ff.

tentionally is acting knowingly are that (1) a person may
intend when he has no awareness of what he is doing, and
(2) he may be aware of what he is doing when he is not
acting intentionally.

First, it may seem that we can have intentions when we
have no knowledge or thought of what we are doing. It
may seem that we cannot discover this element in our
intentions in the way in which we can, say, discover in our
sensation of fear an empty sensation and a thought of
something dangerous. But is there this difference ? The
emotion of fear contains some sort of 'awareness' of the
empty sensation and the thought, but certainly one has no
explicit thought either of this emptiness or of the dangerous
object. One can recognize these elements later, but he
does not identify them explicitly during the experience.
Similarly in intention. One does not have explicit thoughts
of himself and of the event as something which he does, as
contrasted to a thought of the event as something which
merely happens. But he is able to recognize later that he
did know what he was doing. It is on these occasions, and
only on these occasions, that we say that a person acted
intentionally.

Second, it may seem that one may know what he is
doing when he is not acting intentionally. It might be
objected that, according to the present formula, it would
follow that in speaking one would be moving his lips intentionally, for he would know that his lips were moving.
But this premiss is false — that in speaking one knows his
lips are moving. One knows that when he speaks his lips
move ; and he knows at a given moment that he is speaking ; but at that moment he does not know that his lips are
moving, for he does not conjoin this knowledge of the
particular event (that he is speaking) with the knowledge
of the general principle (that in speaking lips move) to get
the conclusion that his lips move. This can be seen in
several ways. First, by *reductio ad absurdum* : if one did
know everything that he could validly infer as a conclusion
from what he knows is now happening, conjoined with the
general principles which he knows, then he would at any
moment be knowing about what he is now doing or what

is now happening an indefinite number of facts, which it seems absurd to think that one does know. For example, one would at this very moment of speaking be knowing all of the physiological conditions of speech which he might on reflection be able to state.

Someone may say that it is no more absurd to say that one now knows this than to say that he now knows whatever general principles of physiology which he could recite. There are two points. One is that what is odd about now knowing the particular physiological facts is that it involves not merely (a) the sort of direct awareness in which one knows that he is now speaking, and not merely (b) the latent possession of general principles, but (c) the inferring of a particular fact (as in (a)), which inferring would itself involve (d) an awareness of general principles. Thus it would involve the simultaneous functioning of several kinds of knowledge, and, what seems most strange, would involve the unconscious performance of a process of inference.[1]

But second, the argument is wrong in supposing that it does in this instance make sense to speak of our knowing general principles in the present moment (which knowledge would of course be necessary for us to know particular facts which were inferred from them). We can sensibly speak of (a) our now knowing, say, the general principles of physiology, but this is not to say that (b) we are knowing them in the present moment. We could appeal to (a) to indicate that the person had learned these principles, such that he 'now' knew them. But to say (b) would have to mean not this but that he was now knowing them, which in turn could only mean either that he was now contemplating them or inquiring about them. But in the case considered the person is not either contemplating or inquiring about these principles. He is neither doing what Aristotle would have us do with general principles, nor is he doing what the experimental scientist would do with such principles. Thus a reference to the present moment is of no relevance in an account of his knowledge of these

---

[1] I was much helped in the formulation of the answer to this objection by the suggestions during the course of an evening's discussion by Professors Donald Davidson, Ammon Goldworth and Herbert Morris.

general principles. The present moment does not give
them exercise, nor does the present situation give them
application. There is nothing about his knowing of the
principles which applies to the 'now'.

A person in 'knowing' what he is doing may, doubtless,
explicitly know general principles as a part of this knowledge of his action. He may know, in terms of a general
principle, that what he is now doing will have a particular
effect. But this shows the subordinate place of such
general knowledge in a person's knowledge of his action.
The action is particular; and it is this particular action
which is the chief part of what he knows. But it may
involve knowledge of principles in so far as he foresees
particular conditions and consequences of his action.

A similar objection is brought up in a case which Professor J. L. Austin presented in a lecture. Suppose a
person, being summoned to quell a riot, leaps in the car
and starts down the driveway. In the path he sees a
child's go-cart. If he stops to move the toy, he will lose
time; while if he does not stop, he will smash it. He does
not stop. Does he break the go-cart 'intentionally'? It is
plain that he knows what he is doing. But Professor Austin
seemed to believe that he did not do the act 'intentionally'.

Whether we agree with Austin, and say that a person
knows he is doing an act which yet he is not doing intentionally, depends on our deciding whether we shall
understand 'intend' with reference chiefly to the noun
'intention' or to the adjective 'intentional'. No one would
want to say that running over the go-cart was his 'specific
intention' or 'intention in acting'. But we would be
willing to say that he did still intend to run over it. We
could explain this by saying that he did know what he was
doing. Ordinary use would sanction our saying that anything which a person did knowingly he did intentionally;
but it clearly would forbid our saying of some such actions
that they were the person's intention or purpose or aim in
acting. An act is a complex of details and consequences:
some of these features of the act may be part of the person's specific intention; other features are recognized and
accepted but not desired (either because their absence is

desired or because the agent is indifferent to them); still other features are not recognized. Plainly the last features are not intended; and the second set are not a part of our 'intention' — but they nonetheless are intended. It is of course somewhat paradoxical to say that a person can do something intentionally which it is not his intention or 'intent' to do. But the paradox arises just out of the two quite distinct uses of 'intend' which we noted earlier, one use being drawn chiefly from the noun 'intention', the other from the adjective 'intentional'. We can perceive the same difference of meaning even in the phrases 'intention to do' and 'intention in acting'. If the person rushing to the riot deliberately runs over the go-cart, this feature of his action is something which we might plausibly say is his 'intention to do', but we could not say that it is his 'intention in acting'. Similarly, we might say that it was 'intentional'.

Whether we should ascribe intending to the act might seem to depend on when the person was asked about his act. Suppose afterwards someone asserts that he has broken the go-cart. He may then reply, 'But I didn't intend to break it; it just happened to be in my way, and there was nothing else I could do'. Now suppose that the person riding with him, seeing the go-cart ahead, exclaims: 'The go-cart! Do you intend to run over it?' He would reply that he did 'intend' to do this. But I think the second use is more standard. We could say the same thing in the earlier case by substituting the word 'purpose'. Moreover, the motive behind this use of 'intend' is to exculpate, but this exculpation is secured as well with the word 'purpose'. The person points out that though he did intentionally break the go-cart, his purpose in acting was not this but to reach the riot, and this purpose justified his intentionally breaking the go-cart. His acting knowingly here was then his acting intentionally.

4. *Intention and Prediction*

Several questions arise as to the account of intention as one's thought of what he is doing (or will do). I want first to consider how what one is doing or will do relates to

what is happening or will happen, and how intention relates
to the expression of intention. These are two questions,
but they have, I think, sometimes been confused in the
asking of the single question: Are intentions predictive?
I think sometimes by the question is meant: Is intention,
like prediction, about the future? and sometimes: Is
intention, like prediction, verbally expressed? So distinguished, we see that the answer to both is negative; for
an intention in the strict sense concerns the present, and
an intention need not be expressed.

First, it is plain that intentions do not exclusively concern the future. One might argue that we ask about present
intention only in order to get information about future
action which we expect will follow from this intention.
But we also ask about past intentions, where there is no
question of what will follow from them. Here we know
what did happen and are unconcerned with what will
happen; we want to know merely whether the person
intended to happen what did happen. Further, not all
intentions are, when they are occurring, merely predictions
of what *will* happen, for they also involve thoughts of what
is happening.

Nor are all intentions expressed. But first, what about
predictions? Is a prediction merely (a) a thought or (b)
an expressed statement of what will happen? As (b), a
prediction is, with respect to a future event, what a description is with respect to a present event (or enduring object)
and what an historical report is with respect to a past event.
We commonly understand by a prediction something which
is uttered, but we do not think this essential to its being a
prediction. For one often says of an event about which
he has said nothing, not even to himself, 'It is exactly what
I predicted would happen'. This may be a loose usage,
and perhaps one ought to replace 'predicted' here with
'foresaw', 'expected', or simply 'thought'. It is true that
the etymology would favor this recommendation. But we
do not need to settle this; for, whether or not predictions
require verbal expression, intentions do not. A person has
manifold intentions which remain unuttered. Further, it
is plain that, whether or not predictions require verbal

expression, intentions are not necessarily predictive; for predictions are exclusively about the future, while intentions are sometimes about the present. Still, what of the intentions which are expressed and are purposes for the future. Are they predictive? The answer is that prediction is not their chief function, but they do entail predictions.

Suppose I either tell someone or record in my diary the sentence: 'I will be at the party tomorrow night'. This is not merely or chiefly a prediction, for its chief use is not to say what will happen. Its difference from a prediction comes out in noticing the different kinds of questions to which the sentence above would function as a prediction and as a statement of intention. It would be a prediction if someone had asked, 'Where will you be tomorrow night?' It would function as a statement of intention (in the sense of purpose) if the question had been: 'What are you going to do tomorrow night?' The concept of intention brings in the concept of the person's action in a way that the concept of prediction does not. A prediction about myself may state solely what will happen to me, while an expression of intention for the future must state what I will do, just as a statement of my intention at the moment is not a description of what is happening to me but of what I am doing. Wittgenstein wrote in the *Philosophical Investigations*: 'Why do I want to tell him about an intention too, as well as telling what I did? — Not because the intention was also something which was going on at that time. But because I want to tell him something about *myself*, which goes beyond what happened at that time' (I, 659).

This respect in which an expressed intention involves prediction can be brought out by considering signals. Signals may be statements of intention, or orders, or commands, or requests. A basketball player may signal a team mate that he *intends* to shoot. A policeman may blow his whistle to *command* a motorist to stop. A golf player shouts 'Fore' to *request* another player to move aside. The order and the request are not in any significant respect reports or predictions. Someone might propose that these

are reports of what the speaker wants, or of what he will
do if the order or request is disobeyed. But neither of
these is a universal characteristic of an order or request.
One can order or request something which he does not
want obeyed, and the disobedience of which he is not
prepared to punish. On the other hand, the basketball
player's signal is, in expressing his intention, also the expression of a prediction. Conceivably the same signal
might also be an order or a request for the other player to
take up a position underneath the basket, but it is not in
this aspect, but only as expression of intention, that the
signal is predictive.

Prediction, then, is not the point of a statement of
intention for the future. But prediction is a necessary
part of such a statement, just as a statement of present
intention is a putative report of what is now happening.
If someone asks what I am doing, and I say 'I am writing
a letter', I imply that a letter is being written. If someone
asks what I intend to do tomorrow morning, and I say 'I
am going to write a letter', I imply that a letter will be
written. The point of a statement of intention is to state
what *I* am doing or will do; while the point of reports
and predictions is to state what *event* is happening or will
happen. But one cannot describe his action and not
describe an event, since his action belongs to the course of
events.

5. *The Evidence for Intentions*

There are other problems about the expression of intention. The knowledge one has of his intentions need
not be formulated or linguistically expressed. But this
knowledge is of a sort that one must be *capable* of explicitly formulating, expressing and communicating. We
should give no heed to a person who said he had intentions
which he could not express. If he told us of intentions
which no one else shared, we would be suspicious, but we
might still say that he had such intentions, only they were
very queer. While if he said he just could not put into
words what he intended, we should think he was lying.
We do not demand that he tell us his intentions — only

very few intentions are worth telling; they are either obvious or trivial. But we do demand that a person not tell us that he cannot tell us.

A person's statement is the final authority in settling whether he was acting intentionally and in settling what his intention was. There is other evidence of intention, but none so conclusive. It follows that we can never be sure whether animals have intentions. We do apply to animals the expressions 'intend' and 'think it is doing such and such'. But we also make judgments of praise and blame about them. Both might be a kind of Aesop's fable. It is important to be clear on this matter, because it is important to know whether we are to hold people responsible only for acts which are knowable from their observable behavior, or whether in holding them responsible we also want to consider what they say about their behavior.

Anscombe evidently thinks that being able to express an intention is not necessary to having one, while Professor Flew thinks that 'the capacity to formulate is absolutely crucial'. In support of this view Flew quotes a statement by the psychologist, G. Allport: 'Without symbols we could not make-believe, dissimulate or lie; we could not make plans for the future; nor hold those schemata in mind that make possible consistency in moral conduct'.[1] But this is doubtful. Animals engage in deception, dissimulation, and, in so far as they play, in make-believe. Further, they do, as Anscombe points out, pursue future objectives, though we would not say that animals 'make plans' for the future. But in any event, knowing whether animals dissimulate or pursue objectives is not the crucial question, for one can in some sense pursue objectives by habit and 'unconsciously', without 'intending' to do so. An agent's intending to pursue an objective is shown in his being able to describe his objective when the question arises. But we cannot put the question to animals.

In most cases of human action the question of intention does not arise. The mere fact of a person's acting at all is

---

[1] A. Flew, 'Motives and the Unconscious' in *Foundations of Science and the Concepts of Psychology and Psychoanalysis*, vol. i, The University of Minnesota Press, p. 155.

taken as showing that he is acting intentionally, unless there
are unusual features about his movements — disconnected-
ness, lack of focus, a blank expression on his countenance,
or the like. These are not sure signs of the absence of
intention, but they raise a doubt. We settle the doubt by
asking the person. Of course we can also doubt his account,
and if there are repeated or marked discrepancies between
what he says he intends to do and what he actually does,
this will be evidence that he is lying. But this does not
show that the behavioral evidence of intention is stronger
than the agent's assertion; it only shows that it is more to
be trusted in a particular sort of case, and in a sort of case
which is not standard. Even here what it shows is not
that the introspective evidence is in this case inferior to
the behavioral evidence, but rather that in this case we are
not given access to the introspective evidence and hence
must go by the inferior behavioral evidence.

However, one might still wish to say that intentions can
exist without the ability to express them. We use the
concept of intention to make certain contrasts, and one of
these contrasts can be made on the basis of behavioral
evidence, namely the contrast between an agent's attempt
and his achievement. But another important contrast
cannot be made, namely the contrast between the agent's
intention and his desire. This question whether an act is
both intended and desired or only intended is (so far as I
can see) of no general relevance to the matter of responsibility. But the question whether intention is ascertainable
by behavioral evidence is of general relevance; and this
question of intention and desire is crucial for that. There
are various ways in which it might appear that we could
make a behavioral test which would enable us to distinguish
merely intentional acts from acts which are also desired;
but on examination each proves inadequate. I shall try to
show this by constructing a series of cases which might be
thought to exhibit the distinction.

(1) Suppose we see a cat crouch in the way it does just
before pouncing on a bird, and then pounce and seize a
bird. In the crouching stage we might say with confidence
that the cat 'intends' to catch the bird, and in the seizing

T

stage we might say that we were right, that it did intend
this. We might equally say that the cat 'wanted' to catch
the bird. There is no feature of the cat's behavior, no
manner in which it crouches and seizes, that might count
as its intending but not its wanting, or as its wanting but
not its intending. Suppose it waits a long time quite
motionless. We might say equally: 'He really does
$\left(\begin{array}{l}\text{intend} \\ \text{want}\end{array}\right)$ to catch that bird'. Or if it shows what we call
signs of impatience, we might say the same thing.

(2) Let us try a different case. An injured bird is
perched on a branch in the midst of a stream; on the bank
a cat runs back and forth, sometimes putting a paw in the
water. We might be inclined to say that the cat wants the
bird but does not intend to get it. But we would have just
as much evidence for saying that the cat wants to get the
bird and intends to get it if it can. We might try to distinguish its wanting from its intending by saying that there
is no doubt about what it wants but some doubt about
what it intends. But this distinction likewise dissolves
when we specify precisely the object of wanting. With
respect to having the bird, we could mark off no differences
in the evidences of its wanting and its intending to have
the bird. With respect to the larger object, getting wet in
order to have the bird, there would be the same doubt or
hesitation about its wanting to do this and intending to
do it.

One might propose, however, that what distinguishes
wanting and intending is that wanting pertains to a specific
delimited (terminal) objective, while intention comprises
steps intermediary to this objective. Of course, intention
does not include all such steps, for becoming aware of some
such steps may lead one to change his intention. A person
may first want to have a thing; next intend to have it;
then, discovering that he must have something else before
he can have it, drop his intention. Still, though the intention does not include all the intermediary steps, it does
often include some of these, while it may seem that the
wanting includes none of them. One may want a drink of
water and intend to have it, and intend to get up and go

get it. Here one's wanting is exhausted by the having of the water. His intending, however, includes these intermediary steps, and this intention arises with the thought that these are necessary means to it. One may say (aggressively) 'I want a drink and I *intend* to go get one'.

We can *imagine* that the same account applies to animals : they want the terminal object, but intend not merely this but some of the intermediary steps. But how can we tell ? In the case of human beings we cannot say that what is wanted is in every case *only* the terminal object of a process. Sometimes one wants not merely to have a drink, but to stretch his legs. How are we to tell whether the cat wants only to seize the bird and not also to perform the act of catching it ? In the case of human beings we can tell this, or at least get some light on it, by letting the person tell us what he wants and wherein this diverges from what he merely intends. The cat cannot tell us.

(3) Consider another case. Suppose we have birds which have been operated on so that they cannot in any way resist the cat's attack, and which are marked so that the cat can distinguish the defenseless bird from a bird of the regular sort. And suppose the cat has been frequently offered both sorts of birds separately, and it has seized or attempted to seize whichever bird has been offered. Now suppose we offer on several occasions at once both sorts of birds, and the cat invariably chooses the defenseless bird. We then deprive it of the defenseless bird and provide only the natural bird, and it now resorts to its old way of attempting to catch the bird. This would provide good evidence that it wanted only the bird and did not want to perform the act of catching the bird. We then conclude that it did perform this act when it did not want to perform it (but only wanted what it obtained by performing it).

But we cannot conclude that it *intended* to perform this act (when it did not want to perform it). What we observe is that it performs what is a means to an end that it wants. But we cannot call all such performances intentional. For human beings come to do through habit and unconsciously acts which are means to ends which they want. If we see a person in a novel situation taking new steps to an end which we have reason to think he wants, we will have evidence that he is acting intentionally. But suppose, as in the animal situation, a person first learns to satisfy a want in one way; then is provided an easier way and adopts that; then is deprived of the easy way while he is still provided with the old way. He might fall into the old way again unconsciously; and our only sure method of knowing whether he were acting intentionally in this situation would be to ask him. In the imagined cat experiment, when we reintroduce the old situation there is no way of telling whether the animal has fallen back into an old habit pattern or whether he is intentionally taking steps to get what he wants.

(4) Consider one more case. Suppose we put the animal in a novel situation which contains the following: an object which the animal wants; none of the usual means of getting it; means which if combined in a certain way would provide the thing wanted. The animal might act in three different ways with regard to these means: (a) ignore them; (b) act toward them in a haphazard way; (c) act toward them in a deliberate way, after the fashion of a human being who is trying to solve a problem. His acting in the third way would provide evidence that he was acting intentionally. Why? Because this is the way human beings act when they are acting intentionally. But this is not the final evidence we use that a person is acting intentionally. Rather this evidence is his saying that he was acting intentionally. We have learned that when a person does know what he is doing then he usually does act in a manner we may call 'deliberate', and conversely. If animals can be shown to act in this way, then we may credit them with intentional action (and then, as Croce says about animals having intuition, if they do, so much the better or so much the worse for them). But until animals learn to talk, we will continue to lack about them what counts as the decisive evidence for the presence of intention in human beings. And if our best behavioral evidence that a person is acting intentionally is his acting in the way he does when he says that he is acting intentionally, then certainly the behavioral evidence is less primary than

the personal report. Though we can infer from his acting that he acted intentionally, and was responsible, we cannot have the certainty about this that he has.

6. *Intending and Trying*

Now let us ask whether intending involves some particular form of trying, or trying in conjunction with something else. This appears to be the view of several writers.

When the cruder versions of 'free will' are put aside, subtler versions appear. Much has been done to show the emptiness of the notion of a special activity of will, distinct from the more everyday occurrences such as intending and trying. But the way these latter notions are treated suggests that the old view still lingers. At least this seems to me to underlie the difficulties of two recent treatments of intention. One account explicates the meaning of intending in terms of trying; the other account introduces the notion of a being able to intend. I shall try to show that both notions are mistaken.

We can first see that (1) intending does not involve trying, nor does (2) trying involve intending. (1) We often intend to do something, and often do something intentionally, which is done effortlessly, without trying. (2) On the other hand, trying usually, but not invariably, involves an intending to try. It is only in an extraordinary case that one could try unintentionally. The reason for this is that trying is ordinarily something one does as a means to an end. It is a means which he adopts, and one can only adopt a means intentionally. But one may also find oneself unconsciously (and unintentionally) trying to do something. While talking to someone I may find myself unconsciously straining to open a drawer even after I have decided that I do not need to open it. Here I was trying, but not intending to try. If I had broken a lock in this way, and only as a result of exerting a fair amount of effort, it still would be right to say that I was not intending to try to open the drawer. Thus trying does not necessarily involve, but usually involves, intending to try.

Recent writers have attempted to analyze or elucidate intending in terms of trying. They have gone at this in a

T 2

rather complex and indirect way. Recognizing that intending does not always involve trying, they propose that it does involve a thought of trying or a belief that one will try. In an essay entitled 'Decision, Intention and Certainty' (*Mind*, 1958), S. Hampshire and H. L. A. Hart wrote: '. . . the minimum force of "I intend to do X" is "I believe that I will try to do X?"' And: '. . . the third person who says that X intends to do a future action is committed to the statement that X believes that he will at least try to do X if the occasion arises' (p. 11).[1] In a review of Anscombe's book Mr. Chisholm tentatively makes the same sort of suggestion: ' "A intends to do something now" means that A is in a state such that, if only an obstacle to the occurrence of B were now introduced, A would make-an-effort-to-do-B'.[2] But this is wrong. Persons intend to do a great many things which do not involve trying and which one has no thought of as involving trying. If someone asks 'What do you intend to do this evening?' and I reply, 'Watch television', I have no thought of trying to do this. Or if asked, when entering the voting stall, 'For whom do you intend to vote?' I reply 'Jones' without any commitment to trying to vote for Jones, or any entertainment or assertion of belief that I will try. Ordinarily no obstacles would arise that could occasion my trying, or exerting an effort, in this direction. But suppose that somehow these activities do become difficult. After dinner I get sleepy; plainly my having intended to watch television does not commit me to trying to overcome my drowsiness in order to do it. Or if, once in the voting stall, I feel qualms about the candidate's record, surely my having intended to vote for him does not now commit me to trying to vote for him. Indeed, one can intend to do things on the supposition that the thing intended may not require effort.

[1] Since writing this chapter Mr. Hampshire's book *Thought and Action* has appeared, and on a most general level our accounts are the same. He writes: 'To say that I did something intentionally is to say that I knew what I was doing when I did it' (p. 145). However, there is considerable difference in our ways of developing this general formula, and many specific points of disagreement — far too many to deal with in a short space. Most important, Mr. Hampshire retains the analysis of intention in terms of trying which he stated in his earlier essay and which I criticize above.

[2] *The Philosophical Review*, January 1959, p. 112.

There is one important use of the expression 'I intend to do X' which does involve a belief that one will try, and a commitment to try, when the opportunity arises. Such intentions are a sort of qualified promise or resolve. Consider: 'Are you coming to the committee meeting tomorrow?', answered by: (1) 'I intend to'. Compare this with the other replies: (2) 'I $\left(\begin{array}{c}\text{certainly}\\\text{fully}\end{array}\right)$ intend to'; (3) 'I will come'; (4) 'I promise to be there'. These latter imply, in ascending orders, the speaker's (a) firmness of belief that he will attend, and (b) assurance that the hearer can count on his attending. Thus there are intentions which are minimal resolves or promises, and these do imply that the speaker is prepared to make some effort to bring about the event. But these are a special variety of intentions. All resolvings or promisings are intendings; but not all intentions are resolves or promises. Let us call this complex variety of intentions 'resolute intentions'.

Still, not even these intentions imply a belief that one will try; what they imply is an intention to try. To say: 'I fully intend to be there' is not to say that I *believe* I will try, but only that I *will* try — that I *intend* to try. It is odd to say 'I believe I will try'. For ordinarily 'trying' is something that is within my control (which I am able to do), and when a future event depends upon an act of mine which is within my control I do not *predict* this event or act but state an *intention* with regard to it. But to say what I *believe* I will do is to predict. An intention, as we saw, implies a prediction, but is something more than a prediction. It is true, I may make a prediction about my trying. I may know that in taking examinations I usually, though not invariably, have exerted effort to make a high score; so, concerning an imminent examination, I conceivably might offer the prediction: 'I *believe* that I will try to make a high score'. Or facing a visit from someone I do not like, I may say: 'I *believe* I will try to be nice to him'. (Of course this literal use of 'believe' must be kept distinct from another common colloquial use such as might be employed in this sentence, the use which we might call the meditative use, and the meaning of which might be conveyed by 'I have a mind that . . .' or 'I allow that . . .'.) These cases are possible, though unusual. It would be more usual to say, 'I *intend* to try to make a high score (or be nice to him)'. But there is one thing we would never say, except as a joke: 'I intend to be nice to him — I mean, I believe I will try to do so'. The second clause, stating only the tentative prediction, adds such a heavy qualification to the first part as in effect to cancel it. About such an utterance the hearer would demand: '*Do* you intend to be nice or not?' or '*Will* you try or not?' The effect is equally ridiculous if we substitute 'know' for 'believe'. To say, 'I know I will try' could only mean either, 'I strongly believe I will try', or 'I intend to (or will) try'. We do use the phrase, as in: 'I don't know whether I'll succeed, but I do know I will try'. But the meaning is simply that the person *intends* to try, the 'I know' functioning to lend emphasis and give assurance of this intention. In such cases the intention to try is but a part of the more general intention to do the act. A person only mentions his intention to try when, having a given intention, he foresees obstacles to accomplishing it. Thus a full expression of his meaning would be: 'I intend to be nice to him, and I intend to do everything in my power to succeed in doing it'.

Thus 'I intend to do X' can never be explicated by putting for 'intend', 'believe I will try', but at most, 'intend to try'; and this of course undermines the analysis of intending in terms of trying. For then the analysans includes the analysandum and a further term as well. It also shows, I think, how writers continue to try to bring in some very special sort of mental event that has affinities to the old concept of 'will'.

7. *Is Intending a Personal Ability?*

Professor Chisholm, having suggested that intending may be analyzable as a belief that one will try, goes on to suggest that (1) whether a person 'can' (is able to) do an act is analyzable in terms of whether the act would be the effect of his intending to do it, and (2) that the problem of 'free will' turns, at least in part, on whether the person 'could intend' the act to occur. Ability to act is analyzed in terms of intention, and 'free will' is analyzed in terms of ability to intend. Chisholm thinks, then, that a 'could intend' or a being able to intend is meaningful. Some acts would depend upon an intention, and evidently some acts would depend upon an ability to intend. Those acts which were, in the older form, dependent on 'free will' would be those acts which we were 'able to intend'. But there is no such thing as a being able to intend. It is not a situational ability, for there is no way in which a situation could affect a person's intending. Nor is it a personal ability. This latter has to be shown in some detail.

First, we do not speak of a person's being able to intend a thing as distinguishable from his being able to do the thing. We simply say that a person is able to do such and such, as to play golf, speak, discriminate colors. Would we have any occasion to say that he was able to intend to play golf, speak, etc.? What if he were hypnotized: might we then say, 'He is certainly able to speak, and he *would* speak if only he were able to intend to speak'? No. Rather we would say, 'He has simply lost control of his normal abilities. He could still speak, if he were to come to his senses.' What we are saying is that he is not now able to speak.

However, this formulation might seem to retain the notion of an ability of intending under the concept of 'control'. (It might seem that an ability to intend or 'control' is a sort of super-ability under whose jurisdiction all the other abilities fall, these other abilities getting exercise only so far as this other super-ability gets exercise.) It is true that 'able to control' is a common expression, where 'able to intend' is not. But they do not mean the same. The former phrase is always a shorthand reference to various specific states of mind or body, or conditions of the environment. We say that he cannot control his feelings or actions (or 'himself', meaning one of these); and we always understand this to mean that he is not able to act in certain ways, not that he is not able to intend to act. Indeed we do think that the person is actually intending to do certain things at the time when he is not able to control what he does.

There may seem to be one use for 'able to intend', namely to refer to the case of a person who has a repressed, unconscious wish, say to hurt a parent. Here we may say that the person cannot intend the act of violence which would satisfy his wish. His disability is not one of action; he may well have the physical powers for doing the act. Nor is the disability one of deliberating and deciding. For it may be that if he recognized his wish he could deliberate upon and choose a particular means of violence. This brings out what the disability is. What he cannot do is to *know*, or believe or recognize, that he has the wish for violence. It is a disability of thought or knowledge of his desire, not of intention to act. It is true that this disability of thought prevents the intention from occurring. But this is not to say that the disability is one of intention. Some activities can be performed only if we can perform other activities, but the ability to perform one is not the same as the ability to perform the other. For instance, we can reason only if we can remember; but the ability to remember is not the same as the ability to reason. Likewise with thinking and intending. To intend we must think, and to intend violence we must have a thought of violence (and perhaps a thought that we want violence). But thinking of violence or thinking we want violence is not intending violence, nor is an ability to think or to think we want violence an ability to intend violence.

There is a further reason for concluding that there is no such thing as an ability to intend. An ability is, at least typically, something which can exist in degrees; but we cannot think of one person as being more able to intend than another, or of a person being more able to intend at one moment than another.

That there are no degrees of the ability to intend is evident in that there are no degrees of intending itself, or, if one wishes, of the 'activity' of intending. One cannot intend more or less intensely, as he can desire, think, try, more or less. Nor can one intend for a longer or shorter time, as he can deliberate long or briefly; not can he intend quickly or slowly, as he can decide quickly or slowly. The only adverbs which seem applicable to intending are 'well' and 'badly', and these are thoroughly deceptive. For they are not ways or manners in which a person can intend, but characterizations of the objects which he intends. There is no intending well which is not an intending of a good thing.

We do say 'I fully intend', but there are two ways of interpreting this, neither of which implies a degree of intending. (1) 'Intend' here may be used in the complex sense of a resolve or promise, or what I have called a resolute intention; and here what occurs in a degree is the resolve or promise. One can firmly resolve or weakly resolve, and he can make a firm or a weak promise. But he cannot accompany the firm resolve with a firm intention; he cannot include within his firmly resolving an additional firmly intending. Any degree of firmness that is present belongs to the resolve, not to the intentional aspect of the resolve. (2) But there is a second way in which we may understand 'I fully intend' — namely in the sense of 'really', or 'truly', 'sincerely', 'earnestly', 'honestly'. All of these qualifiers would be understood in essentially the same way, and what they come to is (as is explicit in the first two of these, 'really' and 'truly') that I *do* intend. The words are brought in to assure someone that I am telling the truth when I say that 'I intend'. They indicate *that* I intend; they do not indicate a *degree with which* I intend.

It is plain why it should be thought that there is a use for 'able to intend'. It seems analytically true that anything which we do we are able to do. We do intend certain things; how could we intend them if we weren't able to intend them? The plausibility here depends upon a special use of the term 'able', namely with the meaning of 'possible'. Obviously we are 'able' to intend, in the sense that it is possible for us to intend; for it is the fact that we do intend. But we cannot give the sense of a personal ability to this notion of being 'able to intend'.

Still intending is something that I do. In order to intend there must be in me a possibility to intend, and a possibility would seem either a definite capacity or devoid of meaning.

Let us consider this same problem with respect to such comparable cases as 'living' and 'being conscious'. Except in a metaphorical sense, these concepts resist union with the concept of ability in the same way that intending does. We say that a person is able to breathe or to digest food, but not, except in a special sense, that he is able to live or be conscious. Rather, we would say simply that he is alive or is conscious, or that he will live or will become conscious. And as in the case of intending, the reason is, I think, that we have no use for the concept of ability where the ability or the act in question cannot be conceived as existing in degrees.[1]

Of course we do sometimes say 'He is very much alive' or 'barely alive', and 'He was highly conscious' or 'dimly conscious'; but in neither of these is the term taken in its normal sense. In the first case we have in mind not degrees of the person's present condition of being alive but degrees of the probability of his remaining in that condition. While in the case of 'conscious' what we have in mind are degrees not of his condition of mental awareness but degrees of his act of perception or attentiveness. We can imagine a case where we might exclaim, 'But he can live!' — the case where we see that his plight is not, as we feared, hopeless. But here either we are not attributing an ability to the person, but to ourselves, who may succeed in snatching him from death's door, or we are attributing to him some other ability than that of living. In this latter case what we have in mind is that his living depends upon his trying to live. We may say simply, 'But you can live!', or 'But you can live, if you *will* try', and not, 'But you can live, if you *can* try', for we may assume — correctly or mistakenly — that he can try. In neither case, then, do we attribute an ability to live. In the first case we attribute an ability to make live or keep alive; in the second, an ability to try. But if we use the phrase 'able to live' in neither of these senses, the only meaning remaining is

---

[1] The act could exist in degrees even when the personal ability to perform it did not exist in degrees, the variations depending upon other cooperating factors in its production. But also I think these acts or conditions are not thought to exist in degree.

'possible to live'. And whatever it might mean to say that such an act is 'possible to a person', it does not mean that this act is the exercise of a personal ability.

We might distinguish, besides the personal and situational sense of 'able', another sense, called the 'general' sense — 'general' in that it attributes the ability not to an individual but to an entire species. Thus we might say that the human being is the only featherless animal which is able to walk upright. Likewise we might say that the human being alone is able to intend. 'Able', however, is in these statements quite superfluous. The point here is just that the human being alone does these things, while other animals do not. The term 'able' gets genuine use only when there is a point in contrasting what he does with what he fails to do, or in estimating what he might do in the future. This sort of interest arises with respect to individuals, not with respect to a species. In describing a species our concern is to state what kinds of things its members do, not what kinds of things they are able to do.

But suppose there were an ability to intend, and one which we all possessed equally; would such an ability do what 'free will' is supposed to do? Not at all. Its being possessed by all equally and in equal degrees would not be sufficient. For the Libertarian requires a kind of action possessing a special sort of personal power. Doing a thing intentionally (as something over merely doing it) does not mean doing it with a special kind of power, but rather doing it with a special kind of knowledge.

8. *Varieties of Non-intentional Acts*

The analysis of 'intention' enables us to understand the varieties of acts from which intention is absent, and for which, accordingly, we do not hold persons responsible. These acts are not limited to the sort we call 'unintentional', but include a considerable variety of acts.

An act is intentional if it involves a thought of what one is doing. What one does is not intentional if he has no thought, as when he is (a) asleep or unconscious, or if the act is (b) by reflex or habit, or (c) 'thoughtless' or 'inadvertent'. But in cases of (a) the question whether the thing were or were not intentional would not come up. Rather the question would be whether some other condition were present, in the absence of which intention could not be present. In cases of (b) or (c) the question might come up. One might ask : 'Did he do it intentionally or instead (b) by reflex or (c) thoughtlessly ?' Affirming (b) or (c) would rule it out as intentional; though what one would say was that it was not intentional, rather than 'unintentional'. (We will return to this distinction presently.)

The major varieties of non-intentional acts are, however, yet another class, which we call 'mistakes' and 'accidents'. These sorts of acts differ from the preceding in that these latter do involve a thought of what one is doing; but for some reason the act goes wrong. This wrongness may arise through (d) a failure of knowledge or (e) a failure of control. We call cases of (d) 'mistakes', cases of (e) 'accidents'. Aristotle says that 'a man makes a mistake when the fault originates in himself, but is the victim of accident when the origin lies outside himself'. But we speak of 'accidents' which are results merely of (e-1) failure of muscular control, as well as of events which are results of (e-2) outside interference. The former are 'accidents' in which the fault none the less originates in the person. Now one might say here that what originates in one's mind and knowledge (or lack of it) more truly originates in the person than what originates in his body and muscles ; and seen in this light we can retain Aristotle's distinction. But the important point is that the basic distinction is between acts that go awry through a fault of knowledge ('mistakes') and those that go awry from some other cause. It also helps to confuse the matter to speak of 'mistakes in performance'. It is true that we speak of things *done* by mistake ; but in these cases the source of the miscarriage in the act is not a muscular lapse or outside interference but a lapse in knowledge.

The difference between mistake and accident comes out in this. It is always a person that 'makes' a mistake; while an 'accident' is something not which one 'does' but which 'happens', often in spite of what one does. We refer to the accidental event by saying, '*It* was an accident' or 'He *had* an accident'. We do say of some events that 'He did it by accident', but we distinguish these from events of which we say, 'It was an accident'. We use the former for the (e-1) sort of events where 'he', the person, is more directly involved in the event, while we use the latter where the event is of the (e-2) type. To take examples of each. Suppose, first, that a driver puts his foot on the brake to stop, but his foot slips and the car crashes into a tree. We may say, 'He wrecked the car by accident'. Suppose now that his foot is put firmly on the brake pedal but the brake mechanism fails. Here we would only say, 'The car was wrecked by accident' or 'The wreck was an accident'.

We have now to distinguish a seventh variety of act, which is most strictly the sort to which we ascribe the word 'unintentional'. This is the act where the event is (f) most strictly contrary to the person's thought of what he is doing. Suppose Smith says something to Jones which would not normally hurt a person's feelings, and which Smith has no reason to think would hurt Jones' feelings, but which does hurt his feelings. We would say that 'Smith hurt Jones' feelings "unintentionally"', not that he hurt Jones' feelings 'mistakenly' or 'accidentally'. What we have in mind is that it is no part of Smith's *thought* that Jones' feelings will be hurt. The contrariety is solely between what happened as a result of his action and what Smith expected to happen. It is not an 'accident', for nothing has gone wrong in Smith's control of his muscles or in the outside circumstances. Nor is it a 'mistake', since it is not due to a lack in Smith's knowledge of the conditions of what he thinks himself to be doing. Suppose Smith, meaning to flatter Jones, mentioned something in Jones' past which involves details of which Smith is ignorant and which Jones in fact regards with shame, so that Jones is insulted. We would then prefer to say that Smith offended him 'by mistake', not 'unintentionally'. An act is 'unintentional' in being contrary to one's thought of our act. An act is 'mistaken' in being based on false beliefs of the conditions under which we act.

9. *Intention as a Condition of Responsibility*

We can now return to the question of intention and responsibility. We commonly think intention is a condition of responsibility. We say: 'Of course he was responsible. He did it quite intentionally'. Or: 'He can't be held responsible, for he didn't do it intentionally'. We do not think intention is a sufficient condition of responsibility; it is also required that the person be able to act. A person may do an act intentionally but under coercion; his responsibility for the act (and for failing to act in a contrary way) is reduced or removed in the degree to which the coercion reduces or removes his ability to act. That we are not responsible for all our intentional acts would, I think, provoke little argument. What does provoke dispute is the contention that intention is necessary to responsibility. Several sorts of counter-instances may be offered.

One is Austin's previously mentioned go-cart case. Although the driver knowingly or intentionally ran over the go-cart we may be inclined to say that he cannot be held responsible for breaking it. We are inclined to say this because we think he should not be blamed. It is true he should not. But the reason is not that he was not responsible, but that what he did was not wrong. Indeed he did the right thing in the circumstances. We excuse him not because he did something for which he was not responsible, but because what he did was justified. It was justified because it was a necessary part of the fulfilling of his primary responsibility. That this is our way of thinking on these matters is shown in that the natural thing to say, in reply to the question, 'Do you intend to smash the go-cart', would be: 'Yes, I accept full responsibility for it'.

Here is another case.[1] Suppose a landlord evicts a tenant who is delinquent in his rent, and as a result of this the tenant experiences considerable hardship. The landlord knows hardship will follow, but takes the stand that

---

[1] This case also was presented by Austin, though I fear I have not remembered the details exactly. It should be noted also that Austin was using these cases not to show that responsibility does not entail intentionality, but rather to argue that the acts in question were not intended.

this is not his affair. What first strikes us is that it would be misleading to say that the landlord's intent was that the tenant suffer. On the other hand, we would not allow the landlord himself to say in excuse : 'I did not intend that he suffer, I only intended to collect my rent'. We would reply, 'But you knew this would happen ; you intentionally did the thing which you knew would lead to his hardship'. This does commit him to some responsibility for the hardship. Again this does not mean that the landlord acted wrongly ; we should need more details in order to judge. But he cannot excuse himself on the ground that his act was not intentional or one for which he was not responsible.

In cases like this one the landlord may want to say : 'But it is the tenant himself, not I, who is responsible for his hardship ; if he had paid the rent, I would not have had to evict him'. This is another evasion. It presupposes, what is plainly false, that two (or more) people may not both be responsible for a single event. The tenant may have been responsible for his own hardship, for he may have known that this would be a result of his action (of not paying his rent) ; but this does not prevent the landlord's also being responsible for the hardship, so long as he did freely and intentionally what led to the hardship.

There is another kind of case which might be offered as an exception to the principle that intention is required for responsibility. Suppose a driver while absorbed in thought runs a traffic signal. Here the case is one in which the person appears to be responsible although he did not act intentionally. He did not know what he was doing, but we feel it right to impose on him the legal penalties. But there are two possibilities : either he was morally responsible, but not for this unintentional act but for a prior intentional act which had this unintentional act as its result ; or he is not morally responsible but only 'practically responsible', in the sense defined in Chapter IV. If we do hold the person morally responsible, it is not for the unintentional act which he committed while in a mental stupor, but for some prior intentional act which led to it. Suppose the driver knows that when he is thinking about philosophy he is apt to act absent-mindedly. We can assume that he knows that absent-minded driving is danger-ous. Then we blame him, not for running the stop sign, but for intentionally driving while in an unfit condition. On the other hand, suppose that he is almost never a victim of this particular sort of mental aberration. Suppose that when he got behind the wheel it never occurred to him that he would not drive with his usual alertness. And suppose that in the past he has taken pains to ascertain what are the conditions of competent driving, and taken pains to fulfill these conditions. Then we would not blame him. This is not to say that we should not impose the usual legal penalties. We may be justified in imposing legal responsibility when we are not justified in imposing moral responsibility. The problem is too complex to con-sider here in detail, and is in any case not necessary. But one thing that is obvious is that the injury done by the suggestion of fault may be so slight as not to warrant the ex-pense involved in assessing with exactness whether the person ought really to be penalized. The driver himself would usually accept this. He would prefer to suffer the minor blame and fine rather than expend even the time required to provide such evidence as the above to show that he was not morally at fault. And it is partly because this is recognized that no moral blame is thought to attach to this sort of infraction. This case, then, does not show that moral responsibility can exist in the absence of intention.

We conclude that intention is a universal condition of responsibility, and that cases which appear to provide ex-ceptions to the principle do not really do so.

We have seen, then, how intention, together with the ability to act, provide grounds for holding people respon-sible. These conditions allow us to pass the judgments of responsibility which the Extreme Determinist would debar us from passing, and which the Libertarian would allow us to pass only if we had a special capacity — 'free will' — which was not subject to natural conditions. We dis-covered no such capacity — neither in intention nor the ability to act; nor in the ability to choose or the ability to will. We saw, further, that though these latter two abilities are occasional conditions of responsibility, they are not, like intention and the ability to act, universal conditions.

It is now also clear that intention and the ability to act, in being conditions of responsibility, are likewise conditions of judgments of obligation. For we hold persons to be under obligation only for acts which satisfy the conditions of responsibility; and the only point of assessing responsibility is to pass a judgment of obligation. Further, because obligation involves value, an ethical concern with intention (and with the ability to act) ultimately leads us back to value — the primary ethical concept. We hold people obligated when they are responsible; we hold them responsible when they act intentionally; and that for which we hold them obligated and responsible is the realization of what is good.

Thus we retrace our steps back to the beginning. The route we actually followed in this essay — from value to intention — was a more natural one, though not so logically necessary as the route from intention to value. For though we cannot consider ethical intention without considering obligation and thence value, we may consider value without going on to consider obligation, responsibility and intention. Our ethical purpose in knowing a person's intention is to judge his responsibility and his obligation. But we may judge the value of something without determining obligation, responsibility and intention. Perhaps most judgments of value are made as a preliminary to determining what someone ought to do. But not every judgment of value leads to a judgment of obligation and responsibility; whereas every judgment of obligation and responsibility must depend on some judgment of value. What gives point to a particular judgment of obligation and responsibility is a particular judgment of value. And what gives us a general concern with obligation and responsibility is our appreciation of value. It is only because we believe that certain things are good that we want to ask — and can ask — what ought we to do and when are we responsible.

INDEX

Ability, 209, 214, 228, 229, 241, 245, 247, 283-5
and freedom, 228
to act, 142, 178, 208 ff., 222, 226-229, 243 ff., 281, 288, 290-1
to intend, 178, 277, 279-82
to will, 226 ff.
Absolutism, 24-5, 52
Act and Action, xiii, 3, 58, 64, 135 ff., 171 ff.
and choice, 55-6, 103, 229, 240, 243 ff.
and desire, 68 ff., 84, 235-6
and intention, 69, 116, 146-7, 209, 211-12, 216, 256 ff., 270
rightness and goodness of, 1, 14, 20, 33, 38, 44, 50, 54-5, 62, 84, 114-15, 129, 137-41, 154-8, 168, 182, 186, 196, 202
Agreement, 25-6, 30, 40-1, 62 ; see also Approval, Blame
Allport, G., 272
Anscombe, G. E. M., 256, 263 n., 264, 272
Approval, 10-13, 141, 148, 201 ; see also Agreement, Blame
Aristotle, 53, 61, 87, 98, 106-7, 116, 190, 208, 266, 286
Austin, J. L., 130, 164, 267, 288
Ayer, A. J., 220 n.

Behaviorism, 71, 74
Bentham, Jeremy, 17, 99, 100, 102, 112, 123
Blame, 165, 170, 216-17
judgments of praise and blame, 5, 6, 13, 129 ff., 169, 199, 210, 217, 239, 241-2, 249, 260, 267, 288, 290
Bouwsma, O. K., x
Bradley, F. H., 112
Brandt, Richard, 20
Broad, C. D., 90

Campbell, C. A., 230 n., 231
Capacity, 31-2, 36, 59, 121, 226-8, 239 ff. ; see also Ability
Carritt, E. F., 151-2

Character, 43, 98-9, 106, 113-17, 141, 151, 153, 163, 165, 201-3, 205, 224-6, 247
Chisholm, R., 264 n., 278 n., 280-1
Choice, ix, xii, 1, 3-6, 9, 41, 54-6, 59, 100, 103, 113, 135, 150, 154-5, 176-8, 184, 217-19
and decision, 193 ff., 200, 204, 206, 218-19, 222, 231, 240
and deliberation, 130, 196-7
Compulsion, see Freedom
Conscientiousness, 55-6, 58, 71, 138-9, 144, 147
Corrective Theory, 143-4, 146, 148-52

Davidson, D., 266 n.
Decision, decide, ix, 4, 13-4, 40-1, 47, 53, 59-60, 123, 168-73, 190 ff., 206, 247-8, 250-5, 277, 282-3
practical, 1-2, 189, 196, 201
technical, 199-201
Deliberation, 13-15, 53, 146, 162, 172, 178, 184, 190, 192, 196-7, 203-4, 247-8, 250-5, 263, 276, 282
Deontology, 125, 154, 167-71, 192, 206
Description, descriptive, 10 ff., 25, 44-5, 70-1, 76, 143-4, 190-3, 221, 238, 263, 269
Desire, ix, 14-17, 29, 56, 61 ff., 85, 125, 146-8, 157, 166, 193, 195-8, 202 ff., 243, 260, 267, 273, 282
and pleasure, 66-7, 93-5 ff.
Determinism, 208, 210, 215 ff., 226, 290
Dewey, J., 51
Disposition, see Capacity
Dostoevski, F., 7
Duty, 36, 55, 70-1, 104, 121, 127, 144-5, 147-8, 156-7, 162, 165, 167-9, 172, 193-4

Ebersole, F., 148 n., 149-50
Emotivism, 10-15, 59, 62, 130, 134, 192
Epictetus, 6

PRINTED BY R. & R. CLARK, LTD., EDINBURGH